The LIFE STORY of ADAM and HAVAH

The LIFE STORY of ADAM and HAVAH

A New Targum of Genesis 1:26-5:5

Shira Halevi

JASON ARONSON INC.
Northvale, New Jersey
London

This book was set in 12pt. Berkeley Oldstyle by Alabama Book Composition of Deatsville, Alabama, and printed and bound by Book-mart Press of North Bergen, New Jersey.

10 9 8 7 6 5 4 3 2 1

Library of Congress Cataloging-in-Publication Data

Halevi, Shira, 1956–
The life story of Adam and Havah : a new targum of Genesis 1:26–5:5 / Shira Halevi.
p. cm.
ISBN 0-7657-5962-4 (alk. paper)
1. Bible. O.T. Genesis I, 26–V, 5—Commentaries. 2. Eden. 3. Adam (Biblical figure) 4. Eve (Biblical figure) I. Title.
BS1237.H27 1997
222'.1106—dc20 96-46018

Manufactured in the United States of America. Jason Aronson Inc. offers books and cassettes. For information and catalog write to Jason Aronson Inc., 230 Livingston Street, Northvale, New Jersey 07647.

To my teachers,
Dr. Harris Lenowitz,
and
Dr. Laurence D. Loeb,
With great esteem and much affection.

And to my fellow student,
Sally Ginsberg,
May her memory be blessed.

"Be diligent in studying Torah . . . and know
in whose Presence you toil."
— *Avot* II.14

Contents

Introduction 1
"In the Bet Midrash, or House of Learning"

1 **"Male and Female"** 33
Genesis 1:26–31

2 **"The Garden of God"** 73
Genesis 2:4b–17

3 **"Under the Huppah"** 121
Genesis 2:18–24

4 **"A Desirable Tree"** 165
Genesis 2:25–3:7

5 **"God Weeps"** 201
Genesis 3:8–3:23

6 **"Good and Evil"** 239
Genesis 3:23–5:3

7 **"Death and Hope"** 283
Genesis 5:4,5

Bibliography 303

Index 307

A Note to the Reader

This is a re-telling and re-interpretation of a story that has profoundly impacted relations between men and women for nearly 3,000 years. The Adam and Havah narrative is the foundation for gender theology within the major Western/Middle Eastern religions of Judaism, Christianity, and Islam, representing, as it does, universal concepts applicable to every man and every woman. This re-telling is formatted as a "targum," consisting of translated scripture interwoven with commentary from a variety of ancient to medieval Jewish sources. This targum includes, but is not limited to, such sources as Philo, the Mishna, the Talmud, Merkavah literature, pseudepigrapha, the Zohar, and Midrash Rabbah. It is also supplemented with Biblical poetry from the Writings, particularly Psalms and The Song of Songs, to enhance the story with emotional expression. The translation itself utilizes both Rabbinic hermeneutical rules and modern techniques, which include poetic structuring and polyvalent reading. The targum is accompanied by "midrash," a fictional debate between two students—a male and female—under the direction of their beloved rabbi. Together, they battle over the targum and its possible interpretations, gender roles, and the essence of tradition itself. This book is not intended to be read as *the* correct reading of this controversial piece of scripture, but as a "mind experience," a splashing-around in the "Sea of Torah," with its myriad of possibilities.

INTRODUCTION
"In the Bet-Midrash, or House of Learning"

Let your house be a meeting-place for the sages.
Sit in the very dust at their feet,
and thirstily drink in their words.

—*Pirke Avot* I.4[1]

Rabbi: What is a targum?

Talmidah: Does it derive from the Hebrew word *tirgem?*

Rabbi: It does.

1. *Avot,* "Fathers," is a tractate in the Mishna and subsequently the Talmud, composed of sayings of the first sages, beginning with Simeon the Just. The sayings are arranged in chronological order from about 200 B.C.E. to 200 C.E.

Talmidah: Then it must have something to do with translation.

Rabbi: What else?

Talmidah: It could also be an interpretation or explanation.

Rabbi: Of what?

Talmidah: Wait . . . is a targum translation, or is it interpretation?

Rabbi: Yes.

Talmidah: So it is a translation *and* interpretation of a text from one language into another.

Rabbi: It would be more precise to say that it is a translation of a text from one language into another, supplemented by interpretation. But the word *targum* is more specific in its application.

Talmidah: A specific text or a specific language?

Rabbi: Yes.

Talmidah: What is the text?

Rabbi: You can derive the answer logically. I will tell you that targums are part of Tradition.

Talmidah: Part of Tradition . . . Torah, midrash, Mishna, Talmud, all that compose Jewish literature.

Rabbi: Would you include medieval Sephardic love poems or secular nineteenth-century Haskalah essays as Tradition?

Talmidah: Yes . . . No. The writings of Tradition are different. How are they different? . . . They comprise sacred writings. But that's not all. They are also the "textbooks" for the *bet-midrash*, or "house of learning." Talmidim[2] spend their lives turning these texts over and over in their minds, debating minute details with other talmidim while learning at the feet of rabbis—teachers of Tradition.

Rabbi: That is all very well, Talmidah. But what do these texts have in common?

Talmidah: They compose the sacred heritage of our people.

Rabbi: More specific.

Talmidah: Most are commentaries on commentaries.

Rabbi: . . . on commentaries on commentaries. Ultimately commentaries on . . .

Talmidah: Torah!

Rabbi: What is Torah?

Talmidah: The first five books of Moses—Genesis, Exodus, Leviticus, Numbers, and Deuteronomy.

2. *Talmidim* is plural for *talmid*, which means "student" or "disciple."

Rabbi: The Prophets[3] and Writings[4] are not Torah?

Talmidah: No . . . yes. All Scripture is Torah.

Rabbi: What does *torah* mean?

Talmidah: Law . . . teaching. Yes, Torah is any teaching based on Scripture. So the commentaries are Torah, too . . . and the commentaries on the commentaries.

Rabbi: By that definition Torah is equivalent to Tradition.

Talmidah: But it is also a specific text, the basic text upon which all Tradition is based. That's it! Targum is a translation and interpretation of Hebrew Scripture into another language!

Rabbi: That is correct.

Talmidah: But into what language is it translated?

Rabbi: That, too, can be derived logically. I will tell you that there is a targum for every book of Scripture except for Ezra, Nehemiah, and Daniel.

---

3. The books of Joshua, Judges, 1 and 2 Samuel, 1 and 2 Kings, Isaiah, Jeremiah, Ezekiel, Hosea, Joel, Amos, Obadiah, Jonah, Micah, Nahum, Habakkuk, Zephaniah, Haggai, Zechariah, and Malachi. These books rank second in status and authority to the Torah itself.

4. The books of Psalms, Proverbs, Job, The Song of Songs, Ruth, Lamentations, Ecclesiastes, Esther, Daniel, Ezra, Nehemiah, and 1 and 2 Chronicles. These books rank third in status and authority behind the Torah and the Prophets.

Talmidah: Ezra, Nehemiah, and Daniel. What do they have in common? . . . They are among the latest books to be written and included in the canon, between 500 and 164 B.C.E. They are all included in the Writings, as opposed to the Torah or the Prophets. So they do not have the same status or credibility as other books of Scripture. Am I getting nearer to the answer?

Rabbi: The era in which they were written may have some relevance. Their status as sacred literature is irrelevant. Remember, we are discussing language.

Talmidah: Language. . . . How do these books differ from earlier books in the language they are written? . . . Late Biblical Hebrew as opposed to the archaic Hebrew of Torah. I don't see how . . . wait! Large portions of these books are written in Aramaic! That's it, isn't it? Aramaic! Targums are translations of Hebrew Scripture into Aramaic, supplemented with interpretation.

Rabbi: That is more or less correct.

Talmidah: Why, that definitely decides the issue for me.

Rabbi: Explain.

Talmidah: Scholars debate whether these particular texts were originally written in Hebrew with portions of them subsequently translated into Aramaic, or vice versa, that they were originally written in Aramaic with portions of them later translated into Hebrew.

Rabbi: Others believe these texts were originally written as we have them today, portions in Hebrew and portions in Aramaic, for purposes about which we can only speculate.

Talmidah: Well, the fact that there are no targums on these books proves they were written in Aramaic. There was no need to translate Daniel into Aramaic because it was already written in Aramaic. Which makes sense because, by the time it was written, Aramaic was the common language of the people. Hebrew was already a literary language that was largely unintelligible to the general population.

Rabbi: That is a reasonable supposition, though unprovable. How do you suppose targums evolved?

Talmidah: I don't know, but I would guess that as the people forgot Hebrew they needed someone to translate the Torah readings during synagogue services.

Rabbi: That is a reasonable guess. The sages of that time determined that Scripture was too sacred to be read in any other language but Hebrew, yet the people could not understand what they were hearing. It became widespread practice for a reader to cant the Hebrew from a Torah scroll, pausing occasionally while a bilingual interpreter, standing to the side, orally translated the passage into Aramaic. The translator would often add explanations of archaic terms or even give interpretation in order to make the passage understandable.

Talmidah: So it was just a matter of time before these oral translations and explanations were written down.

Rabbi: The rabbis actually forbade it, but it was inevitable. Written targums began appearing for several books of Scripture. The rabbis finally commissioned a targum for the Torah themselves in an effort to control the content of translation during synagogue services. *Targum Onkelos*, translated by a Greek convert by that name, was the first to receive official sanction from the rabbis, sometime in the second century C.E. Most targums were written between 200 C.E. and 800 C.E., though some much earlier and later than that.

Talmidah: I can see why the rabbis were concerned about these targums. I mean, a text can be translated several different ways with several different possible meanings. That's risky enough. But to add commentary on top of that is opening Pandora's box.

Rabbi: From a rabbi's point of view, it *is* Pandora's box. Particularly if you have no control over who's opening the box and what items are pulled out.

Talmidah: Wait a minute. If what we're talking about is translation and commentary, I see little difference between a targum and a midrash, except that one is written in Aramaic and the other in Hebrew. Certainly the rabbis did not object to midrash. They fairly reveled in it. They took great delight in debating the various possible meanings of individual words and phrases, as well as the myriad ways in which passages could be interpreted. That is the very heart of Tradition.

Rabbi: If you are equating targum with midrash, you are mistaken. It is true that targum is exegesis or interpretation of Scripture. The very act of translating requires interpretation on the part of the translator. It is also true that a targum supplements the original text with commentary about what the text "means."

Talmidah: But Rabbi, midrash does both of these things. It will play around with different ways to translate a passage and will debate its meaning in the form of commentary.

Rabbi: Ahhhh! Did I say "debate"?

Talmidah: Well, no, but rabbinic debate is very much a part of . . .

Rabbi: Midrash. But not targum. Targum employs the same techniques as midrash for translating Scripture and the same rules of logic to derive meaning, but it presents its translation and commentary in a different form.

Talmidah: What form is that?

Rabbi: You will tell me tomorrow. Here is a copy of *Targums Onkelos*, *Yerushalmi*, and *Palestine*, all targums on the Torah. Read the first few chapters on Genesis and compare them to *Midrash Rabbah* on the same passages. We will meet again at the same time and the same place. I will be prepared to take instruction from you.

Rabbi: What is a targum?

Talmidah: A fraud.

Rabbi: Some would call it a pious fraud.

Talmidah: A contradiction in terms. How can any pious person be a fraud?

Rabbi: You called the targum itself a fraud, not its translator.

Talmidah: What's the difference? A fraudulent document is produced by a fraud. One attests to the other.

Rabbi: So, writing a targum is fraudulent. Explain.

Talmidah: Why, there is no distinction between translated Scripture and added commentary! It's a seamless, interwoven text which disguises interpretation in the form of Scripture itself. No attempt is made to identify or to trace logic or origin of interpretation, nor is there any indication that other interpretations, equally valid, may exist.

Rabbi: There is no debate.

Talmidah: More than that, Rabbi. I mean, in midrash the reader knows who said what—Rabbi Eliezer said this, then Rabbi Ishmael said that—and how they derived their arguments. It tells you that it's quoting a passage from another section of Scripture—"as it is written," "as you read," "as it says." And it literally spells out how a particular rabbi translated a word to derive a different meaning. Most importantly, midrash is wide-open in its style by presenting several different lines of argument, usually contradictory, allowing the reader to continue the debate himself. Targum leaves precious few options for interpretation.

Rabbi: It would be more correct to say that it presents only one line of interpretation.

Talmidah: And it implies that it is the *only* legitimate line because it is fused with Scripture.

Rabbi: Perhaps in the mind of the translator, it *is* the only legitimate line of interpretation. Perhaps in his mind, the commentary he added is a needed explanation of what the Hebrew text really means. In today's scholarly jargon he would call it "nonliteral" translation. What do you suppose is the difference between a literal and nonliteral translation?

Talmidah: A literal translation would attempt to translate each word and phrase into an equivalent word or phrase in the second language. A nonliteral translation . . . I'm guessing the translator tries to find equivalent meaning. I suppose it would be necessary for idiomatic or metaphorical phrases. Unless the two languages shared identical cultural milieus, literal translations of idioms and metaphors would not make sense.

Rabbi: Example.

Talmidah: Well, the Biblical term *know a woman* means to have sexual intercourse with her. A literal translation would not be an accurate one as far as the meaning of the text is concerned.

Rabbi: So you would say that a translator who wrote, "and he knew her, he had sexual intercourse with her" is justified in doing so.

Talmidah: I know what you're getting at, Rabbi. The answer's yes, but there's a fallacy of degree when it comes to targum. These so-called translators go way beyond the reasonable.

Rabbi: Do they? How would you translate *tov?*

Talmidah: "Good."

Rabbi: Is that all?

Talmidah: Well, depending on the context, it could mean "right, fitting, appropriate, happy, healthy, pleasurable, fruitful, prosperous" . . . what else . . . "joyful, desirable, righteous" . . . that's all I can think of at this moment.

Rabbi: Supposing you are a translator who wanted the reader to know just exactly what God meant when He saw all that He had created and said, "It is *tov*. . . . It is good."

Talmidah: I suppose I would pick a more specific term for *tov*.

Rabbi: Why only one term? Suppose by using the word *tov*, God meant several adjectives simultaneously?

Talmidah: How would that work? . . . You mean His creations could be fruitful, happy, and righteous?

Rabbi: Why pick only one meaning? In fact, is it truly accurate to choose only one meaning?

Talmidah: I see what you're getting at. By limiting yourself to one meaning of a word, you lose the other aspects of the word. A single word or phrase can have several meanings, all of which may be applicable. And to translate any one meaning is to rob the reader of a multifaceted perspective of the passage.

Rabbi: It is a polyvalent reading of a text. Hebrew is a particularly fine medium for polyvalency.

Talmidah: Because it is founded on triliteral consonantal roots which relate to one another in meaning.

Rabbi: Why is this important?

Talmidah: Because the original Hebrew text contains no vowel letters or vowel points. These were added by the Masoretes between 800 C.E. and 1000 C.E.

Rabbi: A rather bold form of interpretation I might add.

Talmidah: Because it restricted possibilities for other words. So for over one thousand years the vowels for the text were supplied orally.

Rabbi: Oral reading during synagogue services mandated vocalizing vowels, of course. But the text itself was not voweled.

Talmidah: So you can play around with different vowel letters or vowel points to get different words.

Rabbi: Which in turn could be read polyvalently. A good example is *afar* versus *ofar.*

Talmidah: I remember that from Bereshith Rabbah![5] Instead of reading "God made man from *dust*," you can read, "God made man *a youth*." And from there the rabbis wrote volumes about Adam's youthful physique, both literal and metaphorical.

Rabbi: What does the root *adm* mean?

---

5. XIV.7. A midrash on Genesis, part of a larger collection of exegetical debates compiled between 400–650 C.E., called *Midrash Rabbah* (The Great Midrash).

Talmidah: It can mean "man," *adam* . . . "red," *adom* . . . or "earth," *adama*. Rabbi Eliezer utilized these meanings in his commentary on the word adam. He writes, "Rabbi Yehuda said: Because of the name *adama* (earth) whence he was taken, his name was called Adam. Rabbi Joshua ben Korchah said: He was called Adam because of his flesh and blood,"[6] blood implied by the word "red."

Rabbi: How would a targumist present the same argument?

Talmidah: He wouldn't argue. He'd just translate "red earth man."

Rabbi: Is he a fraud for doing so?

Talmidah: No, of course not. It's actually a literal polyvalent reading of one word. But targumists do more than just play around with vowel points, Rabbi.

Rabbi: Correct. Remember there are more elements in Hebrew you can "play around with." Certain consonants are interchangeable because their sounds are similar.

Talmidah: Like *or*/"skin," and *or*/"light."

Rabbi: Yes. The *ayin* and *aleph* consonants at the beginning of these words are nearly silent, functioning more as vowel markers than "real" consonants.

---

6. *Pirke de-Rabbi Eliezer,* chap. XII. A medieval composition by an anonymous commentator between 650–900 C.E., printed in Constantinople in 1514. The author attributed his work to the famous tanna, Rabbi Eliezer son of Hyrkanos (Eliezer the Great) who lived in the later half of the first century C.E.

Talmidah: So that's where we get the legend that God made garments of light for Adam and Havah, instead of garments of skin.[7]

Rabbi: You forget the midrashic exploitation of these words, Talmidah. Think about the legend once more.

Talmidah: Well, the rabbinic debate on this wordplay is in several places. Some take it literally, that their garments were made of light. Others insist on a metaphorical meaning, that they wore garments of honor or righteousness.[8]

Rabbi: How did they derive these later meanings?

Talmidah: *Light* has metaphorical meanings as well as its literal one. I suppose they could have just as easily picked other words in the same way. I mean, *light* is also a metaphor for knowledge, revelation, or joy.

Rabbi: You are almost ready to enter the debate yourself, Talmidah. You have only to learn how to cite Scriptural passages in which *light* means knowledge, revelation, or joy, and then apply that meaning to our verse regarding the garments of light God made for Adam and Havah.

Talmidah: Using the logic of analogy, one of Rabbi Ishmael's thirteen hermeneutical rules for deriving interpretation.

Rabbi: Continue.

---

7. *Bereshith Rabbah* XIX.8.
8. *Bemidbar Rabbah* IV.8. A midrash on Numbers. See Note 5.

Talmidah: Well, some rabbis use this verse as a proof-text that when God formed man, He made a garment of light or glory . . . glory . . . that's another metaphorical use for *light* . . . for the man. Rabbi Eliezer taught that God made coats of *glory* from the *skin* of the serpent.[9] Some commentaries use the *or* wordplay to prove that the garments God made for Havah and Adam were garments of *honor* worn next to the *skin.*[10] Wait . . . Rabbi, these interpretations are impossible!

Rabbi: Explain.

Talmidah: Either the word is *or*/"skin," spelled with an *ayin,* or it is *or*/"light," spelled with an *aleph*. They can't *both* be right!

Rabbi: Why not?

Talmidah: Because even though the *ayin* and *aleph* are essentially silent and function as vowel markers, they are still consonants. They weren't added later to the text. Either the *ayin* as we have it in the Masoretic text has always been there, or it was mistakenly written down instead of *aleph* by a scribe. Which word is the correct one?

Rabbi: Yes. In the mind of a rabbinic translator or commentator, any possibility is important to the meaning of the text. Now, not only are similar-sounding consonants exchangeable, but similar-appearing consonants as well. For example, the *het* (ח) and *heh* (ה), the *yod* (י) and *wav* (ו), or the *bet* (ב) and *caph* (כ).

---

9. *Pirke de-Rabbi Eliezer,* chap. XX.
10. *Targum Onkelos.*

Talmidah: What about *shin* (שׁ) and *sin* (שׂ)? These consonants have identical symbols, the only difference being a marker added to the right or left of the symbol (שׁ, שׂ).

Rabbi: These markers being added later to avoid confusion. Flexibility is also allowed for consonant groupings, particularly the shifting of letters at the beginning and ending of words to adjacent words. This is acceptable for two reasons.

Talmidah: The original Hebrew text is thought to have been a continual script of consonants, a text with no word breaks at all. This we are taught by Nachmanides.

Rabbi: The existence of such an original text is in question. But even with a text of clearly defined groups of consonants, it is permissible to assume the possibility of scribal error.

Talmidah: You mean in copying the text, a scribe could have mistakenly written letters too close to one another or too far apart, so that letters could easily be attached to a different group of consonants.

Rabbi: Correct. Now we have barely discussed just a few of many possible ways in which a translator can "re-read" a passage of Hebrew Scripture,[11] but I think you have the idea.

Talmidah: Yes. This translating business is confusing. A single word could actually be several different words, each with its own set of literal and metaphorical meanings.

---

11. For a thorough treatment of possible textual emendations as well as a summary of various versions of Hebrew Scripture and their differences, see Emanuel Tov's *Textual Criticism of the Hebrew Bible* (Minneapolis: Fortress Press, 1992).

Rabbi: It makes the text rich in possibilities, Talmidah. You think of the Torah as a rigid, monolithic document carved on two tablets of stone. Not true! It is a fluid, almost living entity, as timely for today as yesterday because any student of Tradition of any age can look into it and see its divine message for him—or her—personally.

Talmidah: By immersing myself in all its possibilities I can emerge with a meaning that applies to me today.

Rabbi: Let us return to the bilingual person orally translating Hebrew Scripture during synagogue service. He repeats the phrase in Genesis, "So God created Man, male and female created He them," then adds, "in other words, God created an androgynous being." Is this person a fraud?

Talmidah: No. But neither is he a targumist. A targumist would not bother adding, "in other words." He'd simply say, "So God created Man, male and female, an androgynous being, created He them." That's fraud.

Rabbi: How so?

Talmidah: Because he makes no distinction between his own opinion and actual text. I can just imagine a fourth-century synagogue service during Simchas Torah.[12] The Torah reader cants the Hebrew portion of Genesis 1:1, roughly translated into English as:

---

12. The celebration marking the end of a one-year reading cycle of the Torah and the beginning of another.

> In the beginning God created the heavens and earth. And the earth was vacancy and desolation, solitary and void; and darkness was upon the face of the abyss, and the Spirit of God breathed upon the face of the waters.

Then the person orally translating the same text into Aramaic proceeds to give his version of *Targum Yerushalmi:*

> *In wisdom* the Lord created. And the earth was vacancy and desolation; solitary *of the sons of men,* and void *of every animal;* and darkness was upon the face of the abyss, and the Spirit of *mercies from before* the Lord breathed upon the face of the waters.

Most of the people sitting in the assembly don't understand Hebrew. They assume that everything the translator says is a literal translation of the Hebrew text. That's the fraud. It's a deception.

Rabbi: Could it be a nonliteral translation?

Talmidah: Certainly. But it is not marked as such. He did not bother to say something like, "Solitary of what? Rabbi Judah the Prince said the earth was empty of human beings and animals. Rabbi Akiva, on the other hand, taught that it was also empty of fish, birds, and plant life, for such were not created yet, as it is written . . ." etc., etc.

Rabbi: You want the translator to present the arguments then occurring in the prominent houses.

Talmidah: It is the only ethical approach to introducing commentary as part of a translation.

Rabbi: When you read through *Midrash Rabbah* on Genesis, how much space is devoted to these first two lines of Torah?

Talmidah: Well, these lines are the sole topic of chapter one of the midrash, which consists of fifteen sections of arguments. But they are included as well in other debates throughout the midrash on Genesis. I'm guessing you could double the first fifteen debates to thirty if you sifted through all the material.

Rabbi: These lines are also extensively commented upon in other midrashes, particularly the one on Psalms. We also find them *derashed* in the Talmud, the Zohar, and commentaries by nearly every rabbi and Jewish philosopher from Philo to Rashi. But to simplify matters, let us assume that *Midrash Rabbah* is the only source of commentary for this text. How long would the translator spend orating these arguments before the Torah Reader was allowed to continue reading the next few lines of scripture?

Talmidah: I see where you're going. Simchas Torah would turn into a reading marathon that would last for days instead of hours. It occurs to me that it would not be appropriate, not just because of the logistics of time, but because of the setting. Midrashic debates, such as we find in the Talmud and *Midrash Rabbah,* evolved from the dynamics of an academic environment and were in turn used in that same environment to stimulate further debate and learning. The purpose is to teach, to instruct and to develop mental abilities among students and their teachers. The synagogue, on the other hand, is a place of worship. Its purpose is to bind community members in a feeling of unity, to strengthen each individual for life outside the synagogue. Instruction is meant not so much to educate the intellect, but to inspire the emotions. For this to happen the Torah reading must be made relevant to those people sitting in the congregation, and must be made simple enough to be comprehended without rabbinic training. In that situation, an oral recitation of midrashic arguments is inappropriate.

Rabbi: A different purpose evolved a different form. But the rules for translation and commentary are the same for both forms.

Talmidah: Midrash outlines the process in detail. Targum merely presents the results. No . . . it actually presents the results of one line of argument.

Rabbi: Which the targumist believes to be the correct conclusion.

Talmidah: Which leaves the possibility open that he is indeed a pious individual presenting what he believes to be the "true" translation and its "true" interpretation. He thinks, "this is what the Torah means." I still don't like it.

Rabbi: Why not?

Talmidah: It's so . . . presumptuous. Who is he to pretend that he knows what Moses intended when he wrote the Torah!

Rabbi: You think Moses wrote the Torah?

Talmidah: Of course! Is it not written, "Moses received Torah from Sinai and handed it on to Joshua, and Joshua to the elders, and the elders to the prophets, and the prophets handed it on to the men of the Great Assembly"?[13] Moses *did* write the Torah, didn't he?

---

13. *Pirke Avot* I.1.

Rabbi: Did he? You will tell me who wrote the Torah tomorrow. There are resources in the library. We will meet at the same time at the same place.

Talmidah: But, I thought Mo . . .

Rabbi: Shalom, Talmidah, until tomorrow.

Rabbi: Who wrote the Torah?

Talmidah: It appears that everybody *but* Moses wrote the Torah. If Moses wrote a Torah it has long since disappeared.

Rabbi: Explain.

Talmidah: There is evidence of several minds at work in the Torah. Leviticus and the first chapter of Genesis, for example, appear to be composed by a priestly writer, whom scholars label "P." Apparently, many of the stories in Torah were written by a scribe whom we call "J" because he consistently refers to God as "Yahweh."[14] The remnant of a second storyteller is also evident, called "E," because he refers to God as "Elohim." Deuteronomy is a product of "D," the Deuteronomist. The work of at least two editors is evident, although the ultimate redactor, "R," is responsible for the final product we have today. So what we basically have is an alphabet soup, à la Torah.

14. The Hebrew word in question begins with a *yod,* which early biblical scholars pronounced as a *j*, even though such a sound does not exist in Hebrew. Modern scholarship pronounces the *yod* as a *y*.

Rabbi: I see. P, J, E, D, and R formed a committee and mixed together a scriptural stew between them.

Talmidah: No, no, no. That's not how it happened! Before the nation of Israel united under King David, each tribal unit had their own traditions about primeval and patriarchal history. Whether these traditions were strictly oral or written down is debatable. I personally believe that Moses wrote a Torah, which was then disseminated among the tribes, each copy undergoing revision or supplementation to incorporate existing tribal traditions. That, however, is insupportable and solely my own feeling.

Rabbi: Because you cherish the Mishnaic tradition of a revelation on Mount Sinai which gave Moses oral and written Torah from the very beginning. Certainly it is your prerogative to defend Tradition, given the lack of evidence either way. Continue.

Talmidah: According to the Documentary Hypothesis first introduced a hundred years ago by Julius Wellhausen,[15] and subsequently refined by scholarship since then,[16] J was a scribe in a Judean court sometime between the reign of King David and King Jehoram, between 1000 B.C.E. and 722 B.C.E.[17]

---

15. 1844–1918. A German biblical scholar. Wellhausen actually represents the culmination of several hypotheses regarding the composite nature of the Biblical text. The first to break from the idea of the Five Books of Moses as a monolithic text written by Moses himself was Jean Astruc in 1753.

16. The specific details of the Documentary Hypothesis utilized by this author are summarized in Richard Elliott Friedman's *Who Wrote the Bible?* (New York: Harper and Row, 1987).

17. Friedman narrows J's scribal activity to between 848–722 B.C.E.

When the Davidic monarchy split into a northern and southern kingdom, the northern kingdom of Israel produced its rival Torah, E, sometime between 922–722 B.C.E. In the meantime, a priestly scribe wrote a Torah which centered on the temple cultus and its seasonal observances, possibly as a polemic against king-centered J and E. It is thought by some that D showed up during the reign of Josiah, between 640 and 610 B.C.E., written by none other than Jeremiah the Prophet as an ethical polemic against P's legalistic Torah and J and E's monarchical Torah. Sometime later, after Judeans returned from their exile in Babylon, Ezra the Scribe redacted all of these versions into one cohesive Torah during the late fifth century B.C.E. R is pretty much the Torah we have today.

Rabbi: The details of this hypothesis change periodically among scholars. But its basic premise continues to hold fast.

Talmidah: The premise being that the Torah is a composite of texts.

Rabbi: How would you describe Ezra's work?

Talmidah: It's a cut-and-paste job. We have pieces of P fused with large chunks of J and bits of E. Leviticus and Deuteronomy are left intact, though there are editorial passages detectable throughout their texts.

Rabbi: Why didn't Ezra start from scratch and write a whole new Torah? Why bother trying to fit conflicting, often mutually-antagonistic texts together?

Talmidah: Scholars theorize that Ezra had to work with texts already regarded as sacred by his people in order to get the final version accepted. Ezra's primary purpose was to unite his people under a priestly government after seventy years of exile under foreign rule. So his final redaction of the Torah helped to supply his new governing body with credibility by combining texts revered by every faction. I suppose you could say that the Torah we have today is a monumental irony.

Rabbi: How so?

Talmidah: Because Ezra—if that who R is—spliced together texts which were originally written as polemics against one another. Certainly their authors would have turned over in their graves to see their work combined with that of their rivals to produce, I'm sure, a text far different from what any of them intended.

Rabbi: That is the second time in two days you have used the word *intended.* Of what relevance is *intent?*

Talmidah: What relevance is intent? Why, it's everything, Rabbi! Particularly when you are translating and commenting upon a text, as we were discussing yesterday.

Rabbi: How so?

Talmidah: The whole purpose of translating and commenting upon a text is to convey to a reader of one language what an author meant to say in another language.

Rabbi: Is it? How do you determine intent, Talmidah?

Talmidah: Well . . . you should be familiar with the author's background, his philosophy of life, his mode of expression, and his other writings if they exist. It would help to know the cultural and social milieu he functioned in, his experiences within that milieu, what contemporary authors were writing, what ideas and texts he may have been exposed to, etc. I mean, the more you know about a writer and his context, the easier it is to understand what he may have intended when he wrote a particular passage.

Rabbi: And how much do we know about J, E, P, D, and R?

Talmidah: Oh.

Rabbi: Much of what you described could be conjectured, based on anthropology, contemporary documents, and the text of the Bible itself.

Talmidah: But nothing can be proven. Nothing concrete or specific. Certainly very little can be found out about these authors as individuals. It's utterly hopeless!

Rabbi: I see. The whole process is a waste of time. Is that what you're saying? Let's throw out the Mishna, the Talmud, every targum, all midrash, and all the commentaries. It's all a colossal waste of time.

Talmidah: No! No, that's not what I meant! It's just that we can't know for sure what the original intent of a document like the Torah may have been. It's too old. Not only that, but it's a composite of many old texts, each with intents we don't know about. Debate is pointless, Rabbi, because there can never be a winner. There's just no way of knowing which translation or which interpretation may be the correct one.

Rabbi: Is a "correct" interpretation necessary? Talmidah, what is the purpose of sacred literature?

Talmidah: It provides me with a system of ethics by which to live my life. And it teaches me the "whys" of life.

Rabbi: . . . as opposed to the "how" of life, which is the purpose of science. But does it really teach you the "whys"?

Talmidah: In a roundabout way. Tradition actually teaches me what sages through the ages have thought as they wrestled with the "whys," and presents a never-ending parade of possibilities.

Rabbi: And how are new "whys" presented?

Talmidah: A sage will attempt to build upon the arguments of previous sages. If there is no precedent for his thought expressed by a rabbinic predecessor, he will *derash,* or derive it from the Torah itself using one or more accepted hermeneutical techniques.

Rabbi: How does he determine which materials he will use in his presentation, and which he will ignore?

Talmidah: Every student of Tradition must sift through the words of the sages, Rabbi. We are taught that in tractate *Avot* in the Mishna.[18] We must sift through their teachings and in that process discard the coarse flour while retaining the fine.

Rabbi: But what determines coarse from fine?

Talmidah: One student's coarse is another student's fine.

---

18. *Pirke Avot* V.15.

Rabbi: You have learned well. Each student must find those bits and pieces of "truth" which answer the "whys" of life for him and combine them together into something cohesive, perhaps new.

Talmidah: The way Ezra did with the Torah.

Rabbi: And the way the targumist did.

Talmidah: I see. You wanted me to understand that a targum is no more fraudulent than the Torah itself. They are both composites of old material, their combination producing something new.

Rabbi: In other words, he presents his new argument in an old form. Why is this process even necessary? Haven't the answers all been hashed out long ago?

Talmidah: I suppose every generation faces its own set of challenges—circumstances, crises, and social conditions unique to itself. To meet the challenges of a changing environment, old ideas must be expanded. A Torah was needed for a new nation struggling to unite itself. Another was needed for a people exiled throughout the world. Still another is needed for a world of technology. I see what you are getting at, Rabbi. It doesn't matter what the original intent of the author was. The important thing is to derive meaningful content from the document today. If a text is capable of yielding "whys" to the questions of life that beset me today in the twentieth century as effectively as it yielded them to a shopkeeper in Jerusalem twenty-five hundred years ago, it is truly the ultimate "teaching."

Rabbi: So the sages taught, "Even that which a gifted student was destined to teach in the presence of his master was already said to Moses on Sinai."[19]

Talmidah: Meaning that all exegesis, even that which has not yet been thought of or written down, is already present within Torah.

Rabbi: Now let us return to our original discussion regarding targum.

Talmidah: I don't see how. . . . Rabbi, targums were relevant to people a thousand years ago who spoke Aramaic.

Rabbi: But do you agree that its form is a legitimate one, as valid as midrash?

Talmidah: I have to agree that every text in Tradition is a composite of texts, including the Torah itself. Targum presents itself the same way the Torah presents itself, as a fluid and cohesive unit, though in reality they are composed of a variety of texts which preceded them.

Rabbi: You did not waste your time at the library. Now, before we meet next time, I want you to write a targum.

Talmidah: What!

Rabbi: Choose a story or logical pericope of Scripture which you are particularly interested in.

---

19. *Peah* 17a, Talmud Yerushalmi.

Talmidah: Me?! You want *me* to translate scripture into *Aramaic?!*

Rabbi: No. I want you to translate Scripture into English.

Talmidah: But a targum is a translation of Scripture into Aramaic.

Rabbi: Why did Onkelos translate the Torah into Aramaic eighteen hundred years ago?

Talmidah: Because Aramaic was the lingua franca of the day.

Rabbi: At least for the Near East. What is the lingua franca today?

Talmidah: English. I see. Aramaic and English are related to one another by analogy.

Rabbi: This is not to be simply a translation.

Talmidah: I'm suppose to lard it with commentary.

Rabbi: Commentary based on precedent or derived logically from Scripture.

Talmidah: I can't believe this is happening to me . . .

Rabbi: You may include commentaries by past sages, so long as they are presented in a way that preserves the character of targum.

Talmidah: Instead of midrash. How long do I have to do this?

Rabbi: Passover starts tomorrow. You have a week and a day. Do as much as you can in that period of time.

Talmidah: *One week!*

Rabbi: And a day.

Talmidah: Anything else? Like parting the Atlantic Ocean? Or making the sun stand still for three days?

Rabbi: I will invite one of my other students to our next session to challenge your work.

Talmidah: Great. Anybody I know?

Rabbi: He will be a worthy adversary. *Hag sameah.*

Talmidah: Happy holiday to you, too . . . Master.

Rabbi: I am gratified to hear you use a much-neglected translation for *rabbi*. Shalom, Talmidah, until we meet again.

[Several hours before meeting with her rabbi at the bet-midrash, Talmidah gave him a copy of her targum for Genesis 1:26–31, to be given in turn to her as-yet-unknown adversary. She provided the following explanatory note.]

> Rabbi,
>
> I formatted my targum so that translated Scripture can be distinguished from commentary. Commentary and scriptural passages from outside my chosen pericope are set apart in

italics. Polyvalent readings of Scripture are singled out by two methods:

1. Slashes (/) between polyvalent readings of a single word. Example: over/upon . . . breath/spirit

2. Polyvalent readings of phrases are indented and aligned with one another. Example: They shall descend among
rule over

"Descend among" and "rule over" are polyvalent readings of the same phrase.

I will see you in session at the time and place agreed upon.

Talmidah

1

"Male and Female" Genesis 1:26–31

Targum

Elohim, Eternal God, said *to the angels who ministered before him,*[1] Gen 1:26

"Let us make mankind in our image, after our likeness
We will prepare earthly man to look like us, to be like us
They shall descend among
rule over
the fish of the sea
the bird of the sky
the beast
all earthly life
even every creeping thing that creeps

1. *Targum Yerushalmi.*

every moving thing that moves
every gliding thing that glides
over/upon the earth"

"What shall his character be?" asked they. "Righteous men shall spring from him," He answered. He revealed to them that the righteous would arise from him, but He did not reveal to them that the wicked would spring from him, for had He revealed to them that the wicked would spring from him, Justice would not have permitted him to be created. The ministering angels formed themselves into groups and parties, some of them saying, "Let him be created," while others urged, "Let him not be created." Love said, "Let him be created, because he will dispense acts of love"; Truth said, "Let him not be created, because he is compounded of falsehood"; Righteousness said, "Let him be created, because he will perform righteous deeds"; Peace said, "Let him not be created, because he is full of strife." While the ministering angels were arguing with each other and disputing with each other, the Holy One, blessed be He, created him. Said He to them, "What can you do about it? Man has already been made!"[2]

Said the ministering angels to the Lord, "Sovereign of the Universe! What is man, that you should regard him, and the son of man, that you should even think about of him? This trouble, for what has it been created?" Said He to them, "What about sheep and oxen, all of them, why were they created? Why were the birds of the air and the fish of the sea created? A tower full of good things and no guests—what pleasure has its owner in having filled it?"[3]

---

2. *Bereshith Rabbah*, VIII.4, 5.
3. *Bereshith Rabbah*, VIII.6. This is an expansion of Psalms 8:5.

The matter may be compared to a king of flesh and blood who built palaces and furnished them, prepared a banquet and thereafter brought in the guests. This refers to Adam and Havah.[4]

Yahweh Elohim formed red earth man *2:7a*
of dust from the earth

Adam/man in the Hebrew tongue signifies "one that is red," because he was formed out of red earth, compounded together; for of that kind is virgin and true earth.[5]

The name for mankind indicates dust, blood and gall.[6]
Afar/dust is masculine, while *adamah*/earth is feminine: a potter takes male dust and female earth in order that his vessels may be sound.[7]

He began to collect the dust of the first man from the four corners of the earth: red, black, white, and pale green.[8] And he took from the four winds of the world, and mixed from all the waters of the world and created him red, black, and white.[9]

And where is it shown that man is the hallah of the world? Thus have our masters taught: Once the woman puts water into the dough, she is to remove her hallah. Thus did the Holy

4. *Sanhedrin* 38a, Talmud Bavli.

5. Josephus, *Antiquities*, I.1.2. Flavius Josephus (born Joseph ben Mat-thias) was a Roman historian who lived between 37 C.E. and about 100 C.E.

6. *Sotah* 5a, Talmud Bavli.

7. *Bereshith Rabbah* XIV.7.

8. *Pirke de-Rabbi Eliezer*, chap. XI.

9. *Targum Yerushalmi*.

One do. Once the Holy One put water on the earth, he immediately removed man as his hallah from the earth.[10]

2:7b And breathed into his nostrils the breath/spirit of eternal life. Thus earthly man became a living soul.

From invisible and visible substances I created man.
From both his natures come both death and life.
And as my image he knows the word like no other creature.
But even at his greatest he is small,
and again at his smallest he is great.
his flesh from earth
his blood from dew and from the sun
his eyes from the bottomless sea;
his bones from stone
his reason from the mobility of angels and from clouds
his veins and hair from the grass of the earth
his spirit from my spirit and from wind.[11]

Six things are said of human beings: in regard to three they are like the ministering angels, and in regard to three they are like beasts. They are like the ministering angels because they have understanding, they walk erect and they can talk in the holy tongue. They are like beasts because they eat and drink, propagate and defecate.[12]

---

10. *Tanhuma Bereshith*. The concept of man as God's hallah is also found in *Bereshith Rabbah* XIV.1. *Tanhuma Bereshith* is part of a larger corpus of midrashic literature attributed to Rabbi Tanhuma. Estimates of its compilation date range from 800 C.E. to 1500 C.E.

11. 2 Enoch 30:8, J recension. A pseudepigraphal work composed in the late first century C.E.

12. *Hagigah* 16a, Talmud Bavli.

Some things are of a mixed nature, like man, who is capable of opposite qualities, of wisdom and folly, of temperance and dissoluteness, of courage and cowardice, of justice and injustice, in short of good and evil, of what is honorable and what is disgraceful, of virtue and vice. Man is the best of all earthborn and perishable productions—a short-lived heaven if one were to speak the truth, bearing within himself many starlike natures. He was born at the same time both mortal and immortal. Mortal as to his body, but immortal as to his intellect.[13]

Since how could the soul have perceived God if he had not inspired it, and touched it according to his power? For human intellect would not have dared to mount up to such a height as to lay claim to the nature of god, if God himself had not drawn it up to himself.[14]

Elohim fashioned mankind in the image *1:27*
in the image of Elohim he fashioned them
male and female
man and woman
He fashioned them.

Male and female He created them
to make known the Glory on high
From here we learn:
Any image that does not embrace male and female
is not a high and true image
Come and see:

13. Philo, *On the Creation*, XXIV, XXVII, XLVI. Philo was a Jewish philosopher who lived in Alexandria from about 20 B.C.E. to 50 C.E.

14. Philo, *Allegorical Interpretation I,* XIII.

The blessed Holy One does not place His abode
in any place where male and female are not found together.[15]

The Lord with his own two hands created mankind; in a facsimile of his own face, both small and great, the Lord created them. And whoever insults a person's face, insults the face of a king, and treats the face of the Lord with repugnance. He who treats with contempt the face of any person treats the face of the Lord with contempt.[16]

"A man's wisdom maketh his face to shine." Who is the wise man? This alludes to Adam. His beauty made his face to shine.[17] There was a lustrous light on both the faces of Adam and Havah.[18]

This is the light that the Blessed Holy One created at first.
It is the light of the eye.
It is the light that the Blessed Holy One showed the first Adam;
with it he saw from one end of the world to the other.[19]
With the light that the Blessed Holy One created on the First Day, Adam could see from one end of the world to the other.[20]

---

15. *Zohar*, pp. 55–56. The *Book of Splendor* was written in Aramaic by a Spanish Jewish mystic named Moshe de Leon in the latter half of the thirteenth century. He wrote in the name of Rabbi Shimon, son of Yohai, a famous tanna of the second century C.E. Page numbers refer to Daniel Chanen Matt's translation.

16. 2 Enoch 44:1–2, J recension.

17. *Bereshith Rabbah* VIII.2.

18. *Pesikta Rabbati*, Piska 23.6. A collection of rabbinic discourses compiled during the ninth century C.E.

19. *Zohar*, p. 51.

20. *Hagigah* 12a, Talmud Bavli.

The light that is revealed is called the Garment of the King.[21]

God made garments for mankind which were like those of the angels.[22]
Clothed in majesty and splendour,
wrapped in light as a garment.[23]
The soul of man is the lamp of the Lord *Prov 20:27*

Then Elohim blessed them, saying to them, *Gen 1:28*
"Be fruitful and multiply
become numerous
become great
Spread abroad and become many[24]
Fill the earth with sons and daughters[25]
and be strong upon it[26]
and master it
descend among
rule over
the flesh of the sea
the bird of the sky
and all life that creeps
moves
glides
over/on the earth

Elohim said, "Lo! I gave to you *1:29*
dedicated to you
entrusted to you

---

21. *Zohar,* p. 187.
22. *Yalkut Shimoni* I.34, as quoted by Ginzberg, vol. 5, p. 104.
23. Psalms 104:2.
24. *Targum Onkelos.*
25. *Targum Yerushalmi.*
26. *Targum Yerushalmi.*

every seed-bearing plant
which is upon the face of the whole earth
and every tree yielding seed-bearing tree-fruit.
This will be your food.

1:30 And to every beast of earth
and to every bird of sky
and to everything that creeps
moves
glides
on/over the earth
in which there is a living, breathing soul
in which there is life's passion/appetite/desire
I give every green plant for food."
And it was so.

So the Lord set everything forth for the sake of mankind, and he created the whole of creation for his sake.[27]

"Behold My works! how beautiful and commendable they are! All that I have created, I created for your sake."[28]

1:31a Elohim perceived
all that he made
prepared
put in order
and lo!
It was very good!
very excellent!
very pleasing and fair!

---

27. 2 Enoch 65:3, J recension.

28. *Qohelet Rabbah* VII.1. A midrash on Ecclesiastes. See note 5, Introduction.

"very"/*me-od* is identical to *adam*/mankind
"And lo! Mankind was good!"[29]

And on the earth I assigned him to be a second angel, honored and great and glorious. And I assigned him to be a king, to reign on the earth, to have my wisdom. And there was nothing comparable to him on the earth, even among my creatures that exist.[30]

This is the book of the generations *5:1*
begettings
accounting
of mankind
At the time when Elohim fashioned mankind.

In the likeness of Divine Ones He shaped them, *5:2*
male and female
man and woman
He fashioned them
He blessed them and called their name Adam
at the time when they were fashioned.

Midrash

> There are four types among those that sit in the presence of the sages: the sponge, the funnel, the strainer and the sifter.
>
> —*Pirke Avot* V.21

---

29. *Bereshith Rabbah* VIII.5.
30. 2 Enoch 30:11–12.

Rabbi: Welcome to our session, Mitnagged. I trust you have had sufficient time to review Talmidah's targum.

Mitnagged: More than sufficient time, Rabbi. A few minutes was sufficient to ascertain enough holes in this pathetic dribble to serve as a strainer for my mother's kitchen, a more apt place for this female intruder on tradition, I might add.

Talmidah: I perceive that you yourself are a strainer.

Mitnagged: You refer to the Mishna's description of four types of students.

Talmidah: The strainer is one who lets the good wine pass through his ears and retains the *drek*, the garbage.

Mitnagged: And you are the funnel, a student who allows everything to pass through one ear and out the other, retaining absolutely nothing. In fact, I object to even calling you a student in the first place. Rabbi, this so-called targum illustrates the wisdom in keeping females out of the bet-midrash. As Rabbi Jeremiah said in the name of Rabbi Samuel, "It is the way of woman to remain at home, and for man to go into the market-place and learn intelligence from other men."[31] Rabbi Eliezer also taught that there is no wisdom for a woman except at the distaff. In other words, at domestic chores. Why? It is written in the Talmud that "women are light-minded."[32] Thus Rabbi Eliezer quoted the Serpent when reasoning his choice between man and woman to deceive, "I will speak to Havah,

31. *Bereshith Rabbah* 18:1.
32. *Shabbat* 33b, Talmud Bavli.

for I know that she will listen to me; for women listen to all creatures, as it is said. 'She is simple and knoweth nothing.'"[33] To teach a woman Hebrew and Aramaic, let alone exposing her to the texts that compose Tradition, is a grave mistake, as warned in the Mishna in tractate *Avot* where Rabbi Yose ben Johanan declared, "So long as a man talks overmuch with women he brings evil upon himself, neglects the study of Torah, and in the end Gehenna is his portion."

Talmidah: You are indeed the strainer, Mitnagged. Rabbi Jeremiah's words are part of his debate with other sages regarding the credibility of female witnesses in court. Rabbi Eliezar disagrees with Rabbi Jeremiah, saying, "She is endowed with more understanding than a man," and cites as proof that the testimony of a 12-year-old girl is allowable, but not that of a boy her same age. The Talmud does state that women are light-minded, but elsewhere in the Talmud it states, "God endowed woman with more intelligence than man."[34] You have cleverly taken Rabbi Eliezer's Serpent monologue out of its entire context. Let me refresh your memory regarding the first part of his reasoning: "The serpent argued with itself, saying: If I go and speak to Adam, I know that he will not listen to me, for a man is always hard to be persuaded, as it is said, 'For a man is churlish and evil in his doings.'" Rabbi Eliezer imputes to Adam stubbornness and evil intentions, whereas to Havah he merely attributes ignorance, ignorance meaning lack of information or knowledge, not lack of intelligence or ability. As to your citing of Rabbi Yose ben Johanan in *Pirke Avot,* you neglect a more logical interpretation of his words. Rashi's

33. Proverbs 9:13.
34. *Niddah* 45b, Talmud Bavli.

students interpret this passage to mean "idle chatter."[35] Menahem ben Solomon ha-Meiri said that this passage refers to conversation which is "entirely unnecessary." I ask you, is Torah "idle chatter"? Do you deem Torah study as "entirely unnecessary"?

Mitnagged: Of course not, but the rabbis taught, "Let the words of the Torah rather be destroyed by fire than imparted to a woman."[36]

Talmidah: The rabbis also taught that every man should teach his daughter Torah.[37]

Mitnagged: In the same debate you allude to, it is written, "Whoever teaches his daughter Torah, it is as though he taught her obscenity."

Talmidah: The sages taught, "If two sit together and the words between them are not of Torah, then that is a session of scorners, but if two sit together and the words between them are of Torah, then the Shekinah[38] is in their midst."[39] When you sit with your mother to eat the meal she prepared for you, do you share words of Torah with her?

Mitnagged: Of course not! She is not a fellow talmid!

---

35. *Machsor Vitry*, a compilation of commentaries written between 1040–1105 C.E.

36. *Sotah* 19a, Talmud Bavli.

37. *Sotah* III.4, Mishna.

38. The presence of God.

39. *Avot* III.3.

Talmidah: And whose fault is that? According to R. Hananiah, you are a scorner. Is it just you and your mother who eat at the table?

Midnagged: No, I have a sister and a younger brother. I fail to see what relevance my dinner conversation with my family has to this discussion.

Talmidah: When all of you are gathered together as a family at the dinner table, do you talk Torah?

Mitnagged: Of course not! Such conversation is entirely inappropriate for women and children.

Talmidah: According to Rabbi Simeon, you eat sacrifices to dead idols everytime you eat with your family without speaking Torah.

Mitnagged: What!

Talmidah: He said, "When three eat at one table and do not speak words of Torah there, it is as though they had eaten of the sacrifices to dead idols, as it is said, 'For all tables are full of filthy vomit, when God is absent.'[40] But when three eat at one table and do speak words of Torah there, it is as though they have eaten from the table of God, blessed be He, as it is

---

40. Cites Isaiah 28:8. According to rabbinic tradition, Torah study substitutes for temple worship. The table around which sages and their disciples discuss Torah symbolizes the temple altar. Words exchanged across the table are sacrifices. Depending on the quality and nature of the discussion, these "sacrifices" are either "sweet-smelling" to God, or sacrilegious "vomit."

said, 'And He said unto me, this is the table that is before the Lord.' "[41]

Mitnagged: This is outrageous! The sages never meant their words to be applied to anyone other than Rabbis and their *male* students.

Talmidah: Is that so? Where does it say that in the Mishna?

Mitnagged: It is implied in the Talmudic prohibition against women studying Torah.[42]

Talmidah: You refer to positive commandments from which a woman is *exempt,* not prohibited. A man must be commanded to study Torah. A woman may do so if she so desires.

Mitnagged: Such study is not to impede her domestic duties, which should be her most urgent priority.

Talmidah: Is that so? Suppose I define Torah as a vital and even the most important of my domestic duties, considering the fact that my table is an altar and the words I speak over the meal I prepared is an offering to the Holy One? I would assert that the words of Rabbi Hananiah and Simeon apply to *everyone.* Everytime you sit down with a woman and refuse to talk Torah with her, you prove yourself a scorner of tradition. Not only that, but you are guilty of idle chatter and worthy of Gehenna. But everytime you sit down with a woman and talk Torah with her you invite the Shekinah.

---

41. Ezekiel 41:22.
42. *Kiddushin* 1.7.

Mitnagged: You take the words of the sages and twist them to mean the opposite of their original intent.

Talmidah: Intent? Of what relevance is "intent" in a . . .

Rabbi: Ahem. That issue has already been discussed with both of you. As curious as I am to hear its finer points debated between you, I am more curious to hear Talmidah's targum discussed.

Talmidah: You mean attacked, shredded, and thrown away. This . . . Neanderthal has no interest in studying the merits of my targum at all. His only interest is in proving that a woman is too weak-minded to contribute anything worthwhile to Tradition.

Rabbi: Which guarantees a thorough examination of your work, Talmidah. Do you think the sages laid aside their personal antagonisms, rivalries, and prejudices when debating Torah among themselves?

Talmidah: Up to this moment I enjoyed the underlying personality conflicts running through the Talmud and midrashic texts. Now they are not so amusing.

Mitnagged: Because they are vicious? Argument and counterargument is the jousting tournament in Jewish Tradition. It is our version of bloody encounters between rival knights, each testing the strength, training, and intelligence of his opponent. *His* opponent. Such a battleground is no place for a lady, as you are beginning to see. If you do not like the taste of blood, get off the field.

Rabbi: In this case the tournament master has paired unseasoned, fledgling knights of equal weakness, inexperience, and ignorance.

Talmidah: You consider *him* my equal? He belongs in the stable shoveling manure from the tournament horses, for such is the material he loves to throw around. He is not worthy to be your student, Rabbi!

Rabbi: And *you* are?

Mitnagged: Hah!

Talmidah: Hand me my lance! Prepare to die, you wobbly-kneed black knight, for the black night that blinds your eyes with darkness will deliver you to the sharp edge of my tongue!

Mitnagged: A pointed tongue whose aim is pointless and therefore foolish and meaningless. It will require but one easy thrust to unhorse you.

Rabbi: Deliver the blow.

Mitnagged: This is not a targum.

Talmidah: What?

Rabbi: Explain.

Mitnagged: I base my judgment on the targums given to me by Rabbi to review: *Targum Onkelos, Targum of Palestine,* and *Targum Yerushalmi.* Your fantasy departs from these targums in two significant ways. First, and most importantly, you changed the Torah text itself. You deleted whole passages in your pericope, namely the last half of 1:31 and verses one through six in Chapter Two. You then rearranged the text by plugging 2:7 after 1:26 and tacking on 5:1–2 to the end of your composition. A targum maintains the integrity of the scriptural text it is translating by presenting *all* verses in *sequential* order as they appear in our Torah. A targum may supplement scripture with nonliteral translation and interpretation, but it may not break up scripture into bits and pieces to be arbitrarily rearranged. Even though we here may agree that Torah is a composite of texts, a targumist does not treat it as such. A targum assumes that the text it is translating is monolithic in nature, whole and complete as it stands. Is this not correct, Rabbi?

Rabbi: You are correct.

Talmidah: But in order for me to isolate a particular pericope—in this case the life story of Havah and Adam—it was necessary for me to extract it from P's Creation Account that overlapped it. For example, 1:31b through 2:4a makes no sense unless I began translating from the very beginning of the Torah—Genesis 1:1, which begins a numerical sequence of creative acts. I couldn't suddenly talk about the sixth and seventh days of the Creation Week without going through the other five days as well.

Mitnagged: Why not start with Genesis 1:1?

Talmidah: Because P's Creation Account is a cosmic description of the creation of heaven and earth which climaxes in Shabbat. J and E centers on mankind and humanity's relationship with God. Well you can read P's agenda for yourself, as it says in 1:31b–2:4a:

And there was evening and there was morning, the sixth day.

The heaven and the earth were finished, and all their array.

On the seventh day God finished the work that He had been doing, and He ceased on the seventh day from all the work that He had done.

And God blessed the seventh day and declared it holy, because on it God ceased from all the work of creation that He had done.

Such is the story of heaven and earth when they were created.[43]

I would have spent the entire week combing through commentaries on Shabbat—and there are *tons* of material on it, believe me—not to mention each of the creative acts with their commentaries on seasons, festival days, and all the elements of nature. I would have found myself walking down a path not of my choosing.

Mitnagged: But it would have been a path marked by Scripture.

Talmidah: No! It would have been a path marked by a priest interested in hallowing the Temple cult, a path that guarantees job security for him and his successors. Besides, this particular piece of my targum does not cover 1:26–2:7. It covers 1:26–31a. Verses 2:7 and 5:1–2 are scriptural midrashim dropped in to strengthen my line of interpretation. Verses 2:4b–2:6 are translated *in sequence* at the beginning of the next segment of my targum.

Mitnagged: What happens to 1:31b–2:4a?

43. JPS translation (Jewish Publication Society).

Talmidah: They are part of P's Creation Account and therefore irrelevant to my pericope.

Mitnagged: Your logic . . . or illogic . . . astounds me. Throw out five verses, just like that. It's nothing short of . . .

Rabbi: Redaction.

Talmidah: Redaction?

Rabbi: What letter of the alphabet do scholars assign Ezra?

Talmidah: R.

Mitnagged: For "Redactor."

Rabbi: Precisely. A redactor attempts to combine several versions of the same text through an editorial process which involves deletion, rearrangement, and transitional additions.

Midnagged: Which is precisely what we have here!

Rabbi: Not precisely.

Mitnagged: Then it is a targum on a redaction. A duck-billed platypus if I ever saw one.

Rabbi: I doubt you've ever seen one. Now, Talmidah raises two interesting issues. First, what precisely is her pericope?

Mitnagged: 1:26–2:7. She claims it only covers 1:26–31a.

Talmidah: No, I don't. I said this particular *piece* of my pericope covers 1:26–31a. The pericope I am translating is much larger—1:26–5:5.

Rabbi: If we confine our judgment to the document before us, which Talmidah spent Passover week translating and editing, I would have to side with Mitnagged. This is not a targum. It is a redaction of Torah supplemented with commentary. If we reserve our judgment until we have the entire pericope, as Talmidah defines it, we may decide otherwise. We shall table the matter until we see the entire text.

Mitnagged: You mean there's more of this vomit to lay on the altar of Torah?

Talmidah: It is vomit only to a dog that cannot digest human food.

Mitnagged: Human food? This is not fit even for swine.

Talmidah: You should know.

Rabbi: The second issue Talmidah addresses is the insertion of other scriptural passages as midrashic commentary. Is this allowed?

Mitnagged: No!

Talmidah: Yes! For all Torah is teaching, and therefore commentary which can be applied to Torah.

Mitnagged: A classic example of circular thinking.

Talmidah: A circle being complete and whole.

Mitnagged: A never-ending cycle of non sequiturs. Look, interscriptural citation as midrash does not occur in a targum.

Talmidah: Perhaps not in *Targum Onkelos, Palestine,* or *Yerushalmi,* though you could argue that allusions to other scriptural passages abound. But it does occur in other targums, particularly those on the Writings.

Mitnagged: Then you admit it does not occur in a targum on the Torah!

Talmidah: What is *Torah?*

Rabbi: Ahem. . . . We've already covered that issue.

Talmidah: But it is important! Rabbi, you told me that the status of scriptural text is irrelevant when we discuss targum. But I did not find this to be true. It seems that the lower the status, the more expanded the targum, the more commentary, and intrascriptural allusions and outright quotations are employed to interpret them. In targums *Job* and *Song of Songs,* for example, commentary and citations from other bodies of Scripture expand the original text fivefold. The nature of targum becomes more . . . how do I put it? . . .

Mitnagged: Irresponsible. . . .

Rabbi: Uninhibited. . . .

Talmidah: Open to inter- and intratextual interpretation.

Mitnagged: You touch on my second reason for rejecting this as a targum. The fact that this is not so much Scripture supplemented by interpretation as Scripture *drowning* in commentary. One could lose your eyesight looking for strands of Scripture floating in a vast sea of midrash.

Talmidah: I can understand your predicament, Mitnagged. Your eyesight would qualify you for the esteemed occupation of Blind Beggar at Jaffa Gate. Look, the issue is one and the same. What is *Torah?* Ancient targumists treated the Torah, Prophets, and Writings differently.

Rabbi: Mitnagged, do you agree with her assessment of the way targumists treated different levels of Scripture?

Mitnagged: How can I make such a judgment? You only gave me targums on the Torah.

Rabbi: I gave you what I gave Talmidah. It is a poor student who does not go beyond what his teacher gives him.

Mitnagged: I will be better prepared next time.

Rabbi: For your sake, I hope so, for Talmidah is about to puncture your armor.

Talmidah: I chose to treat my pericope of Torah the way ancient targumists treated other books of Scripture.

Mitnagged: But you can't do that! They are different!

Talmidah: What is *Torah?* Torah is not only a specific text—the Five Books of Moses—but it is all Scripture.

Mitnagged: But the Five Books of Moses are more sacred and therefore must be treated in a more conservative manner.

Talmidah: Why?

Mitnagged: Because Moses wrote . . .

Rabbi: Yes?

Talmidah: Who wrote the Torah?

Mitnagged: Never mind!

Rabbi: The other question before us is whether Talmidah's creative placement of 2:7 and 5:1–2 should be considered the editorial activity of a redactor, or commentary-via-citation by a targumist. This should be easily determined, for both of these passages are part of Talmidah's self-defined pericope. Mitnagged?

Mitnagged: How can I determine this? I don't have the rest of her composition.

Rabbi: Ask the pertinent question.

Mitnagged: Very well. . . . In your so-called targum, do you actually present these same passages again in their proper sequence?

Talmidah: 5:1–2 occurs again in the "right" place, namely between 4:26 and 5:5.

Mitnagged: And 2:7? . . . I can't hear you, Talmidah. Stop mumbling and say it louder.

Talmidah: No.

Mitnagged: Hah!

Talmidah: I put it in a more logical place.

Mitnagged: You certainly did! You eliminated the source of many a rabbinic debate over the past nineteen hundred years—the fact that there are *two* accounts of the creation of man. You collapsed two separate stories into one account. How convenient!

Rabbi: So far you have both managed to deal impressive blows upon your opponent. I am not disappointed. Now to particular matters of translation. Mitnagged?

Mitnagged: I don't understand what you want me to do.

Rabbi: Are there no specific words or phrases in Talmidah's translation that you feel compelled to challenge?

Mitnagged: I didn't know I was supposed to do that.

Rabbi: What did you *think* you were supposed to do?

Mitnagged: I thought I was supposed to challenge Talmidah's targum. Since it is not a targum, there is nothing to challenge.

Rabbi: I see. It was easier to attack the whole composition rather than to analyze its specific components. How convenient.

Mitnagged: I will be better prepared next time.

Rabbi: I hope you survive your foolish negligence. Now I shall do what you should have been prepared to do today, and which I expect you to do next time we meet. I shall question Talmidah concerning three specific phrases which I view as unusual and significant in their interpretative implications. Talmidah, in verse 1:26, you translate *ve-iredu-be* polyvalently. Explain.

Talmidah: This phrase is traditionally translated "rule over" or "have dominion over," based on the word *radah*/"rule." But it could also be read "descend among," based on the word *yarad*/"descend." This is possible because these words both contain vowel letters, *yod* and *heh*, which often disappear when these words are conjugated.

Rabbi: Mitnagged, do you have any objections to Talmidah's additional reading of "descend among" in this verse? No? It happens to be extremely significant.

Mitnagged: It is?

Talmidah: It is?

Rabbi: The verse now reads that the first man and woman *descended.* To where did they descend?

Talmidah: To where the animals and birds were . . . to the earth.

Rabbi: And where did they descend *from?* Mitnagged?

Mitnagged: Well . . . they . . . they couldn't have descended from anywhere. Man was created from the dust of the earth, as it is written in 2:7, "God formed man from the dust of the earth." Having been formed of the earth at his creation, he was already *on* the earth. As for Woman, she was created from a rib of Man, as it is written in 2:22, "And the Lord God fashioned the rib that he had taken from the man into a woman." Since she was created from Man, who was already on the earth, she too was already on the earth at the time of her creation.

Rabbi: Talmidah?

Talmidah: I don't know.

Rabbi: You don't *know?*

Talmidah: I was just experimenting with different readings of a Hebrew root, Rabbi. I thought it was a clever double-reading so I put it in. It sounded good.

Rabbi: To which meaning of *tov* do you refer?

Talmidah: Rabbi, please. I don't understand what the big deal is.

Rabbi: That is quite obvious. You accidentally translated a Hebrew root into a word that could change the meaning and direction of your entire pericope. Your enemy is lying helplessly ignorant at your feet while you stand there with a lethal weapon in your hand, unable to deliver the blow because of your own ignorance.

Talmidah: What is its significance?

Rabbi: I will not do your work for you, Talmidah. I will say that the word *descend* has significance in ancient Merkavah literature.

Talmidah: Merkavah . . . "chariot" . . . mystical accounts of prophets and patriarchs ascending to the chariot, or throne, of God.

Mitnagged: Based on scriptural accounts of chariot visions by Daniel and Ezekiel.[44]

Talmidah: They were ascenders to the throne of God. Only, the odd thing about it is that they called themselves *yoradim*, "descenders." Anyway, merkavah visionary accounts are considered the predecessors of Jewish mysticism.

Mitnagged: Kaballah? I don't get it.

Talmidah: I don't either. Rabbi, why are you putting your head on the table?

Rabbi: Funnels. Both of them. Funnels.

Talmidah: Wait a minute. Where is the Chariot of God?

Mitnagged: In the inner chamber of the Heavenly Temple, located in the seventh, or highest, heaven.

Talmidah: That's right!

Mitnagged: Oh no . . . you don't seriously . . .

Rabbi: The light dawns.

---

44. Daniel 7, Ezekiel 1.

Talmidah: Well, this certainly puts a different slant on the origin of man . . . and woman.

Mitnagged: This is clearly heretical.

Rabbi: Prove it, next time we meet. As for you, Talmidah, you must either support or retract your alternate reading of this word, with all its implications. If you are able to retain it, it will prove most helpful to the remainder of your targum.

Talmidah: How?

Rabbi: Are you asking how to support your translation, or how your translation will support your targum?

Talmidah: Yes.

Rabbi: That is for you to work out.

Talmidah: But I haven't even translated the whole pericope yet. And I don't see anything in what I've done so far that seems to need "descend" to support it.

Rabbi: I suggest you apply yourself more vigorously. I trust Mitnagged will do so.

Mitnagged: I most certainly will.

Talmidah: I have a better idea. Let *him* write a targum, and let *me* be on the offensive for a change.

Rabbi: Ahhh, but this is far more interesting. I am curious to see how you manage this narrative, Talmidah. I find the female voice to be most intriguing.

Mitnagged: I find it to be most nauseating.

Rabbi: Yes, well, we shall see. Now for a less controversial, yet interesting translation of the word *chaim* in 2:7, normally translated as "life," but which you translated as "eternal life." Explain your logic.

Talmidah: Well, *chaim* is actually a plural form of the word *chai*. I remembered how the rabbis explained the plural *Elohim* as a title for God, and why verbs applied to this plural are singular. According to them, a plural form of a singular entity conveys the concept of "multiple," "on-going," "never-ending."[45] In other words, "eternal."

Rabbi: The sages then derived the meaning of "justice" from this word, based on this concept of God as unchangeable and everlasting in judgment.

Mitnagged: While "Yahweh" expresses his attribute of mercy.

Talmidah: I applied the principle of analogy. If the concept of "eternal" can be applied to a plural-singular in one passage of Torah—in this case Gods/God—it can be applied to another plural-singular in another passage.

Rabbi: The sages employed a similar logic for explaining the plural form of "holy" in Joshua 24:19: "For he is a holys/holy God." As it is written, "He is holy/all kind of holiness," the perfect, eternal kind of holiness applicable only to God.[46]

---

45. *Bereshith Rabbah* VIII.9.
46. *Beracot* 13a, Talmud Bavli.

Mitnagged: There are other midrashim on the word *chaim* as "lives." The one that comes to my mind is the notion that man has more than one soul.

Tamidah: Five . . . the *nephesh,* the *ru'ah,* the *neshamah,* the *yehidah,* and *cayyah.* That's kabbalah.

Rabbi: It is also rabbinic and neoplatonic. They are utilized by various sectors of Judaism to symbolize abstract concepts unique to their religious philosophy. Kabbalah does, however, exploit the idea of five souls in the most detailed, imaginative fashion, integrating them in an elaborate scheme of the cosmos.

Mitnagged: Seems like we keep bumping into mystic concepts.

Rabbi: That is because the originators of Jewish mysticism followed the same hermeneutic rules to derive meaning from the Biblical text as do our more "down to earth" interpreters. I am curious why you did not choose that line of interpretation, Talmidah. It is rich with possibilities regarding the psychological makeup of humanity.

Talmidah: Rabbi, you know I am not partial to kabbalah or any other form of mysticism, ancient or modern.

Rabbi: You do not seem to object to Jewish philosophy, as represented by Philo in your targum. If you study him more vigorously, I think you will find shared symbols between the two extremes of mysticism and philosophy, though interpreted differently. In fact, one could argue that mysticism founds itself on the ideas and symbols of philosophy.

Talmidah: Perhaps I am being too hasty. I shall do as you say. In any case you told me to write a targum, which means presenting the line of interpretation I feel most comfortable with.

Mitnagged: Right. The one that all but declares that Adam and Havah descended from the throne of God.

Rabbi: It was not so obvious to you at first, Mitnagged—not to you or to Talmidah.

Talmidah: It would only occur to someone steeped in Merkavah literature.

Rabbi: Or unconsciously to someone who would like to rewrite the story of Adam and Havah so that the status of women might be elevated.

Talmidah: I hadn't thought of that. In fact, I don't think it's coincidental that I felt drawn to this particular pericope of Scripture.

Rabbi: It was no surprise to me at all. I would say that the majority of rabbinic arguments regarding women are derived from the Adam and Havah narrative. The brief exchange of semi-intelligent debate between you and Mitnagged regarding female character at the beginning of our session serves as a case in point. Nearly every argument presented by you and your opponent can ultimately be traced to these particular scriptural passages.

Mitnagged: Of course. As the primal ancestors of humanity, Adam and Havah represent every man and every woman. The whole narrative is symbolic of universal truths about men and women and their relationship with each other and God. You would do well to study it carefully, Talmidah. Its conclusions are inescapable.

Talmidah: As presently translated, I can understand your rooster's crow. Woman is made from a man's bone, making her part of him, completely dependent on him for life, yet utterly dispensable to him. She is the weak and foolish one who succumbs to her evil inclinations at the moment of temptation, while Adam stands impregnable to the whisperings of sin. Because of these shortcomings, Man is perfectly justified in dominating and even abusing Woman. After all, it's *her* fault, and therefore *my* fault, that we suffer grief, pain, and death. No wonder female voices were not welcome in the bet-midrash before modern times! Heaven forbid that a chicken should dare challenge the rooster's song of self-adoration! I shall indeed study this pericope with care, Mitnagged, and when I'm done I shall choke your crow into a croak.

Rabbi: That would be most disappointing. I was hoping for a harmonizing duet.

Mitnagged: Rabbi, have you ever heard a chicken "sing"? It's a screeching cackle.

Rabbi: I prefer to think of men and women as court musicians—she on the lyre, he on the pipe—praising the Name of the King together.

Talmidah: You have been pushing us into a fowl fight from the very beginning, Rabbi. How can we act like human troubadors if we are compelled to peck and claw each other's eyes out like foul chickens?

Rabbi: Ahhh, but the secret to such debate is to remember that it is an academic exercise for getting at "truth," or at least exploring every possibility of truth. The jousting tournament is not a war, talmidim.

Talmidah: It is a game.

Rabbi: Precisely. It is a game that arouses emotion and stimulates thought, but when it is over contestants remember that they are fellow knights serving the same King, to whom they owe loyalty and love. Attack her targum vigorously, Mitnagged. And you, Talmidah, defend it vigorously. But in your translation and commentary, let your prime motivation be the love of humanity and God, not the decapitation of a particular *chaver*[47] whom you find repulsive and hateful.

Mitnagged: I don't see that she can do much with this narrative to change its message that Man is a superior being to Woman.

Rabbi: You may be right. But your premature dismissal of her piece of targum serves you ill, Mitnagged. Do you not recall her use of Zohar imagery to assert divine origin *and* divine approval of both male and female?

Male and female He created them
to make known the Glory on high
From here we learn:
Any image that does not embrace male and female
is not a high and true image
Come and see:

47. Fellow student, literally "comrade."

The blessed Holy One does not place his abode
in any place where male and female are not found together

Mitnagged: I confess I did not catch her use of mystic symbolism—out of context I might add—to interpret 1:27. Once again, I protest allowing a woman to distort Scripture in this manner. Her motive is obvious!

Talmidah: And the motives of the sages who interpret this narrative to your liking are pure and completely objective? As men, how could they not be motivated by desires to confirm their dominant status over women!

Rabbi: On to the task at hand. My third and final question, Talmidah, regards 1:27. In this verse you translated a masculine-singular possessive, *be-tsal-mo*/"his image" into a simple definite noun, "the image." Later, in the same verse, you translated a masculine-singular object pronoun, *oto*/"him" into a neuter-plural, "them."[48] These are severe violations of Hebrew grammar.

Mitnagged: I'll say. Instead of reading, "in the image of God he created *him*," we suddenly learn that "in the image of God he created *them*."

Rabbi: A grammatical "mistake."

Mitnagged: A deliberate fraud which attempts to include woman in the Divine Image.

48. Hebrew words are either feminine or masculine. Masculine plurals are ambiguous, because they can refer to a group of masculine entities or a group of mixed genders. Masculine plurals which include both feminine and masculine entities are often called neuter-plurals.

Talmidah: I followed Dr. E. A. Speiser's logic when he translated 1:26 for the Anchor Bible. He translated a first-person plural, *na-a-seh*/"we will make," to a first-person singular, "I will make." He also translated two nouns with first-person plural suffixes, *be-tsal-me-nu*/"in our image" and *kid-mu-te-nu*/"after our likeness" to "in *my* image" and "after *my* likeness." So instead of the traditional translation, "And God said, 'Let us make men in our image, after our likeness,'" he translates, "And God said, 'I will make man in my image, after my likeness.'" How does he justify this "grammatical fraud"? He says there are no other divine beings mentioned in the text. He further points to the following verse, 1:27, which uses singular suffixes and pronouns throughout, as evidence that God is speaking of himself alone. "The point of issue," he says, "is one of grammar alone, without a direct bearing on the meaning."[49] In other words, Speiser opted to smooth over grammatical differences between 1:26 and 1:27 in order to make them conform to one another. He justifies his choice of singular over plural by pointing out that the title for God, "Elohim," is a plural-singular, as we discussed earlier, which may account for a scribal error in 1:26 which applied plural verbs and suffixes to a plural noun. But one could easily use Speiser's argument to do the opposite—to change the singulars of 1:27 into plurals to conform to the plurals of 1:26. He argues that no other divine ones are mentioned in the text. I disagree. Verse 1:26 itself implies other divine beings. The rabbis, as noted in my targum, assumed that Elohim counseled with his ministering angels, which allows for divine beings other than God, without challenging his supreme Oneness. You can also read *elohim* in 5:2 as "divine ones." "In the likeness of divine ones He shaped them." Note the plural "*them*"!

49. Anchor Bible, p. 7, note i.26.

Mitnagged: You yourself said earlier that *Elohim* means "Eternal God."

Talmidah: Yes! But it has other meanings as well. As it is written,

El elohim, Yahweh, El elohim
God of gods, Yahweh, God of gods[50]

and elsewhere,

El elohim, Yahweh, diber
God of gods, Yahweh, is speaking[51]

Many words in Hebrew are like this, Mitnagged, you know that. *Adam* can be a proper noun—the name of the first man. It can also mean "a man," or "mankind/humanity," a collective noun.

Mitnagged: You have a lot of chutzpa twisting the logic of an imminent scholar like Speiser.

Talmidah: I am grateful to him for supplying me the justification I needed to translate 1:27 in a more egalitarian light.

Mitnagged: If he were still alive today he'd turn you over on his knee and . . .

Rabbi: Ahem. Talmidah, I am disappointed. There is no need to rely on the creative manipulations of a single sage, may his memory be blest, to justify your translation. I expected you to counter my grammatical objection with a grammatical argument.

Talmidah: I don't understand.

---

50. Joshua 22:22.
51. Psalms 50:1.

Rabbi: Make her do it, Mitnagged.

Mitnagged: With pleasure. Talmidah, you violated grammatical rules in 1:27.

Talmidah: I did not.

Mitnagged: Did so.

Talmidah: Did not.

Rabbi: Children! That's what you are! Children! I've seen better exchanges in a *kheyder!*[52]

Mitnagged: What's wrong?

Rabbi: Try being a little more specific.

Mitnagged: *Be-tsal-mo* is a noun with a third-person masculine-singular possessive suffix. *Oto* is a third-person masculine-singular object pronoun.

Talmidah: I don't deny either of these facts. My treatment of *be-tsal-mo* is a simple matter of disagreeing with masoretic voweling. The unvoweled phrase reads *btslm.* I revoweled this phrase to *be-tselem,* "in the image," just as the same word, repeated, is voweled immediately afterwards. So the verse literally reads:

> Fashioned Elohim mankind in the image
> in the image of Elohim He fashioned them.

52. A children's school for learning Hebrew.

An A-B-C-D-D-B-A-C chiasm, "the image" serving as a pivot in our poetic parallel.

Rabbi: You don't even have to eliminate the vowel letter *vav*, Talmidah.

Talmidah: But I have to, Rabbi. It's the *vav* that functions as a third-person masculine-singular possessive suffix.

Rabbi: That is its function at the end of a noun.

Talmidah: I see! If I shifted it over to the next word, so that it is at the beginning of a word, it becomes a conjunctive! It can mean "and," "so," "then," "even," "while," "or," etc.

Rabbi: Any of those meanings. Remember that letters at the beginning or end of a word can be shifted to surrounding words. This is an acceptable translation technique which assumes scribal error during transmission of the text.

Talmidah: If I keep the *vav* and shift it to the next word, the verse could read

> Elohim fashioned mankind in the image,
> even the image of Elohim he fashioned them.

Mitnagged: Correction.

> Elohim fashioned man in the image
> even the image of Elohim, He fashioned *him*.

You still have the little problem with *oto,* Talmidah. There's no *mem*[53] following that word to justify changing it from a masculine-singular into a neuter-plural.

Talmidah: We both know that third-person masculine-singular nouns, verbs, suffixes, and pronouns can serve more than one function. They can apply to a male person—he, his, him—or to a neuter item—it, its.

Mitnagged: Of course. Any idiot knows that. But they cannot apply to neuter-plurals, as you have done.

Talmidah: But they *can* be applied to collective nouns, in which case they can be logically translated into English as neuter-plurals.

Mitnagged: Agreed. But what collective noun does *oto* refer to? Surely not "Adam"?

Talmidah: Why not? In fact, *ha-adam* can be treated as a collective noun two different ways. "Mankind" is a collective, as is "the Couple," meaning Adam and Eve together.

Mitnagged: You are calling the first couple "Adam"?

Talmidah: Of course. In much the same way we call couples by their last name—"the Orens" or "the Sterns." Better yet, "the Oren family," since we're not using plural forms for that title. Look, you don't have to take my word for it. God Himself called the first couple "Adam" in 5:2:

53. The neuter-plural object pronoun would be *otam*.

> In the likeness of Elohim He shaped them, male and female. He blessed them and *called their name Adam.*

Rabbi: It appears that Talmidah has justified her grammatical innovations both through precedent and syntax, thanks to you, Mitnagged.

Talmidah: Thank you.

Mitnagged: Please don't mention it . . . ever.

Rabbi: We shall meet again this time next week to review Talmidah's next installment of her targum.

Mitnagged: I won't ask how well we did today.

Rabbi: That is most wise. You would find my response . . . disappointing.

Talmidah: I will be better prepared next time.

Mitnagged: As will I.

Rabbi: We shall see. Shalom *yeladim.*[54]

---

54. "Children."

2

"The Garden of God"
Genesis 2:4b–17

Targum

At the time when Yahweh Elohim made land and sky *Gen 2:4b*
there was not yet any plant of the plowed field *2:5*
or grain of the plowed field in the land
for Yahweh Elohim had not sent rain upon the land
and there was no earthly man
to work/plow/serve the earth
Instead, a flow would well up from the land *2:6*
and water all the surface of the earth.

Yahweh Elohim planted an enclosed garden in Eden *2:8*
a garden of delight
in the east
from ancient times

before the creation of the world[1]
and there he placed the earthly man whom he had formed.

The Lord planted a garden in a region of pleasantness in the time of the beginning, and He made to dwell there the man whom He had created.[2] God had fashioned mankind as one being with two faces, male-and-female. Then He split/divided/separated into two.[3]

Adam: When God created me out of earth along with Havah your mother, I used to go about with her in a glory which she had seen in the aeon from which we had come. Then God, the ruler of aeons and the powers, separated us. We became two aeons, and the glory in our hearts deserted us, me and your mother Havah, along with the first knowledge that used to breathe within us.[4]

The Lord God took the man away from the mountain of worship, where he had been formed, and made him dwell in the Garden of Eden, to do service in the law, and to keep its commandments.[5] The first man entered the Garden of Eden, and the ministering angels were praising before him, and dancing before him, and escorting him into the garden of Delight.[6]

Enoch: And that place is inconceivably pleasant. I saw the trees in full flower. And their fruits were ripe and pleasant-smelling,

---

1. *Targum of Palestine.*
2. *Targum Onkelos.*
3. *Midrash Tehillim* CXXXIX.5. A midrash on Psalms.
4. *The Apocalypse of Adam* I:2, 4–5. A pseudepigraphal work originally written in Greek between the first and fourth century C.E.
5. *Targum of Palestine.*
6. *Pirke de-Rabbi Eliezer,* chap. XVIII.

with every food in yield and giving off profusely a delightful fragrance. And there were three hundred angels, very bright, who look after Paradise; and with never-ceasing voice and pleasant singing they worship the Lord every day and hour.[7]

Yahweh: And I created a garden in Eden, in the east, so that he might keep the agreement and preserve the commandment. And I created for him an open heaven, so that he might look upon the angels singing the triumphal songs. And the light which is never darkened was perpetually in paradise.[8]

And he knew that the Garden of Eden was the holy of holies and the dwelling of the Lord.[9]

Yahweh Elohim caused to grow out of the earth *2:9a*
every kind of tree enticing to look at
desirable for vision/perception/revelation
also good for food

The word Paradise, if taken literally, means a place thickly crowded with every kind of tree; but symbolically taken, it means wisdom, intelligence both divine and human, and the proper comprehension of the causes of things.[10] He exhorts the soul of man to derive advantage not from one tree alone, nor from one single virtue, but from all the virtues; for eating is the symbol of the nourishment of the soul, and the soul is nourished by the reception of good things.[11]

---

7. 2 Enoch 8:1, 8, J recension.
8. 2 Enoch 31:1–3, J recension.
9. *Jubilees* 8:19. A pseudepigraphal work composed during the second century B.C.E.
10. Philo, *Questions,* I.6.
11. Philo, *Allegorical Interpretation I,* XXI.97.

2:9b with the Tree of Eternal Life in the middle of the garden

And in the midst of them was the Tree of Life, at that place where the Lord takes a rest when he walks about in paradise. And that tree is indescribable for pleasantness and fine fragrance, and more beautiful than any other created thing that exists. And from every direction it has an appearance which is gold-looking and crimson, and with the form of fire. And it covers the whole of Paradise, having something of every orchard tree and every tree.[12]

For the law is the Tree of Life. Whoever keeps it in this life lives and endures like the Tree of Life. The law is good to keep in this world, as the fruit of the Tree of Life in the world to come.[13]

But the Tree of Life signifies Torah, the word of God, as it is said, "It is a Tree of Life to them that lay hold upon it."[14]

The more Torah, the more life.[15]

2:9c and the Tree of Knowing/Discerning good and evil
right and wrong
health and injury
joy and misery
pleasure and pain

12. 2 Enoch 8:2.
13. *Targum Yerushalmi.*
14. *Pirke de-Rabbi Eliezer,* chap. XII.
15. *Avot* II.7.

by which all things are known and distinguished from one another, whether they be good and beautiful, or bad and unseemly, or in short, every sort of opposite is discerned.[16]

And another tree, the Tree of Mercy, is near it, an olive, flowing with oil continually.[17]

A river flows out of Eden, "Delight," *2:10*
to water the garden
and from there divides into four headwaters
The name of the first is Pison, "spreading out" *2:11*
It winds all through the land of Havilah, "Life"
where there is gold,
the gold of the land being pure. *2:12*
There also is the lapis lazuli
and the onyx gem.

You were the seal of perfection *Ezek*
full of wisdom and flawless in beauty *28:12*
You were in Eden, the Garden of God *28:13*
Every precious gem was your covering:
cornelian, chrysalite and amethyst
beryl, lapis lazuli and jasper
sapphire, turquoise and emerald
and gold beautifully wrought for you
I fashioned you as a cherub *28:14*
with outstretched shielding wings
and you resided on God's holy mountain
You walked among stones of fire

16. Philo, *Questions*, I.11.

17. 2 Enoch 8:3–4. "The Tree of Mercy" is an added phrase, this identity of the third tree coming from "Vita Adae."

28:15 You were blameless in your ways
from the day you were fashioned

Gen 2:13 The name of the second river is Gihon, "bursting forth," the
one which winds all through the land of Cush, "Sated."
2:14 The name of the third river is Hiddekel, "pressing in," the one
which flows along Eastern Asshur, "Happiness."
And the fourth river is Prat, "Fruitful."

Paradise is between the corruptible and the incorruptible. Two streams come forth, one a source of honey and milk, the other a source which produces oil and wine. And it is divided into four parts, which wind around quietly and serene. The four rivers flow past with gentle movement, with every kind of garden producing every kind of good food.[18]

2:15 So Yahweh Elohim took the man away
and set him down in the enclosed garden of Eden
the garden of delight
in order to serve it
and to preserve it
have charge over it.

With love abounding did the Holy One, blessed be He, love the first man, inasmuch as He created him in a pure locality, in the place of his Temple, and He brought him into his palace. From which place did He take him? From the place of the Temple, and He brought him into His palace, which is Eden.[19]

18. 2 Enoch 8:5, 7, J and A recension.
19. *Pirke de-Rabbi Eliezer,* chap. XII.

Adam stood on his feet and was adorned with the Divine Image. He began to gaze upwards and downwards. He saw all the creatures which the Holy One, blessed be He, had created: and marveling in his heart, he began to praise and glorify his Creator, exclaiming, "O Lord, how manifold are thy works!"[20]

Adam: And I poured out to God exultation, praise, and song for His works.[21]

You have brought me joy, Yahweh, by your works *Psalms*
at the works of your hands I cry out, *94:4*
"How great are your works, O Yahweh!" *94:5*
Let the heaven and earth praise him! *69:34*
the seas, and all that move within them
The heavens declare the glory of God *19:1*
The vault of heaven proclaim his handiwork
Acclaim Yahweh, all the earth! *98:4*
Burst into shout of joy and sing praise!
Let the sea thunder, and all that it holds *98:7*
the world and all who live in it
Let the rivers clap their hands *98:8*
and the mountains shout for joy together!
Yahweh, our Lord *8:2*
How majestic is Your name throughout the earth
You whose splendor is celebrated all over the heavens!
When I behold Your heavens, the work of Your fingers, *8:4*
the moon and stars that You set in place
What is mankind that You are mindful of him? *8:5*
or the son of man that you take note of him?
for you have set him a little lower than Divine Ones *8:6*

20. *Pirke de-Rabbi Eliezer,* chap. XI.
21. *Midrash Tehillim* 92:10.

and adorned him with glory and majesty
8:7 You have made him master over Your handiwork
laying the world at his feet
8:8 sheep and oxen, all of them
and wild beasts, too
8:9 the birds of the heavens, the fish of the sea,
all that travel the paths of the sea
8:10 Yahweh, our Lord
how majestic Your name throughout the world!

Gen 2:16 Then Yahweh Elohim commanded the man, saying,

"You are free to eat of any tree of the garden
2:17 but you may not eat from the Tree of Knowing Good and Evil
for in the day you eat from it you will certainly die,
because it is fatally dangerous for you.[22]
Dying you shalt die[23]
Consuming you shalt be consumed"[24]

Yahweh: I gave him his free will. I pointed out to him the two ways—light and darkness. And I said to him, "This is good for you, but that is bad," so that I might come to know whether he has love toward me or abhorrence, and so that it might become plain who among his race loves me. Whereas I have come to know his nature, he does not know his own nature. That is why ignorance is more lamentable than the sin, such as it is in him to sin.[25]

---

22. *Midrash Tehillim* 92:14.
23. *Targum Onkelos.*
24. *Targum Onkelos,* Samaritan version.
25. 2 Enoch 30:15, 16, J recension.

Midrash

> Keep warm at the fire of the sages, but beware of their glowing coal, or you will be scorched. For their bite is the bite of a jackal, and their sting the sting of a scorpion, and their hiss the hiss of a serpent. All their words are like coals on fire.
>
> —*Pirke Avot,* II.10

Rabbi: So we meet again to review Talmidah's offering for this week.

Mitnagged: A burnt offering. Similar to the meal my mother burnt to a crisp not too long ago because she neglected a basic rule in food preparation—any good thing can be overdone, and then it's not fit for anything but the garbage heap.

Talmidah: You honor me greatly, Mitnagged. As it is written, "It was a burnt offering for a pleasing odor, an offering by fire to the Lord."[26]

Mitnagged: I was thinking more along the words of Isaiah, "Instead of a pleasing odor, a stinking stench; burning instead of beauty."[27]

Rabbi: And what do you have to offer today, Mitnagged, besides water for the altar?[28]

Mitnagged: Before questioning Talmidah's outrageous commentary on the so-called separation of man and woman, I wish

26. Leviticus 8:21.

27. Isaiah 3:24.

28. A reference to the water Elijah poured on his altar to prevent the burning of sacrifice by human hands, 1 Kings 18:33–35.

to go back and address the issues we left hanging around the word "descend" last week.

Rabbi: You wish to challenge the root *yarad*/"descend" used in Talmidah's translation of 1:26.

Mitnagged: I have no objection to the translation itself, only to its interpretation . . . or implied interpretation.

Talmidah: You do not demand a retraction?

Mitnagged: Totally unnecessary. Rabbi, you asked, "From where did man descend?" We read in the *Targum of Palestine*, "The Lord took the man from the mountain of worship where he had been created, and made him dwell in the Garden of Eden." It is a simple solution. God fashioned man upon a mountain. In order for man to enter the garden he had first to descend from the mountain.

Talmidah: I am gratified to hear you quoting a passage which I selected for this week's segment of my targum.

Mitnagged: I noted its presence *and* its misuse.

Talmidah: Before launching your tirade against my reading of 2:15—namely that Adam was taken from Havah's side to live alone in the garden—I wish to clarify just one small detail in your theory about the place from which Adam descended.

Mitnagged: Proceed.

Talmidah: Was this just any old mountain?

Mitnagged: A "mountain of worship," whatever that means.

Talmidah: According to the same targum it was "the house of the sanctuary." *Bereshith Rabbah* claims that man "was created from the place of his atonement."[29] Rabbi Eliezer is quite specific in his commentary on 2:15: "From what place did he take him? From the place of the temple."[30]

Mitnagged: So it was Mount Moriah. That makes perfect sense. It is the location for several holy events—the first land to appear during the Creation, the place where Abraham bound Isaac and the place where the temple was built. It's still a mountain, nonetheless, solid and "earthly." Mystic "descensions" are not implied in any of the commentaries you cited.

Talmidah: Nor are they discounted. None of these texts explicitly names Mount Moriah, nor do they talk about a future, unbuilt temple. It is "the House of Sanctuary," "the Place of Atonement," or "the Place of the Temple."

Mitnagged: Perhaps the sages you selected were not specific as to location, but I recall a midrash on Psalm 92 that leaves no doubt:

> Adam was driven out, and he went forth out of the Garden of Eden and abode on Mount Moriah, for the gates of the Garden of Eden are close by Mount Moriah. God had taken Adam thence, and thither He returned him, returned him to the place whence he had been taken. From what place had He taken him? From the place where the Temple was to stand.[31]

---

29. XIV.8.
30. Chap. XII.
31. *Midrash Tehillim* 92:6.

There is only one place where the temple can stand. And the first temple was not built until 950 B.C.E., Talmidah, quite some time after the creation of man. It had to be Mount Moriah, the site for the future temple.

Talmidah: The temple King Solomon built was *not* the first temple to be built, nor was the first temple built on Mount Moriah.

Mitnagged: What are you talking about!

Talmidah: I am referring to the Tent of the Tabernacle that Moses built in the desert during Israel's exodus from Egypt. It had all the structural and functional elements of a temple, Mitnagged. It had outer, inner, and holy courts, the sacrificial altar, the brass laver, the veils of cherubim, the menorahs, the ark of the covenant, everything. Priests were anointed and clothed in sacred garments, performed sacrifices, received offerings and interfaced between Israel and God within the holy of holies. In fact, you must agree that the so-called first temple was patterned after the Tabernacle, the true first temple.

Mitnagged: I had not thought of the tabernacle as a temple before.

Talmidah: Because it was made of skins and cloth instead of stone? Because it moved around instead of remaining permanently in one sacred spot?

Mitnagged: I shall concede your point regarding the tabernacle. But I see little difference in timing. A few hundred years earlier still misses the Creation by at least twenty-five hundred years.

Talmidah: The word for temple in Hebrew is *bet-miqdash*, "House of Holiness." It is a holy place where God dwells, which means it can be anywhere, as it is written, "The Holy One, blessed be He, is the place of His universe, but His universe is not His place."[32]

Rabbi: Hence one of His names, *ha-makom*.

Mitnagged: "The Place."

Rabbi: Meaning that He encompasses space, but space does not encompass him.[33]

Talmidah: Or another way to put it is that God's house is not confined to a single geographical spot. You can't take a map and put an *X* on the place where God dwells.

Mitnagged: Just what are you driving at, Talmidah?

Talmidah: I'm saying that it's just possible that some of the sages were ambiguous as to the location of the holy place where man was formed in order to allow for the presence of more than one holy place. There's no question that according to Tradition, Mount Moriah is the place where man was formed. But ancient literature speaks of another tradition, the tradition that God dwells in a heavenly temple, accessible to man through vision.

---

32. *Bereshith Rabbah* LXVIII.9.

33. A citation of A. Cohen's explanation of "The Place" as a name for God, *Everyman's Talmud* (New York: Schocken Books, 1975), p. 8.

Mitnagged: You refer to ascension accounts in Merkavah literature.

Talmidah: Right! Since Merkavah accounts were being written about the same time as the Mishna, the earliest of rabbinic writings, it is conceivable that both places were implied.

Mitnagged: There is little evidence of any connection between Merkavah and rabbinic circles. But putting that aside for the moment, I see nothing earth-shattering about the existence of Merkavah ascension accounts and their strong allusions to temple structure and ritual. I would even add to this literature *hekhalot*[34] ascension accounts, composed contemporaneously with the earliest copies of the Talmud.

Rabbi: These were somewhat different.

Talmidah: Magical textbooks on how to achieve an ascension experience.

Mitnagged: Featuring credible sages like Rabbi Ishmael as a prototype "descender."

Talmidah: Can't say I'm crazy about that literature. But it does add to the evidence that ancient Jews believed in a heavenly temple.

Rabbi: Or believed in a state of being represented by the temple.

Talmidah: I don't understand.

---

34. "Palace/temple chambers."

Rabbi: Hekhalot descenders tried to achieve a state of holiness by putting their heads between their knees, repeating certain Hebraic formulas, and basically hyperventilating.

Mitnagged: You say that with much disgust.

Rabbi: Short cuts do not impress me. Talmudic sages advocated another, more rational application of temple symbology.

Talmidah: Ethical behavior, pious observance, and the study of Torah.

Rabbi: Yes, the achievement of holiness through old-fashioned toil—the effort of learning Torah and the challenge of living it in our daily lives.

Mitnagged: Prayers and learned words substituting for sacrificial offerings.

Talmidah: As well as service to God and acts of loving kindness.

Rabbi: Haven't you ever wondered why Rabbi Ishmael was called a "High Priest"?[35]

Talmidah: Yes, I have. He was a child when the temple was destroyed. He couldn't possibly have been a high priest.

---

35. Ishmael ben Elisha, a sage of the first and second century C.E. and a descendant of a wealthy priestly family in Upper Galilee. His teachings are found throughout the Talmud, but he is most known for drawing up the thirteen hermeneutic rules by which Scripture may be interpreted.

Rabbi: Ahhh, but if you think of Torah study as a way to ascend to the presence of God, his title makes perfect sense.

Mitnagged: As a great teacher, he guided his students through progressively higher levels of learning, much as a high priest symbolically leads Israel through progressively more sacred chambers of the *bet-miqdash*.

Talmidah: Hmmmmm. *Bet-miqdash, bet-midrash*. Very similar-sounding.

Rabbi: Talmidah, you have a habit of stringing together unrelated fragments of information.

Mitnagged: Yes, her fictional "separation" being the all-time . . .

Rabbi: You will have your chance, Mitnagged. But first we must finish this line of thought. The sages did not oppose an ascension of the soul to a state of holiness and ecstasy. They only disagreed with contemporary mystics as to how such a state should be achieved. A story is told in *Tractate Hagigah*[36] in Talmud Bavli about how Torah study—specifically the study of the Chariot, or throne, of God—can lead to such an experience.

Mitnagged: The story of Rabbi Yohanan ben Zakkai.[37]

---

36. 14b.

37. First century C.E. A prominent sage before and after the destruction of the temple. After the fall of Jerusalem in 70 C.E., he succeeded in procuring permission from Vespasian to spare Yavneh, where most of the sages of that generation were living and teaching. He actively worked

Talmidah: Also given the title High Priest by his disciples.

Rabbi: Be that as it may. Do you recall the story?

Talmidah: Not offhand. I remember something about singing trees, rainbows, and angels.

Mitnagged: I remember an ass, a stone, and a tree.

Rabbi: According to the Talmud, Rabbi Zakkai was riding on an ass, which one of his students, Eleazar ben 'Arak, was prodding from behind. Eleazar begged his master to teach him about the Chariot. "Look," Zakkai answered, "didn't I teach you that you can't talk about the Chariot unless you are speaking with a sage?" In other words, "Sorry, you don't know enough." Eleazar didn't give up. He said, "OK, let me do the talking, then. I'll talk about the Chariot with the knowledge you have already taught me." Zakkai agreed. The sage then immediately got off the ass, sat on a stone under an olive tree . . .

Talmidah: An olive tree!

Rabbi: . . . an olive tree and wrapped himself up in his tallit. Eleazar stood there, puzzled. "Why did you do that?" he asked. "Is it proper for me to be sitting on an ass," Zakkai replied, "while you are expounding on the Chariot, knowing that the Divine Presence and ministering angels are with us?"

---

towards a renewal of Judaism through rabbinic rulings emerging from the *bet-midrashim* in Yavneh.

Talmidah: I remember the next part! As soon as Eleazar began his discourse on the Chariot, fire came down from heaven and surrounded the trees in the field. That's when they began to sing.

Rabbi: And when Eleazar had finished his discourse, Zakkai got up, kissed his talmid on the head and exclaimed, "Blessed be the Lord God of Israel, Who gave a son to Abraham our father who knows to speculate upon, investigate, and expound upon the Chariot!"

Mitnagged: I didn't hear anything about rainbows in that story.

Rabbi: Talmidah must be confusing this story with its sequel, which follows immediately afterwards. You see, when two of Zakkai's other students heard what happened to Eleazar, they decided to try it for themselves. As soon as one of them began his discourse on the Chariot the sky swiftly filled with clouds and a rainbow appeared. In addition, ministering angels gathered to listen to Rabbi Yeshua and Rabbi Yosi discuss the Chariot of God.

Talmidah: So they experienced a kind of ecstatic joy and feeling of holiness from the teachings of Torah regarding God's throne, rather than actually trying to ascend, or descend, physically or mystically to the throne itself.

Rabbi: That is correct.

Mitnagged: Back to the Garden of Eden. I fail to see how any of this has any relevance to this pericope of Scripture.

Talmidah: The point, as I said earlier, is that a temple can be anywhere God chooses to dwell, whether it's a palace constructed by a king, a bare mountain, a house of learning, or a place of vision called heaven.

Rabbi: Or the human body itself.

Talmidah: What!

Rabbi: You are fond of Philo. Did he not say regarding Adam's body, "For it was an abode, or sacred temple, for a reasonable soul which was being made, the image of which he was about to carry in his heart, being the most God-like looking of images."[38]

Talmidah: OK, as long as the thing and people in a particular place are consecrated as "holy" or "pure" and apply basic temple metaphors to the way they see themselves, their behavior, and others around them, it's a temple. As Rabbi Abba bar Kahana said, "If He is in a temple above, I will come to His abode; and if He is in a temple below, I will come to His abode."[39] The point is that mankind descended from a holy place. As Rabbi Eliezer said, "He created him in a pure locality."[40]

Mitnagged: You are jousting with a straw man of your own making, Talmidah. I do not reject your "descend among" translation. I merely disagree with your interpretation of it. I say man was created of the earth and *on* the earth, and that his descension was simply that from mountain to garden. In fact,

38. Philo, *On the Creation*, XLVII.
39. *Tanhuma Bereshith* 1.13.
40. Chap. 12.

I would say that our discussion so far regarding rabbinic attitudes towards mystical ascent, or descent, confirms a more "on-the-earth" explanation. But even if your temple theory was correct, I would point out that in all these commentaries, nothing is said of woman descending from the mountain. She's not even in the picture.

Talmidah: Then you do not object to the notion of temple topology superimposed on a landscape which is not made of stone?

Mitnagged: An odd way of asking a simple question. Do I agree that any place where God dwells, whether you think of that in concrete or metaphorical terms, is a holy place and therefore a temple, the answer is yes.

Talmidah: Thank you.

Mitnagged: So what's your point?

Talmidah: Nothing.

Mitnagged: Nothing. Why is it that I feel an icy chill when you say "nothing"?

Rabbi: Your instincts do not deceive you. If my hunch is correct, you will feel the blade between your shoulders next week when Talmidah presents her targum on the rib story.

Talmidah: Don't worry about it, Mitnagged. The Rooster doesn't know he's going into the pot until the *shokhet*[41]

41. Ritual slaughterer.

suddenly runs the blade across his neck. Enjoy your last week among the living. As for your statement that woman has not yet entered the picture, you conveniently forget 1:27:

> Elohim fashioned mankind in their image
> in the image of divine beings He fashioned them
> male and female
> man and woman
> He fashioned them

Quite astonishing considering the fact that we discussed this verse in great detail only last week.

Mitnagged: She has not entered the *second* time. You are the one who suffers amnesia, Talmidah. The Torah, *unredacted,* contains two separate accounts of the creation of humanity. In the first account, 1:26–27, we have a general preview of the fashioning of man and woman. Later, we get the details—first the man from "the dust of the earth" in 2:7, then second, the woman from the rib of man in 2:21–22. You failed to justify your placement of 2:7 immediately after 1:27. Remember?

Talmidah: I will yet prove that such a placement is logical, particularly given the fact that there *is* no second creation account for Woman.

Mitnagged: Of course there is! I just cited it—2:21–22!

Talmidah: We shall see. For the moment you may enjoy the illusion of victory.

Rabbi: Let us move forward into Talmidah's treatment of 2:4b–17. Mitnagged.

Mitnagged: About this "separation" business . . .

Rabbi: First things first, Mitnagged. First, you must analyze the translation itself. Once that is accomplished you can move into commentary.

Mitnagged: I did not detect anything particularly obnoxious in the translation itself.

Talmidah: You have no objections to my translation?

Mitnagged: Should I?

Talmidah: There are two words for which I want to be doubly sure that we are in agreement.

Mitnagged: Meaning there are two words which you deem vital to your overall targum. If they turn out to be as harmless as *descend* I fear nothing. There is nothing to fear from a weak mind, as it is written, "I fear no harm, for you are with me."[42]

Talmidah: It is also written, "I will laugh at your calamity, and mock when fear comes upon you."[43]

Mitnagged: Shoot your little darts.

Talmidah: I will not shoot them . . . yet . . . only confirm their existence. In verse 2:8 I translate *mikedem* polyvalently to mean not only "in the east," but "from ancient times," which

42. Psalms 23:4.
43. Proverbs 1:26.

Targum of Palestine boldly translates, "before the creation of the world."

Mitnagged: It is not so bold. We find the Garden of Eden listed as one of the seven wonders created before Creation, both in *Midrash Tehillim*[44] and in Rabbi Eliezer's commentary on the Creation.

Talmidah: You have no objection to this even though it disagrees with *Jubilees* II.7, which says that the Garden was created on the third day of Creation?

Mitnagged: No. If it means something to you, Talmidah, it will undoubtedly mean something different to me.

Talmidah: In 2:9, I translated *le-mar-eh*/"to look at," an infinitive verb, also as *le-mar-ah*/"for vision/revelation," a noun preceded by a preposition.

Mitnagged: Had you not included Philo's interpretation of this verse I would have been startled. But I find his rational explanation of the garden as a place where a variety of types of wisdom are available for the nourishment of Man's soul quite satisfactory.

Rabbi: Suppose you only had the translation before you, Mitnagged, without Philo's commentary?

Mitnagged: It could be read that the trees were sources of prophetic visions and revelation.

44. 90.391.

Rabbi: Like Isaiah or Jeremiah?

Talmidah: Or perhaps Daniel or Ezekiel?

Mitnagged: That would make Adam a prophet. We are not going beyond Tradition here. Not at all. Adam is listed among prophets in *Seder Olam Rabbah.*[45]

Talmidah: It is also written, "Adam received five crowns: he was king, prophet, high priest, his countenance shone in heavenly splendor, and God revealed torah to him."[46]

Mitnagged: I am not disputing Adam's status as a prophet.

Talmidah: Do you also agree that Havah ate from the same tree as Adam?

Mitnagged: Wait a minute . . .

Talmidah: Do you dispute that Havah also ate from the trees in the garden? I'll take your scowl as a *yes*. So we have a man and a woman deriving wisdom and prophetic revelation from identical sources.

Mitnagged: Hold it . . .

Talmidah: Don't worry, Mitnagged. That's not the point I wanted to make with this word. The thought just slipped into my mind.

45. Chap. 21.
46. *Shu'aib ki-Tissa,* 39c, as quoted by Ginzberg, V.5, p. 78, note 21.

Mitnagged: What *is* your point?

Talmidah: I told you. I'm saving it.

Rabbi: Proceed with your analysis Mitnagged.

Talmidah: You mean nonanalysis.

Rabbi: I stand corrected. *Do* you have anything to say about Talmidah's targum?

Mitnagged: I most certainly do. Though I concede that your translation is noncontroversial, your selection and manipulation of commentary, particularly for 2:8, can only be described as incredibly fraudulent. You misquote *Midrash Tehillim* 139.5 as follows:

> God had fashioned mankind as one being with two faces, male-and-female. Then He split/divided/separated into two.

It truly reads:

> Rabbi Samuel taught: God created man as a single creature with two faces and then split him in two, making a back for each part.[47]

Talmidah: A difference in translation. I clarify "man" as the collective noun "mankind", and reword "single creature" as "one being." I added "male-and-female" because that is part of Rabbi Eliezer's commentary just preceding it, thus informing the reader over what issue they were debating. "For it is said,

---

47. This same midrash is also found in *Bereshith Rabbah* VIII.1, and in *Berakhot* 61a and *Eruvin* 18a in Talmud Bavli.

'male-and-female created He them.'" The image of "a back for each part" did not appeal to me as a metaphor.

Rabbi: Ahhhh . . . It does not appeal to you. What kind of argument is that, Talmidah?

Mitnagged: The argument of a toddler rejecting green beans in favor of ice cream. Her repugnance is understandable, considering the fact that Rabbi Eliezer's commentary, when cited *fully*, is quite explicit about what "one being" actually means.

> Rabbi Eliezer taught: Adam and Havah were created as an androgyne, for it is said, "male-and-female created He them."

R. Levi in this same debate also makes it clear just which part of this androgynous creature is most important.

> "You fashioned me behind and before" (Psalm 139). Why is it said "behind and before"? Because at the first Adam and Havah were created as a single creature with two faces Adam's face in front and Havah's in back.

You mutilate the text so badly that one easily misses the image of Man as the Rabbis envisioned for 1:27: an androgynous being which God afterward literally pulled apart. You are attempting to portray some romantic image of a man and woman holding hands together, which God then separated, presumably leaving Havah behind with God.

Talmidah: You prefer that ridiculous idea of Adam and Havah as Siamese twins?

Mitnagged: I said nothing about what I envision for 1:27. I am merely pointing out that you are using a text out of context to make it mean something it doesn't. You shore up a fictional reading of rabbinic commentary by softening "split" to "separate" and fusing it with an excerpt from a decidedly antirabbinic text.

Talmidah: Before attacking my use of a passage from a gnostic text, let me first address your objection to my citation of Rabbi Samuel's commentary on 1:27. First of all, since his commentary is part of a *debate* with other rabbis, including Eliezer and Levi, regarding the meaning of Psalm 139, you cannot assume that his opinion is in harmony with theirs. Quite the contrary. If they are in the midst of a debate, it is more likely that he is in disagreement. In either case, you cannot include the arguments of other sages to prove what Rabbi Samuel "meant" when he said, "one being," or even what he meant when he said "making a back for each one." Rabbi Eliezer and Rabbi Levi obviously believed that the male-and-female God fashioned was an androgynous being. It does not automatically follow that R. Samuel thought the same thing. For all we know he thought of the first couple's oneness in metaphorical terms, that they were constant and heretofore inseparable companions who (Shall we dare say it?) loved each other. I prefer to think of their "oneness" as the ultimate *yehud,*[48] as it is written:

> Neither man without woman
> nor woman without man
> and neither of them without the Divine Spirit[49]

Mitnagged: I seriously doubt that R. Samuel had such "oneness" in mind.

---

48. Perfect oneness.
49. *Bereshith Rabbah* VIII.9.

Talmidah: Perhaps not. But we cannot know for certain. And so his commentary is open for alternate interpretation.

Mitnagged: An interpretation supported by gnosticism!

Talmidah: No! An interpretation supported by a single concept within a gnostic text.

Mitnagged: I fail to see the difference.

Talmidah: You object to the passage I inserted from *The Apocalypse of Adam,* a text believed to be part of gnostic literature. I will not challenge that assumption. Nor will I deny that the overall gnostic approach to Scripture is clearly anti-rabbinical.

Mitnagged: You do not deny that it portrays Yahweh as a demiurge, an evil one at that, inferior to a higher God.

Talmidah: No. Nor do I deny that the Serpent is portrayed in a benevolent light, as is Cain, who committed the first murder. It exploits the Greek word *gnosis* as "secret knowledge" of heavenly mysteries available only to its disciples. It is obviously an "upside down" kind of theology which I neither advocate nor believe in.

Mitnagged: Then why do you include its filth in your targum?

Talmidah: I would call it mud. I sifted through the mud and found a few pearls, Mitnagged, pearls which cannot be found among your favorite rabbinic texts.

Mitnagged: Namely?

Talmidah: A beautiful and intelligent image of Havah. And the way her husband regards her—wise and glorious.

Mitnagged: The text all but makes her into a goddess. A blasphemous . . .

Talmidah: It does not! The text describes how Adam regarded his wife. Just because a man sees his wife as a goddess does not make her one. I would hope one day to see a goddess in the eyes of my future husband when he looks at me.

Mitnagged: Romantic *drek.*

Talmidah: A romantic ideal.

Mitnagged: *It is not in the text!*

Talmidah: It is implied. God fashions a man and a woman together, at the same time. Next thing we know, the man is alone in a garden all by himself. What happened? The text says God "took him away" and "put him in the garden." Took him away from where? Took him away from whom? What happened to the woman? She was left behind. Left behind where? Wherever they were together before they were separated.

Mitnagged: This is illogical! Why would God separate them and then reunite them? What is the point?

Talmidah: They were separated so that the man might experience loneliness, that he might find out for himself that life with a woman in a mortal world—with all its growing pains—is infinitely preferable to a life in Paradise without her.

Mitnagged: A decidedly feminine interpretation.

Rabbi: It does not conflict with rabbinic attitudes toward marriage. Your portrayal of God in this interpretation is interesting.

Talmidah: As Teacher? I suppose you could say that He is the ultimate Rabbi.

Rabbi: Let us go back to Talmidah's amazing rationale for slicing off the last phrase in Rabbi Samuel's commentary on Psalm 139. It did not appeal to her. This brings up the question of intertextuality and the liberties with which a commentator may quote other commentators, or even Scripture, out of context, in order to introduce a new concept.

Mitnagged: You chastised her for misquoting another commentator.

Rabbi: No. I chastised her for not justifying it properly.

Mitnagged: How can you justify it?

Talmidah: How do I justify it? Precedent?

Rabbi: A promising possibility.

Talmidah: Rabbi Natan's commentary on *Avot.*[50] I can justify textual alteration by citing examples of similar emendations performed by Rabbi Natan on the Mishna.

---

50. Rabbi Natan ha-Bavli was a tanna of the mid-second century C.E. who wrote a commentary on *Avot,* called *Avot de Rabbi Natan* (The Fathers According to Rabbi Natan). He also wrote *The 49 Hermeneutical Rules of Rabbi Natan,* an extended version of Rabbi Ishmael's list. Along with his contemporary, Rabbi Judah ha-Nasi, who compiled the Mishna, Rabbi Natan is considered to be the last of the tannatic sages.

Rabbi: An excellent choice, considering we recently studied this text.

Talmidah: You assigned me the task of analyzing Rabbi Natan's overall treatment of *Avot* and specifically tracing allusions and direct citations from the Talmud in chapters 1–4 of his commentary.

Mitnagged: I was given a similar assignment.

Rabbi: Both of you carried out your assignment to my satisfaction. Excellent. Now we have a common frame of reference. Briefly summarize your analysis, Talmidah.

Talmidah: The first thing I noticed about Rabbi Natan's commentary is that he ignored half of the sayings in *Avot*.

Mitnagged: Forty-eight percent. He commented on 51 of 97 *mishnayot*.[51]

Talmidah: This process of picking and choosing automatically selected those portions of *Avot* worth contemplating and those which are not so important.

Rabbi: Where else do we find this process taking place?

Talmidah: Every commentary does it to some extent or another.

Rabbi: Even the Talmud?

---

51. Chapters or sayings.

Talmidah: Especially the Talmud. The Talmud is a commentary on the Mishna, yet it fails to provide commentary for half the Mishna.

Mitnagged: Talmud Bavli provides *gemara*[52] for thirty-six and a half of sixty-three tractates of Mishna, while Talmud Yerushalmi provides *gemara* for thirty-nine.[53]

Talmidah: Yes, that's right. Talmud Bavli ignored agricultural laws tied to the land of Israel, which makes sense because they were irrelevant to people living in Babylon. On the other hand, Talmud Yerushalmi ignored purification laws and rulings connected with the temple, probably because the temple was gone and the sages living in *Eretz-Israel*[54] saw no use for studying temple cultus.

Rabbi: What did they retain in the selection process?

Mitnagged: Practical matters.

Rabbi: Such as?

Mitnagged: Festival observances, civil law, and religious law centered in the home and community.

---

52. "Commentary" or legalistic debate. *Gemara* largely deals with legal rulings, both religious and civil, as opposed to midrash, which is largely composed of biblical exegesis.

53. These figures are based on analysis performed by H. L. Strack and G. Stemberger in *Introduction to the Talmud and Midrash* (Scotland: T & T Clark, 1991).

54. "The land of Israel."

Talmidah: The selection of some Mishnaic tractates over others in the Talmud determined the whole course of rabbinic Judaism thereafter.

Rabbi: What about the Mishna itself?

Mitnagged: Rabbi Judah the Prince compiled the Mishna from rulings and exegesis emerging from the major Houses of Learning in his day. Since we do not have access to the original transcripts he worked from, we cannot ascertain just what he judged to be irrelevant and what he esteemed as supremely important.

Talmidah: There are definite biases detectable, however, which suggest a great deal of selection.

Rabbi: Such as?

Talmidah: Well, Rabbi Judah's preference for the School of Hillel,[55] for example. You must admit that Hillel's rival, the School of Shammai, does not look good in the Mishna. When I read the Mishna, I get the feeling that Shammai's weakest arguments are pitted against Hillel's best. Hillel's arguments always seem more reasonable than Shammai's, so that a reader inevitably comes away pro-Hillel. One wonders what the real debate must have been like, for we know that both schools enjoyed equal prestige and a large following of disciples.

55. Founded by Hillel, "The Elder," a sage during the first century B.C.E. He served as Nasi, the spiritual leader of the Jews, between 30 B.C.E. and 10 C.E. His teachings and legalistic rulings were generally more lenient and milder than those of his rival Shammai.

Rabbi: That is an astute observation, particularly when you realize that Hillel's sayings and arguments outnumber Shammai's at least five to one.

Talmidah: Hillel's sayings are worth careful study on your part, Mitnagged, for he advocates teaching *anyone* who wants to learn Torah, regardless of social status, economic conditions, level of education or even motive. It is he who said, "Be of the disciples of Aaron, loving peace and pursuing peace, loving mankind and drawing them all to the Torah."[56] The "bad guy," Shammai, is the one who preaches exclusivity in the *bet-midrash*.

Rabbi: In any case, Hillel's prestige and importance in the eyes of Rabbi Judah are attested by the amount of space devoted to Hillel's teachings. What about you, Talmidah?

Talmidah: Me?

Rabbi: How did you use the selection process in your targum?

Talmidah: Well, my selection of Genesis 1:26–5:5 is a commentary in and of itself as to the importance of Adam and Havah's story.

Mitnagged: You also selected "out" Genesis 1:1–1:25, which many would consider part of that story.

Rabbi: Mitnagged is correct. You ignored P's Creation Account as irrelevant to your commentary. That is significant.

56. *Pirke Avot* I.12.

Mitnagged: I'll say. It magnifies man's creation as the most important, arguably the only important, step of creation.

Talmidah: We discussed this last week, Mitnagged. You know there is more to my decision than *that*.

Rabbi: Continue your analysis, Talmidah.

Talmidah: While chasing down Rabbi Natan's use of other commentaries in chapters 1–4, I discovered some very creative interpolations. He cited forty-five sages, most out-of-context. He applies phrases and scriptural exegesis used in one kind of debate to support arguments for which they were not originally applied. But more interesting to me were the thirty-four cases of *uncited* passages of talmudic commentary interwoven into his own writing. Sometimes he "lifted" entire arguments, practically quoting them word-for-word only to add an original twist at the end to change its entire meaning. Sometimes he changed story lines to better suit his illustrations. Sometimes he deleted arguments from a debate that he didn't agree with. For example, Rabbi Natan preached that a *niddah*[57] should not make herself attractive. He supports it with arguments we can find in *Shabbat* 64b in Talmud Bavli, but conveniently deletes Rabbi Akiva's ruling that allowed a *niddah* to apply makeup and wear attractive clothing.

Rabbi: The deletion of detestable material. Mitnagged, did your analysis uncover similar instances of deletion?

---

57. The time during which a menstruating woman is "impure" is called a *niddah* period (the time she is menstruating plus seven days). Consequently, a woman in this condition is often called a *niddah*.

Mitnagged: Many. Rabbi Natan was obviously not interested in presenting a true midrash. It was probably the earliest example of a rabbinic text which represents our modern notion of biblical commentary—namely the presentation of one man's interpretation in a given monograph. Contradictory opinions were simply not presented.

Talmidah: But it was not "modern." Perhaps a step towards modern, but still a mile away.

Rabbi: Explain.

Talmidah: He did not dare use his own words. Another technique I found in his commentary was the mixing of various phrases and sentences from various sages on different topics to form a single thought or even sentence.

Mitnagged: The words of the sages but not their thoughts. If you are comparing your cut-and-paste job to Rabbi Nathan's, you are suffering brain disease. His sources all derive from the Talmud.

Talmidah: Wait a minute, Mitnagged. Rabbi Natan wrote his commentary scarcely a generation after the Mishna was complete. The Talmud was only just beginning to form, a process which would take well over four hundred years. There was no monolithic text called "the Talmud" when he wrote his commentary. Mishna was still being debated in the houses of learning, arguments were still under way, perhaps distributed in different communiques, but certainly not unified under one book. That means he picked up his "talmudic" arguments, homilies, phrases, and stories from a source available to both himself and his talmudic peers.

Mitnagged: Regardless, his material was all well embedded in rabbinic tradition.

Talmidah: We can't be sure. There's much in his commentary which cannot be traced to common rabbinic sources. Where did *they* come from?

Mitnagged: His own head.

Talmidah: Perhaps. Perhaps not. Suppose that what we assume to be "original" commentary is really a series of selected passages from sources rejected by his talmudic peers? Texts which no longer exist, or which we do not yet recognize?

Mitnagged: We cannot determine that. We *can* determine that traceable citations and allusions are talmudic, which means, until otherwise proven, untraceable allusions are likewise derived from talmudic-type texts which we may not have today. We certainly don't see any trace of gnosticism in his composition.

Talmidah: Perhaps not. But that does not disallow unconscious influence from other cultural and literary genres.

Mitnagged: Your gnostic citation is hardly unconscious. In fact, your entire collection of source material amazes me. Besides acceptable sages speaking from talmud and midrash, your assembly of teachers includes a Greek philosopher, a pro-Roman historian, an apocalyptic visionary, a prekabbalah mystic and a gnostic heretic! The only thing they share in common is that they all had a Jewish mother.

Talmidah: Except Onkelos.

Mitnagged: The rabbi who wrote *Targum Onkelos*?

Talmidah: A proselyte.

Mitnagged: I change my mind about you, Talmidah. You are not a funnel. You are a sponge, soaking up absolutely *everything*, producing a gastric nightmare both bizarre and revolting!

Rabbi: It appears that Mitnagged no longer objects to your "Rabbi Natan" technique, Talmidah, only to your sources.

Talmidah: Then we are at a standoff.

Rabbi: When precedent fails, you must *derash* your idea from Scripture.

Talmidah: I did not come prepared to do that.

Rabbi: A most unfortunate blow to your targum.

Mitnagged: You went too far. Like Icarus who flew too close to the sun with his man-made wings. The heat from the sun melted the wax holding his wings together, and thereby sent him falling down to his death. Your fantasy about the "separation" of Adam and Havah melts under the heat of analysis.

Talmidah: Why, Mitnagged, I'm surprised at you. I had no idea you believed in polytheism.

Mitnagged: What are you talking about!

Talmidah: It's obvious from your allusion to a Greek myth that you adhere to Greek paganism with its pantheon of decadent gods and goddesses.

Rabbi: She draws an analogy between the way you used the story of Icarus to the way she used an excerpt from a gnostic text.

Mitnagged: It's not the same thing!

Talmidah: And why not?

Mitnagged: Because I did not use the myth as a commentary on Scripture.

Talmidah: What about the stories, legends, and parables the rabbis used constantly to illustrate their arguments? You can't say it all came straight from orthodox sources. There must have been a great deal of improvising with the literature of the culture they lived and grew up in.

Mitnagged: Prove it.

Talmidah: I did not come prepared to do that today.

Rabbi: Most unfortunate.

Talmidah: I will be better prepared next time.

Mitnagged: And I will be prepared to counter any Torah argument with a stronger one.

Rabbi: We shall see. Any other observations you wish to make on her commentary, Mitnagged?

Mitnagged: Yes. Why include a third specially-named tree in the Garden?

Talmidah: You refer to the Tree of Mercy.

Mitnagged: Yes, the one flowing with olive oil. It does not seem relevant to your translation.

Talmidah: It will become relevant towards the end of my targum. It also serves as an additional metaphorical tie between Garden and Temple. Olive oil, after all, has historical significance in the anointing of kings and priests.

Mitnagged: Ahhh. You suggest that the Garden of Eden was some sort of primordial temple?

Talmidah: The evidence is overwhelming.

Mitnagged: So far I am not overwhelmed by your idea of overwhelming evidence.

Talmidah: Alright, let me spell it out for you. First of all, the Garden is set up topologically like a temple in the following ways:

1. It is an enclosed space, separate from the rest of the world. This is implied in its Persian name *paradise,* which by definition is an enclosed park sealed off from the wild lands beyond to prevent the encroachment of dangerous animals and noxious plants. The Garden of Eden is likewise sealed from the encroachment of the world by divine sentinels with flaming swords, as it is written, "He stationed in front of the Garden of Eden the cherubim and the flaming sword whirling

to and fro to guard the way."[58] These same cherubim are embroidered on the veils which separate the temple chambers from the outer courts.

2. It is divided into three concentric spaces, just like a temple, as it is written, "The Garden of Eden has three walls around it, all on fire."[59]

3. God dwells there, as it is written, "And he knew that the Garden of Eden was the holy of holies and the dwelling of the Lord."[60] So it is a holy place, a "House of Holiness."

4. The Tree of Eternal Life corresponds to the temple menorah. In fact, as described in Exodus 25:31–33, we find the menorah fashioned like a tree, with branches, almond blossoms, and petals. And just as the menorah is made of gold and burns with fire, so does the Tree of Eternal Life, as it is written, "And from every direction it has an appearance which is gold-looking and crimson, and with the form of fire."[61]

5. The Garden is sweet-smelling, "ripe and pleasant-smelling" and "giving off profusely a delightful fragrance."[62]

Mitnagged: What does fragrance have anything to do with the temple?

Talmidah: I'm not finished. What fragrances permeate the Garden? Frankincense, galbanum, stacte, and spices.[63] Incense, Mitnagged, such as were offered in the temple, as it is written, "And the Lord said to Moses: Take the herbs stacte,

---

58. Genesis 3:24.
59. *Bet ha-Midrash,* vol. 3, "The Order of the Garden of Eden."
60. *Jubilees* 8:19.
61. 2 Enoch 8:2.
62. 2 Enoch 8:1, 8.
63. *Jubilees* 3:27.

onycha, and galbanum—these herbs together with pure frankincense; let there be an equal part of each. Make them into incense, a compound expertly blended, refined, pure, sacred. Beat some of it into powder, and put some before the Pact in the Tent of Meeting, where I will meet with you; it shall be most holy to you."[64]

6. God's throne is said to be set under the Tree of Life, flanked by angels, just as the Ark of the Covenant is flanked by Angels in the holy of holies. "And the throne of God was made ready where the Tree of Eternal Life was."[65]

7. Sacred rivers flow from the Garden, as it does in Ezekiel's temple, a source of healing and prosperity to the land to which they flow. As it is written by the hand of the prophet Ezekiel, "He led me back to the entrance of the temple, and I found that water was gushing from below the platform of the temple."[66] And again, "It will be wholesome, and everything will live wherever this stream goes. All kinds of trees for food will grow up on both banks of the stream. Their leaves will not wither nor their fruit fail; they will yield new fruit every month, because the water for them flows from the temple. Their fruit will serve for food and their leaves for healing."[67]

Rabbi: Ahhhh. I begin to understand your translation of the four headwaters issuing from Eden and the names of the places they water.

---

64. Exodus 30:34–36, JPS translation.

65. *Apocalypse of Moses* 22:4. A pseudepigraphal work written during the first century C.E. Translated from a Greek text believed to be originally composed in Hebrew.

66. Ezekiel 47:1.

67. Ezekiel 47:12.

Talmidah: Yes. The names of the rivers echo Ezekiel's description of water "gushing" from the temple. So we have water "spreading out," "bursting forth," and "pressing in." The places they water reflect the healing and fruitful effects of God's holiness: "Life," "Sated," "Happiness," and "Fruitful." Note Ezekiel's strong allusion to the garden in his use of the phrases "all kinds of trees" which "serve for food," the same kind of language used in Genesis 2:9 to describe the Garden of God. Conversely, the description of lands noted for gold and precious stones in 2:11–12 trigger associations with the gold and precious stones with which the temples on Mount Moriah were adorned.

Rabbi: Mitnagged, how are the names for these rivers and places normally translated?

Mitnagged: Normally the names Pison, Havilah, Gihon, Cush, and Asshur are not translated. They are simply left as proper names. Hiddekel and Prat are commonly translated nonliterally as Tigris and Euphrates, to indicate the probable rivers referred to by these headwaters.

Rabbi: In other words, they are normally translated, and therefore interpreted, as geographical features which can be located on a modern map. Talmidah translated, and therefore interpreted them metaphorically. You did not challenge her deviation from traditional readings.

Mitnagged: At the time I did not see it as a metaphorical translation, only as clarification of possible Hebrew roots underlying the proper names of real geographical features.

Rabbi: But it is a targum. She would have been justified in translating it thus: "The name of the third river is Hiddekel,

'Pressing In,' known today as the Tigris." She did not do this. Did that not raise a question or two in your mind?

Mitnagged: Only the supposition that she was ignorant of scholarly consensus concerning the identity of this river.

Rabbi: It is never wise to underestimate your opponent.

Mitnagged: How was I supposed to know that it was some grand allusion to Ezekiel's vision of a future temple! This whole temple business is preposterous. The presence of temple imagery in a primordial narrative is a weird anachronism.

Talmidah: I'm not finished. The Garden is oriented to the east, just like the temple. As it is written, "Yahweh Elohim planted a garden eastward in Eden."[68] Now, not only do we find temple topology superimposed on the Garden throughout Tradition, but we discover Adam and Havah functioning as high priests.

Mitnagged: Hold it. I'll concede the point for Adam, but not Havah. Adam is called a high priest in *Seder Olam Rabbah*. He is said to function as one in *Bereshith Rabbah*[69] and *Bemidbar Rabbah*,[70] wearing the garments of a high priest and offering sacrifices to the Lord. *Nobody* talks about Havah in such a role.

Talmidah: When and where did Adam receive his high priestly vestments?

---

68. Genesis 2:8.
69. XVI.5.
70. IV.8.

Mitnagged: In the garden, when God clothed him in garments of skin, as written in Genesis 3:21.

Talmidah: Let me quote it for you. "Yahweh Elohim made garments of skin for the man *and his wife* and clothed *them*." We both agree the rabbis reasoned among themselves that these garments were priestly garments. So let's extend the debate a little further. The sages reasoned that because Yahweh clothed Adam in the garments of a high priest, Adam must have functioned as a high priest. Right?

Mitnagged: They don't say that.

Talmidah: They most certainly do!

> When Adam offered his sacrifice, he donned high priestly garments; as it says, "And the Lord God made for Adam and for his wife garments of skins and clothed them." They were robes of honor which subsequent firstborn used. When Adam died he transmitted them to Shet.[71]

Now, I ask you, why was Havah honored to wear high priestly clothing? To what purpose did she put them? To whom did she bequeath her clothing? What happened to the garment Yahweh made for Havah? Tradition is silent regarding these questions.

Rabbi: Perhaps these questions were never asked.

Talmidah: I ask them today, but I will not attempt to answer them today. I did not come prepared for that kind of midrashic discussion. I wish to go back and prove that the association

71. *Bemidbar Rabbah* IV.8.

between Eden and temple is not a "weird anachronism." In addition to its topology, Tradition alludes to the Garden of Eden as a temple directly, as cited in my targum: "And he knew that the Garden of Eden was the holy of holies and the dwelling of the Lord";[72] "From which place did He take him? From the place of the Temple, and He brought him into His palace, which is Eden."[73] The "Palace" of God, His House, is equivalent to his temple, the "House of Holiness." In addition, we have several descriptions of Paradise, as the future abode of the righteous, divided into three "courts" of progressively more sacred spaces within which the righteous are assigned to live according to the merits they earn in this life.

Mitnagged: You confuse the Paradise reserved for the righteous after they die with the Garden of Eden, a place of ancient times where the first man and woman lived.

Talmidah: They are one and the same. The Garden story tells of our expulsion from the presence of God, from his holy place. Paradise promises our return in the life to come.

Mitnagged: They exist in polarity, Talmidah, both in time and space. One existed at the beginning of time, the other will exist in the future. One was a physical reality on the earth, the other a conception of life in heaven.

Talmidah: Ahhh, but you agreed that time does not exist in the Garden.

Mitnagged: What!

---

72. *Jubilees* 8:19.
73. *Pirke de-Rabbi Eliezer,* chap. XI.

Talmidah: You agreed that the Garden was created before the Creation, before time existed.

Mitnagged: You can't be referring to your *mikedem* translation.

Talmidah: The Garden as paradise for Adam and Havah, or paradise for the righteous, is literally timeless, Mitnagged. And because it is timeless we can talk about past, present, and future in one breath. Collapsed time. Anything you say about one, you say about the other. They exist in the same time warp, so to speak.

Mitnagged: Please don't drag Einstein into this.

Talmidah: Einstein's theory of relativity? I don't think that's necessary, though I do think it is intriguing that he was a Jew. In any case, Paradise is also placeless.

Mitnagged: Placeless?!

Talmidah: Where did God put it? He had not yet created anything to put it in or on.

Mitnagged: Are you suggesting that Paradise is in some kind of "Twilight Zone"?

Talmidah: In a way it is. It's, well, it's very much like God Himself.

Mitnagged: You said you were not partial to mysticism.

Talmidah: I'm not. I *am* partial to metaphors and looking for universal truisms within those metaphors. You, on the other hand, are looking at the garden much too literally.

Mitnagged: Are you saying the Garden never existed?

Talmidah: Of course not. It is all too real. I'm just saying that the Garden serves the same purpose as other temples. It represents, simultaneously, the estrangement and reconciliation of man and God.

Mitnagged: You're saying man was formed in God's temple and then taken to God's temple to live. Makes no sense at all.

Talmidah: I didn't say it. Rabbi Eliezer said it. "From which place did He take him? From the place of the Temple, and He brought him into His palace, which is Eden." You agreed with me that a temple is any holy place where God dwells. He took man from one holy place and put him in another holy place.

Mitnagged: For what purpose? And what is your obsession with temples, Talmidah? They're everywhere! On the mountain, in the garden, up in the sky. For a woman who expressed absolute contempt for P and his temple cult, you have certainly made a 180 degree turnabout. Of what relevance is any of this to your targum?

Rabbi: I believe you will soon discover the answers to your questions. We shall meet at this same time next week.

Mitnagged: I think it's obvious who won today's round. Talmidah came out of the field reeling with drunkenness, a victim of confused thinking.

Rabbi: You think so? We shall see.

3

"Under the Huppah"
Genesis 2:18–24

Targum

Then Yahweh Elohim declared, *Gen 2:18a*

"It is not good that the man be alone
It is not right/fitting that the man be isolated/separated
The man is not happy
not fruitful
not joyful
because of his aloneness/isolation/separateness"

He who has no wife dwells without good
without help
without joy
without blessing
without atonement

without peace
without life

He is incomplete[1]

2:18b I will prepare/provide/appoint a partner equal to him
resembling him
corresponding to him

But He did not provide her until the man expressly demanded her.[2]

2:19 Now Yahweh Elohim had fashioned all the wild animals
and all the birds of heaven from the earth
These He brought to the man,
according to their kinds, both male and female,[3]
to see what he would name them.
And whatsoever the man named each living creature,
that was the name thereof.
2:20 So the man gave names
to all the cattle
all the birds of heaven
and all the wild animals.
But no suitable partner was found for the man.

Now the man was observing all of these, male and female, according to every kind which was on the earth, but he was alone and there was none whom he found for himself, who was like himself.[4]

1. *Bereshith Rabbah* XVII.2.
2. *Bereshith Rabbah* XVII.4.
3. Josephus, *Antiquities,* book I:I.2.
4. *Jubilees* 3:1.

He wondered at the other animals which were male and female.[5]

Then God paraded them, the animals and birds, again before him in pairs, male and female. Said the man, "Every one has a partner, yet I have none."[6] He being alone in the luxuriant plantation of the garden desired conversation, and prayed to behold another form like his own.[7]

The Holy One, blessed be He, had compassion upon the first man.[8]

Yahweh Elohim caused a visionary trance *2:21a*
to fall upon the man.

Adam: I was carried off into the Paradise of Righteousness, and I saw the Lord sitting and his appearance was unbearable flaming fire. And many thousands of angels were at the right and at the left of the chariot, God's throne.[9]

And while he slept *2:21b*
he perceived One/She from His temple side-chambers
  whom He enclosed in flesh below
  whom He delivered up in flesh to the wedding chamber
  he received joyous tidings of marriage.

---

5. Josephus, *Antiquities*, book I:I.2.
6. *Bereshith Rabbah* XVII.4.
7. *The Sibylline Oracles*, book 1, line 26. This passage from the oracles is among the oldest, believed to be written by a Jewish sibyllist around the turn of the era, shortly before the destruction of the Second Temple.
8. *Pirke de-Rabbi Eliezer*, chap. XII.
9. *Vita Adae*, 25:3. A Latin text based on an Hebrew original composed during the first century C.E.

Then the Holy One, blessed be He, called to him, "Adam! Adam!" When he awoke from his sleep he saw her standing opposite to him.[10] Whereupon Adam recognized her when she was brought to him.[11]

When he saw her, he was suddenly greatly amazed in spirit, rejoicing. Such a wonderful maidenly spouse![12] Such exquisite and desirable beauty and endowed with such excessive life and grace![13] And he rejoiced at the sight, and approached her and embraced her. And she, in like manner, rejoiced also, and addressed him in reply with modesty. And love being engendered, as it were, uniting two separate portions of one being into one body, adapted them to each other, implanting in each of them a desire to connect one with the other.[14] And they conversed with wise words which flowed spontaneously.[15] And both of them were wise in their glory.[16]

2:22a Then Yahweh Elohim built the side chamber
from where the man took to wife
from where the man married

He made the walls of the wedding canopy of gold and the covering of precious stones and pearls. He even made him hooks of gold. What think you, that He brought her to him from under a carob tree or a sycamore tree![17]

---

10. *Pirke de-Rabbi Eliezer*, chap. XII.
11. Josephus, *Antiquities*, book I:I.2.
12. *The Sibylline Oracles*, book 1, lines 29, 31, 32.
13. Philo, *Questions*, I.28.
14. Philo, *On the Creation*, LIII.
15. *The Sibylline Oracles*, book 1, lines 33, 34.
16. *Targum Yerushalmi*.
17. *Bereshith Rabbah* XVIII.2.

Rabbi Levi said, "The Holy One joined together thirteen wedding canopies over Adam in the Garden of Eden." According to Rabbi Simeon ben Lakish, it was eleven wedding canopies, and according to the majority consensus of the Rabbis, ten.[18]

Regarding the wedding canopy which God built for Adam and Havah: Imagine a king who gave his daughter in marriage and arranged a bridal chamber and a home for her, which he plastered, panelled, and painted. He saw it and it pleased him. "My daughter, my daughter!" he cried to her, "May this bridal chamber find favor before me at all times just as it has found favor before me at this moment."[19]

And He brought her to the man *2:22b*
He gave her to the man in marriage[20]

"And brought her to Adam" teaches that the Holy One, blessed be He, acted as groomsman for the first man.[21]

Do you want to know that all the Holy One's ways are loving kindness? At the beginning of Torah He adorned the bride.[22]

---

18. *Pesikta de-Rab Kahana,* Piska 4; *Pesikta Rabbati,* Piska 14.9. The Jewish tradition that God built a wedding canopy (in some cases, several canopies) for Adam and Eve in the Garden of Eden permeates Rabbinic literature. Besides the sources cited above and in note 17, we find it in *Tanhuma Bereshith* and *Pirke de-Rabbi Eliezer* (chap. XII).

19. *Bereshith Rabbah* XVII.2.

20. "*Ye-va-ah*/brought her" can be taken literally or as an idiomatic term meaning to give a bride away during a marriage ceremony.

21. *'Eruvin* 18b, Talmud Bavli.

22. *Tanhuma Bereshith.*

The Holy One, blessed be He, braided Havah's hair, and brought her to Adam.[23] The Holy One adorned Havah with twenty-four ornaments. And not only that, but He took her by the hand and brought her to Adam.[24] Then the Holy One, blessed be He, took a cup of blessing and blessed them.[25]

The Holy One, blessed be He, said to the ministering angels: Come, let us descend and render loving service to the first man and to his companion. So the ministering angels passed to and fro, walking before the man like friends who guard the wedding canopies. And the Holy One, blessed be He, was like a Chazan.[26] What is the custom observed by the Chazan? He stands and blesses the bride in the midst of her wedding chamber. Likewise the Holy One, blessed be He, stood and blessed Adam and his companion.[27]

2:23a Then the man said,

> "This One at last
> is bone of my bones
> and flesh of my flesh."

---

23. *Tractate Berakot* 61a, Talmud Bavli.

24. *Tanhuma Bereshith.* Rabbinic tradition insists that God personally groomed Havah as a bride by plaiting her hair and adorning her with jewels, a wedding custom still prevalent in the Middle East today. Besides the sources cited above and in notes 25, 26, and 27, this teaching is also found in tractates *'Eruvin* and *Shabbat* in the Talmud Bavli (18a and 95a respectively).

25. *Bereshith Rabbah* VIII.13.

26. "Cantor."

27. *Pirke de-Rabbi Eliezer,* chap. XII.

When a man takes one of his relations to wife, of him it is said, "Bone of my bones and flesh of my flesh."[28]

[Groom:] You ravish my heart *Song of*
my sister, my promised bride! *Songs 4:9*
How beautiful you are, how charming, *7:7*
my love, my delight!
In stature like the palm tree, *7:8*
its fruit-clusters your breasts.
I have decided, "I shall climb the palm tree, *7:9*
I shall seize its clusters of dates!"
May your breasts be clusters of grapes,
your breath sweet-scented as apples,
and your palate like sweet wine. *7:10*
You are wholly beautiful, my beloved, *4:7*
and without blemish.
[Bride:] How beautiful you are, my beloved, *4:1*
how beautiful you are!
My love is fresh and ruddy, *5:10*
to be known among ten thousand.
His head is golden, purest gold, *5:11*
his locks are palm fronds
and black as the raven.
His eyes are like doves *5:12*
beside the water-courses,
bathing themselves in milk,
perching on a fountain-rim.
His cheeks are beds of spices, *5:13*
banks sweetly scented.
His lips are lilies,
distilling pure myrrh.

28. *Bereshith Rabbah* XVIII.4.

5:16 His conversation is sweetness itself,
he is altogether lovable.
Such is my love, such is my friend.
4:10 [Groom:] What spells lie in your love,
My sister, my promised bride!
How delicious is your love, more delicious than wine!
How fragrant your perfumes,
more fragrant than all spices!
4:11 Your lips, my promised bride,
distil wild honey.
Honey and milk
are under your tongue.
2:8 [Bride:] I hear my love.
See how he comes
leaping on the mountains,
bounding over the hills!
2:9 My love is like a gazelle,
like a young stag.
2:10 My love lifts up his voice,
he says to me,
"Come then, my beloved,
my lovely one, come.
2:11 For see, winter is past,
the rains are over and gone.
Flowers are appearing on the earth.
The season of glad songs has come,
the cooing of the turtledove is heard in our land.
2:13 The fig tree is forming its first figs
and the blossoming vines give out their fragrance.
Come then, my beloved,
my lovely one, come."
4:12 [Groom:] She is a garden enclosed,
my sister, my promised bride;

a garden enclosed,
a sealed fountain.
Your shoots form an orchard of pomegranate trees, *4:13*
bearing most exquisite fruit:
nard and saffron, *4:14*
calamus and cinnamon,
with all the incense-bearing trees;
myrrh and aloes,
with the subtlest aromas.
Fountain of the garden, *4:15*
well of living water.
[Bride:] Awake, north wind, *4:16*
come, wind of the south!
Breathe over my garden,
to spread its sweet perfume around.
Let my love come into his garden,
let him taste its most exquisite fruits.
[Groom:] I come into my garden, *5:1*
my sister, my promised bride,
I pick my myrrh and balsam,
I eat my honey and my honeycomb,
I drink my wine and my milk.
[Bride:] Come, my love, *7:12*
let us go to the fields.
In the early morning we will go to the vineyards. *7:13*
We will see if the vines are budding,
if their blossoms are opening,
if the pomegranate trees are in flower.
Then I shall give you
the gift of my love.
The mandrakes yield their fragrance, *7:14*
the most exquisite fruits are at our doors;
the new as well as the old,
I have stored them for you, my love

8:6 [Bride and Groom:] Set me as a seal upon your heart
as a seal upon your arm.
6:3 I belong to my love
and my love to me

Psalms Oh come! Let us sing to the Lord!
95:1 Let us make a joyful noise!
98:1 for He has performed wonders!
98:5 Play to the Lord on the harp
98:6 to the sound of trumpet and horn!
98:4 Make a joyful noise to the Lord!
Make a loud noise!
Rejoice and sing praise!

Gen 2:23b She shall be called Holy Fire
Divine One
Woman
Wife
because she came from Holy Fire
Divine One
Man of Holiness

We find in the Torah, the Prophets, and the Writings that a man's marriage partner is from the Holy One, blessed be He.[29]

2:24 In this manner an elevated man will
loosen the bonds of his father and mother
forsake the sleeping house of father and mother[30]
And cleave/cling/adhere to his wife

---

29. *Bereshith Rabbah* LXVIII.3.
30. *Targum Onkelos.*

be lovingly devoted to his woman
his Divine One
And they shall be as one flesh
one body

Neither man without woman
nor woman without man
and neither of them without the Divine Spirit[31]

Blessed be the Name of the Lord of the world, who taught us His righteous way. He taught us to unite the bridegroom and the bride in marriage, as He united Havah to Adam.[32]

Midrash

The timid cannot learn, the short-tempered cannot teach
—*Pirke Avot,* II.6

Rabbi: Mitnagged, I presume you have examined this week's portion of Talmidah's targum.

Mitnagged: A most disagreeable dish of sour grapes. My teeth are still set on edge,[33] as when my mother serves sour lemonade.

Talmidah: You dislike my drink offering of wine.[34] That is not surprising. It is not meant for babies, as it is written:

---

31. *Bereshith Rabbah* VIII.9.
32. *Targum Yerushalmi,* Deuteronomy 34.
33. A reference to Jeremiah 31:30.
34. A reference to Levitical laws regarding offerings of wine in the temple cultus.

"To whom expound a message?
to those newly weaned from milk?
just taken away from the breast?"[35]

Mitnagged: It is also written, "Wine is a scoffer, strong drink a roisterer; he who is muddled by it will not grow wise."[36] And again, "Do not ogle that red wine! Your eyes will see hallucinations; your heart will speak distorted things."[37]

Talmidah: But it is also written, "Wine cheers the hearts of men,"[38] and "their hearts will be cheered as through wine."[39] This is a joyous piece of targum! Admit it!

Mitnagged: I enjoy a wedding bash as much as the next man. But "A season is set for everything, a time for every experience under heaven."[40] This is not the time for celebrating a fictional marriage ceremony. It is the time for interpreting the creation of woman from the rib of man. Rabbi, surely even you could not have anticipated this complete rewrite of a story unchallenged by sages, ancient and modern, for two millennia! Even the most virulent critics of this assertion of biblical patriarchy do not challenge the existence of the story itself, only its interpretation and application.

Rabbi: I must admit that when I read this piece of targum, I "drank the wine of astonishment."[41]

---

35. Isaiah 28:9.
36. Proverbs 20:1.
37. Proverbs 23:31, 33.
38. Psalms 104:15.
39. Zechariah 10:7.
40. Ecclesiastes 3:1.
41. Psalms 60:3.

Talmidah: I thought you knew where I was going, Rabbi. You acted as though you did.

Rabbi: I knew by the look in your eye that you had a weapon under your robe which Mitnagged failed to detect. Even with that anticipation, however, I was completely surprised by the nature of your attack.

Talmidah: How can you call this an "attack"? This is no attack! It's an embrace! It celebrates the mutual adoration which should exist between men and women. It defies the gender war by proclaiming with passion, "We need each other." It is a relationship blessed by the Holy One. Where are the daggers in this targum? I see none. It is the singing of male and female musicians in the court of the King—she on the lyre, he on the pipe—as you suggested yourself, Rabbi.

Mitnagged: It is an attack on Tradition. Your textual interpolations aside, there is not a single commentator, including those you cited in your targum, who did not repeat the rib story and subsequently interpret it. No one else translates the word *tsela* as a "temple side-chamber" in this story. Everyone translates the word as "rib" or "side," and reads this pericope to mean that woman was fashioned from a bone taken from the side of man. And *no one* translates *ish* as "Man of Holiness" to imply that Woman came from God rather than Man.

Talmidah: Agreed. But I feel confident that I can *derash* it from the Biblical text itself. In fact, I know that my translation is much more supportable under textual analysis than the one that has been circulating for two thousand years. I do *not* concede that my translation is an attack on Tradition. Quite the contrary. I will yet prove in this session that almost all sages agree that God performed a wedding ceremony in the Garden of Eden for Havah and Adam.

Mitnagged: What?

Talmidah: It's true, as you will soon see for yourself. It is also true that Tradition supports my interpretation of this story—namely that men and women need one another equally. I cited the passage from *Bereshith Rabbah* in my targum regarding the unhappy state of an unmarried man. In addition to that, it is written in the Talmud, "An unmarried man is not a man in the full sense,"[42] and "the unmarried person lives without joy, without blessing and without good."[43] And I shall repeat my favorite passage at the end of this piece of targum:

> Neither man without woman
> nor woman without man
> and neither of them without the Divine Spirit

Mitnagged: Before you can interpret a text, you must prove that the text you are interpreting actually says what you say it says, Talmidah. Get down from the clouds and face the reality of the text. Let's start with *le-bado*, "alone" in 2:18, which you translated polyvalently as "isolated" and "separated."

Rabbi: A most unwise strategy, Mitnagged. You will find that her translation of such words as *le-bado* and *e-eseh*, normally translated as "alone" and "make" in this verse, as well as *tardemah*, "sleep" in 2:21, which she translates as "visionary trance," are amply supported in Biblical Hebrew. There are

42. *Yevamot* 63a, Talmud Bavli.
43. *Yevamot* 62b, Talmud Bavli.

analogous passages elsewhere in Scripture where these words are utilized the way she has done so in this pericope.

Mitnagged: How did you know which words I was going to challenge?

Rabbi: Because those are the words which support her major piece of creative translation.

Mitnagged: You *agree* with her translation?

Rabbi: My initial reaction to it is negative. It is too startling to accept without convincing argument. She must prove to me that it is a viable translation, a translation at least possible.

Mitnagged: What strategy do you suggest?

Rabbi: I told you once, first things first. This must be the exception to that rule. In this case, I strongly advise you to begin at the middle with 2:21–22, for it is upon these two verses which most of Talmidah's other unusual alternate readings in this pericope depend for coherency.

Mitnagged: Very well. Talmidah, in 2:21 how do you justify your translation of *tsalot* as "temple side chambers"?

Talmidah: *Tsalot* is the plural of *tsela,* which is how it appears in 2:22. I checked every instance in the Hebrew Bible where a plural or singular form of *tsela* appears. Did you know that of the thirty-two places where it occurs, 2:21–22 is the *only* place where it is translated as "rib," meaning a bone from the rib cage of a living being? Nowhere else in Hebrew scripture does *tsela* refer to a human body part. In one case it refers to a hillside.[44] In *all* other cases, *tsela* is part of the construction of the tabernacle, temple, or Ark of the Covenant. It refers to a "plank," "beam," "wall," "chamber," or "side-chamber," all specifically referring to structural elements of a temple.

Mitnagged: The rabbis noted the analogous relationship between "plank" and "rib."

Talmidah: Yes. They justify the rib translation by comparing a plank to a rib. But there is another anomaly in these two verses, Mitnagged. The word *banah* in 2:22, which translators conveniently read as "fashioned" or "made." As far as I know, only one English translation gives *banah* its true meaning—"built." "The Lord God built up the rib into a woman."[45] I checked every instance where *banah* occurs in Hebrew scripture—which took a while, by the way—and guess what? The idea of "building" a living being is found nowhere else in Scripture. In 368 other instances *banah* describes the act of constructing man-made—in rare cases, God-made—structures such as cities, houses, walls, towns, gates, altars, shrines, and temples.[46] The word *banah* makes no sense in the context of creating a living being, particularly when three other, more appropriate words are used throughout the Creation account in Genesis 1 and 2, just before this verse, to describe the fashioning of plant life and living creatures, including mankind: *bara*, *yatzar*, and *asah*.

44. 2 Samuel 16:23.

45. NEB translation.

46. These include all grammatical forms of *banah*, as well as its Aramaic form in Ezra and Daniel.

Mitnagged: The word *banah* often occurs as a metaphor for building families or nations. You can hardly call a family a concrete, man-made structure.

Talmidah: There are fourteen such instances,[47] hardly "often." And applying *banah* to families and nations is logical, because the universal symbol for these collective entities is "house," meaning "household," which includes all individuals belonging to a *bet-av* or "father's house." It makes poetic sense to "build" them up. But individuals are never called houses by themselves, alone. "Building" them makes no sense.

Mitnagged: The rabbis disagree. They came up with several explanations for use in 2:22 of *build* to describe the creation of woman. In the Talmud we read that God "built" Havah in the shape of a storehouse, its shape accommodating her reproductive functions.[48]

Talmidah: You conveniently ignore the other two commentaries explaining the word *built* in this verse. "*And the Lord God built the rib* teaches that the Holy One, blessed be He, endowed the woman with more understanding than the man."[49]

Mitnagged: How did they derive that meaning?

Rabbi: The particle *wa-* attached to the imperfect form of *banah*, normally translated as the conjunctive "and," is here

47. 1 Sam. 2:35; 2 Sam. 7:27; 1 Kings 11:38; 1 Chron. 17:10, 17:25; Deut. 25:9; Ruth 5:11; Jer. 24:6, 31:4, 33:7, 42:10; Psalms 28:5; Gen. 16:2, 30:3.

48. *Eruvin* 18a–b, Talmud Bavli.

49. *Niddah* 45b, Talmud Bavli.

read as an arithmetic term. So *wa-yiben* means "one more than the previous number." In other words, God made Havah "one up" from Adam.

Mitnagged: Incredible.

Talmidah: There's a third explanation for what is meant by "building" the woman, which is by far the most popular. It is cited four times in the Talmud and in several major commentaries thereafter. Apparently, in ancient times there was a custom among people who lived in sea-towns—wherever those might have been—to call an elaborate braided hair-style a "building." Based on this custom, the rabbis derived the idea of building a woman's hair. According to this interpretation, God braided Havah's hair and adorned her for her marriage.[50]

Mitnagged: You certainly exploited that interpretation in your targum—all out of context as usual. So you have generously provided three metaphorical applications for this word from rabbinic sources. You don't need me here, Rabbi. Talmidah is quite effective in stabbing herself. In fact, she seems to enjoy it.

Talmidah: The problem with all three of these interpretations is that they equate *tsela* with "woman." In the minds of the sages, "built the *tsela*" is identical to "built the woman." But the text itself does not read built the woman. It reads "built the *tsela*," which in three other passages of Scripture means "built the side-chambers." As it is written,

50. *Eruvin* 18a; *Niddah* 45b; *Shabbat* 95a; *Berakot* 61a, Talmud Bavli.

> And against the wall of the house he *built* chambers round about . . . and he made *side-chambers* round about.[51]

Again it is written,

> And he *built* the *side-chambers* of the house within. . . .[52]

And finally,

> Then he *built* a terrace against its walls round both the sanctuary and the inner shrine. He made *side-chambers* all around. . . .[53]

All of these verses, by the way, refer to Solomon's construction of a temple. So if we buy into the traditional translation of this passage, Mitnagged, we are faced with not one, but two anomalies. Genesis 2:22 is the only verse which translates *banah* as "fashioning" a human being, and 2:21–22 is the only passage in Hebrew scripture where *tsela* refers to a body part. In terms of objective textual analysis, our traditional translation of this verse cannot be supported.

Mitnagged: There is no other Hebrew word which means "rib," Talmidah.

Talmidah: There is no Biblical Hebrew word for "rib," period.

Mitnagged: Come on, Talmidah! Any Israeli child will tell you that *tsela* means "rib"!

---

51. 1 Kings 6:5.
52. 1 Kings 6:15.
53. 1 Kings 6:45.

Talmidah: An Israeli child learns Modern Hebrew, a different language from the ancient language spoken by Israelites three thousand years ago. The word *tsela* as "rib" was written into Israeli vocabulary by the man who "reconstructed" conversational Hebrew a hundred years ago—Rabbi Eliezer ben-Yehuda. Guess where *he* learned Hebrew? In a yeshivah.[54] And what did his rabbi teach him *tsela* meant when they translated this passage together?

Mitnagged: What rabbis have been teaching their students for a thousand years.

Talmidah: Exactly. It's an assumed meaning which does not bear up under textual analysis. Look, there are more logical ways to write the rib story in biblical Hebrew. J—whoever that was—could have written that God took an *atsmah*/"bone" from Adam's *tsad*/"side." Both of these words are used liberally throughout Hebrew Scripture to refer to body parts. There is no need to use an obscure temple term as an analogy to a man's rib cage. Now there is yet another way J could have written this passage to mean what you and every other male want it to mean. In 2 Samuel there are four accounts of murder in which the attacker stabs his victim with a knife or spear "under the fifth."[55] Translators universally add "rib" to aid the reader. We read, "under the fifth *rib*," even though a word for rib is not actually present in Hebrew. Now if *tsela* meant "rib" to people speaking ancient Hebrew, why didn't these accounts read "under the fifth *tsela*"? Or, if J meant Adam's rib, why didn't he write that God took Adam's "fifth"—or "second" or "third," for that matter?

---

54. Advanced school for religious studies.
55. 2 Samuel 2:23, 3:27, 4:6, 20:10.

Mitnagged: J was writing a primeval story. The scribe of Second Samuel wrote an historical chronicle.

Talmidah: What difference does that make? According to the Documentary Hypothesis, they were contemporaries. They may have been writing about different periods of history, but they shared the same language tools and cultural background. They used the same vocabulary. Either one of them—keep in mind these were supposed to be well-educated courtly scribes—either one of them didn't know what the word for rib was, or one of them didn't know the idiomatic formula for referring to a rib, namely by its numerical position in the rib cage.

Mitnagged: I don't see that your translation offers a better alternative.

Talmidah: My translation is supported by the Hebrew text in three ways. First, it translates the words *banah* and *tsela* as they are commonly translated elsewhere in Scripture—"built" and "chamber"—within the context of constructing some kind of structure. Second, as noted earlier, these two Hebrew words are found together in three other places in the bible. I remind you once again that each of these cases refer directly to side-chambers in a temple. Finally, the idea of God building a side-chamber in His temple is found elsewhere in Scripture, in Ezekiel 40–42. Check out 41:5–11 in particular. Ezekiel observes, with meticulous detail, the construction of temple side-chambers by a divine being. And it takes place in a vision, Mitnagged, *while he is sleeping.*

Rabbi: Hence your translation of *tardemah* in 2:21 as "visionary trance."

Mitnagged: Which everyone else translates as "a deep sleep."

Talmidah: Not everyone. At least one translation reads "trance."[56] And that's admissible! The sages taught that there are three different meanings for *tardemah:* the torpor of sleep, the torpor of unconsciousness, and the torpor of prophecy.[57] You'll find the last of these meanings elaborated in your lexicon. It is a stuporous state caused by a supernatural agency. A torpor of prophecy precedes a vision while the visionary is sleeping.

Mitnagged: You typecast a lone man—and I mean the *only* human being on earth—as a prophet receiving visions from God. Who does he prophesy to, Talmidah? The squirrels? The rabbits?

Talmidah: You yourself called Adam a prophet.

Mitnagged: I did not!

Rabbi: I'm afraid so. Last week. During your nonanalysis of her reading of *le-marah,* "for vision/revelation," in connection with the trees from which Adam ate.

Talmidah: Yes, and you kindly provided rabbinic evidence that Adam is listed among the prophets. And I will further support your own statement. In my targum, I cited a passage from a text that describes an ascension vision experienced by Adam.

---

56. NEB.
57. *Bereshith Rabbah* xvii.5.

Mitnagged: Out of context—*again*. The document you extracted this piece of visionary experience from places the event at his deathbed, over nine hundred years later. You place it at the beginning of his life, not the end.

Talmidah: Totally irrelevant, Mitnagged. The important point made is that Adam *did* have a vision.

Rabbi: One might add that, according to Tradition, Adam was shown all generations of mankind while yet a golem. He was not even fully created when he reached this vision.[58]

Talmidah: Besides the fact that a Merkavah account for Adam exists, there is another important detail in this excerpt. Adam's description of God and the throne He sits upon is consistent with other ascension accounts given both in Scripture and Merkavah literature. "I saw the Lord sitting and his appearance was unbearable flaming fire. And many thousands of angels were at the right and at the left of the chariot." Compare that to Daniel's vision in 7:9–10:

> While I was watching,
> thrones were set in place
> and One most venerable took his seat.
> His robe was white as snow,
> the hair of his head as pure as wool.
> His throne was a blaze of flames,
> its wheels were a burning fire.
> A stream of fire poured out,
> issuing from his presence.

---

58. *Bereshith Rabbah* XXIV.2; *Pesikta Rabbati*, Piska 23.1.

A thousand thousand waited on him,
ten thousand times ten thousand stood before him.[59]

And Ezekiel's vision in 1:26–27:

High above was what appeared to be a throne
upon which was what appeared to be a human being.
I saw a brilliance like amber, like fire,
radiating from what appeared to be the waist upwards
and from what appeared to be the waist downwards,
I saw what looked like fire,
giving a brilliant light all around.
The radiance of the encircling light
was like the radiance of the bow in the clouds on rainy days
The sight was as the glory of Yahweh.[60]

You will see parallel descriptions in ascension accounts attributed to Enoch, Abraham, Isaac, Jacob, Levi, Moses, Isaiah, Zephaniah, and Baruch.[61] They all view God as glorious beyond description, like *fire,* sitting on a throne made of *fire,* surrounded by myriads of bright and shining angels.

Mitnagged: You are once again alluding to the holy of holies, where the throne of God—represented by the Ark of the Covenant—is flanked on either side by gilded angels, and where incense, "fire," burns continually.

59. NJB translation.

60. NJB translation.

61. 1 Enoch, 2 Enoch, 3 Enoch, Testament of Abraham, Testament of Isaac, Testament of Jacob, Testament of Levi, Ascension of Moses, Ascension of Isaiah, Apocalypse of Zephaniah, Apocalypse of Ezra, Apocalypse of Baruch.

Talmidah: That and the idea . . .

Mitnagged: Very nice. Except that *it is not in the text.* You're propping up a piece of commentary, which in turn props up a dubious translation of Scripture, which by itself makes no mention of any kind of Merkavah vision.

Talmidah: I didn't finish. I'm pointing out that all of these visionary accounts associate Yahweh with fire.

Mitnagged: Now we're moving into your polyvalent reading of *ish* as "holy fire" and "Man of Holiness" in 2:23. This had better be good.

Talmidah: Verse 2:23 is traditionally translated, "She shall be called Woman, because she was taken from Man." The Hebrew word for man in this verse is *ish,* not *adam,* as you pointed out. This is the first time *ish* occurs in the Torah. Up to this point in Scripture, *man, Adam,* and *mankind* are consistently represented by the word *adam.*

Mitnagged: What difference does that make? *Ish* and *adam* both mean "*man.*"

Talmidah: In many cases in Scripture there is no difference. They are both generic terms for "man." But there are other levels of meaning for these two words, which make a significant difference in this pericope of Scripture. We all agreed that *adam* shares the same root letters as "earth," "dirt," and "red," and that it's OK to tie these meanings together in order to describe what kind of "man" *adam* is. He's "earthly," made of "dirt" and "blood." *Midrash Tehillim* draws upon all of these roots to imply that *adam* is a lower kind of man. As it is written, "Whenever one finds in Scripture the word *adam,* it refers to a man of low degree."[62] Circumstances in which the word *adam* is used in other passages of Hebrew Scripture support this idea of "lower man" as applied to the word *adam*. *Adam* is often found in parallel phrases with animals, as it is written, "And every living substance was destroyed which was upon the face of the ground, both *adam*/man and cattle."[63] And did you know that a dead body is always the carcass of an *adam*, never an *ish?* The dead body of an *adam* is a source of defilement for anyone who touches it, as it is written, "He who touches the dead body of any *adam* shall be unclean seven days."[64] When we apply the same rules for deriving meaning for *ish* as we did for *adam,* we discover that *ish* means "man" alright, but an entirely different kind of man. The word shares consonants with *esh,* which means "fire." But not just any kind of fire—holy fire, like the *esh*/fire that burnt up sacrificial offerings on the altar,[65] or the *esh*/fire that burnt the bush on Mount Sinai—so holy that Moses was commanded to take off his sandals in its presence.[66] And the presence or even wrath of God was often manifested with great pillars or blasts of *esh*/fire.[67] The biblical connection between the words *ish*/man and *esh*/fire and their joint association with the Divine is best portrayed in a story about Elijah the prophet in the first chapter of 2 Kings. King Ahaziah sends a captain with fifty soldiers to arrest the prophet, who happens to be sitting on a hill. As the captain approaches Elijah, he exclaims, "Hey you! *Ish*/Man of God! The king says, 'Come down!'" Elijah retorts:

62. 9:16.

63. Genesis 7:23. Also Genesis 6:7, 7:21; Exodus 9:25, 12:12, 13:13, 15; Leviticus 24:21, 27:28; Numbers 3:13.

64. Numbers 19:11.

65. I.e., Leviticus 6:12, 13.

66. Exodus 3:2.

67. I.e., Exodus 24:17, Numbers 11:1–3.

If I be an *Ish*/Man of God,
then let *Esh*/Fire come down from heaven
and consume you and your fifty!

What happens? "And there came down *esh*/fire from heaven and consumed him and his fifty."

Rabbi: Elijah was not a patient man.

Talmidah: Not only do we have shared consonants between *ish* and *esh*, but we find certain uses of *ish* in Scripture in which *adam* is never used. I used my Hebrew concordance to chase down every instance where *ish* or *adam* occurs in the Torah and the book of Joshua. I discovered that such men as prophets, patriarchs, priests, temple workmen, royal officials, and men of wisdom are always called *ish*—never *adam*.[68] The difference between an *ish*/man and an *adam*/man is further stated in Psalms 62:9, where an *adam* is described as "a man of low degree" and an *ish* as "a man of high degree." In other words, an *ish* is an elevated man, often holy. A literal translation for this level of meaning would be "higher man," "holy man," or "man of holiness."

---

68. *Prophets*: Exodus 11:3, 18:7, 32:1; Numbers 12:3; Deut. 33:1; Joshua 14:6 (Moses); Joshua 10:14 (Joshua); 1 Kings 17:18; 2 Kings 1:9–13, 4:16, 21, 22, 25, 27, 40 (Elijah); 2 Kings 4:9, 5:8, 14, 15, 20, 6:6, 9, 10, 15, 7:2, 17, 18, 19 (Elisha); 1 Samuel 9:6, 10 (Samuel); 1 Kings 12:22 (Shemaiah); 1 Samuel 2:27; 1 Kings 13:1, 4–8, 20:28 (anonymous prophets). *Patriarchs*: Genesis 6:9 (Noah); Genesis 20:7 (Abraham); Genesis 24:65 (Isaac); Genesis 30:43 (Jacob); Genesis 39:2 (Jospeh); Genesis 42:25, 35, 43:21, 44:1, 11, 13 (Joseph's brothers). *Priests*: Numbers 7:5; Lev. 7:10, 10:1, 21:9, 22:4; Deut. 33:8. *Temple Workmen*: Exodus 36:1, 2, 4; Numbers 19:9, 18. *Royal Officials*: Genesis 42:30, 33, 43:3, 5, 7, 13, 14, 17, 19, 24; Exodus 7:12; Numbers 1:4, 44, 27:16; Deut. 1:23; Joshua 3:12. *Men of Wisdom*: Genesis 41:33, 38, 44:15.

Mitnagged: But they are still quite human.

Talmidah: *Ish* also refers to angels or divine messengers, as it is written,

> When Joshua was near Jericho, he looked up and saw an *ish*/man standing in front of him, grasping a naked sword. Joshua walked towards him and said to him, "Are you on our side or on that of our enemies?" He replied, "On neither side. I have come now as the captain of the army of Yahweh." Joshua fell on his face to the ground, worshipping him, and said, "What has my Lord to say to his servant?" The captain of the army of Yahweh answered Joshua, "Take your sandals off your feet, for the place where you are standing is holy."[69]

Rabbi: Almost the same words Yahweh spoke to Moses as he approached the burning bush on Mount Sinai.

Talmidah: Alit with *esh*, holy fire. One other type of man described in Hebrew Scripture is always referred to as an *ish*/man rather than *adam*/man. God Himself is compared to an *ish*/man, as it is written, "The Lord is an *Ish*/Man of war: the Lord is his name."[70] So what do we have? Adam sees, in vision, his future wife in the place where God, the Man of Fire, dwells. What does Adam call her? If he meant to name her after himself, he would have named her *Adamah*, the feminine counterpart to his own name. Instead, he calls her *Ishah*, the feminine counterpart to *ish*, with all its allusions to holiness and fire.

---

69. Joshua 5:13–15. See also Genesis 32:24 and Judges 13:6, 8.
70. Exodus 15:3. See also Deut. 1:31, 8:5, and Exodus 33:11.

Mitnagged: The feminine counterpart to god is goddess. Talmidah. Are you calling the woman a goddess?!

Talmidah: Of course not! I am not calling her a goddess, and neither did Yahweh. *Adam* called her *ishah*. He called her *ishah* to acknowledge her origins, as it is written, "She shall be called *ishah,* 'holy fire' or 'Divine One,' *because* she was taken from *Ish,* 'Holy Fire' or 'Divine One'."

Mitnagged: Your argument hinges on your interpretation of *ish* as it occurs for the first time in Torah. Where does it occur the second time?

Talmidah: Verse 2:24.

Mitnagged: Immediately following 2:23. Do you also translate *ish* in this verse as "Man of Holiness" meaning "God"?

Talmidah: No, I do not. You did not disagree with my assertion that there are three levels of meaning for *ish. Ish* can be a generic term for "man." It can mean an elevated man of importance—a prophet, patriarch, or man endowed with wisdom, for example. Or it can refer to a divine being, an angel, or even God Himself. There is yet another meaning for *ish,* a meaning never labeled *adam* in Scripture—a man who marries a woman. Very often a woman's *ish* is translated into English as a woman's "husband."[71] I would argue that these meanings are interrelated. When an *adam* marries an *ishah,* a woman, his status is immediately elevated to that of an *ish*—a man of

71. Genesis 2:24, 29:32*, 34*, 30:15*, 20*; Numbers 30:7*; Deut. 21:15, 22:16, 23*, 24:2, 3*, 28:56. Starred verses are places where the Hebrew word *ish* is typically translated as "husband."

higher degree. He becomes more like the Divine Being in whose image he was created.

Mitnagged: How so?

Talmidah: Without a woman a man cannot engage in the most godlike activity available to human beings—making life.

Rabbi: Nor can a woman.

Talmidah: Nor can a woman do what?

Rabbi: Make life. A woman without a man cannot make life.

Mitnagged: Look how she blushes!

Talmidah: I am *not* blushing. One cannot study Torah and be squeamish about sex. Half the laws in Exodus and Leviticus address sexual behavior.

Rabbi: It is also a minor theme throughout all the narratives, as well as the subject of numerous proverbs, psalms, and prophetic tirades.

Mitnagged: You are nevertheless embarrassed. Shall we say then that a woman without a man is a field without a plow? It will never produce a harvest?

Talmidah: Then we shall say that a man without a woman is like a plow without a field. It hangs in the shed, small and limp.

Mitnagged: This is disgusting. Rabbi, why do you allow this conversation to go on?

Rabbi: I find it amusing to listen to children discussing a subject of which neither one has any experience. Ahhh . . . now your faces truly match one another—a uniform color of beet-red.

Talmidah: Let us go back to a more elevated plain.

Mitnagged: Agreed.

Talmidah: The man called his wife by a honorific title, *ishah,* because she came from a holy place, from the side of the Holy One, "Man of Fire," to the place where the man dwelled. And there they were united, once more, as a couple.

Mitnagged: Reunited in a side-chamber.

Talmidah: That's right.

Mitnagged: Look, a side-chamber by definition is built into a wall, is part of a building. We're talking about a freestanding room without walls. It is an impossible structure as well as an absurd anachronism!

Talmidah: You imagine a chamber made of stone. But you must remember two things from last week, points which you eventually conceded, Mitnagged. First, a temple, or its elemental parts, does not have to be made of stone. The *tsalot* in Moses' tabernacle, for example, were necessarily made of cloth or skins. Second, the garden of Eden is conceived by many sages to be a temple itself—or at least characterized by temple topology and function. I don't find it difficult at all to imagine a *tsela* standing in the middle of a garden—a room of cloth without walls.

Rabbi: A *huppah.*

Talmidah: That's right. A wedding canopy.

Mitnagged: A *huppah* is not a *tsela!*

Talmidah: A tree is not a menorah. A garden is not a building.

Mitnagged: If J meant to say *huppah,* he would have written *huppah,* not *tsela.*

Talmidah: I'll spare you another argument over intent and its irrelevance to exegesis, and appeal to precedent. You say that a structure that is not specifically named a *huppah* is not a *huppah,* even though it may look like one and function like one.

Mitnagged: That is correct.

Talmidah: Then you defy rabbinic logic, for the sages had no problem identifying a *huppah* by another name. We even find a consensus among them that such a *huppah* existed in the Garden of Eden.

Mitnagged: What are you talking about?

Talmidah: I am talking about the word *masekah,* "covering," in Ezekiel 28:13. "You were in Eden, the Garden of God. Every precious gem was your *masekah,* your covering." I quoted the entire passage in last week's portion of targum. The rabbis debated endlessly about this passage. What was the *huppah* made of? How many *huppahs* were there? One? Three? Ten? Thirteen? There were no arguments presented by anyone against equating *masekah* to *huppah*. It is upon this passage, by the way, that the sages derived their exegesis that God performed a marriage ceremony for Adam and Havah under a *huppah*—or several *huppahs*—in the Garden of Eden. This idea is never disputed. Their debates were not over whether this event actually occurred or whether there actually was a *huppah*, but over how *many huppahs* God built and what the *huppah* was made of. Now, there is a parallel line to "You were in Eden" in verse 14 in our Ezekiel passage: "You resided in God's holy mountain"—another allusion to temple, as we agreed last week. This allusion was not lost on the sages. As cited in my targum, *Bereshith Rabbah*'s description of the *huppah* God built for Adam and Havah strongly alludes to the description of temple chambers in Scripture. The *huppah* in the garden was made of gold, held together with "hooks of gold." So it is written in Exodus 26:37, which gives instructions for making the desert sanctuary of Moses, "You will make five poles of acacia wood and overlay them with gold, with hooks of gold."

Mitnagged: Then you admit that the rabbis did not derive their exegesis from an alternate reading of 2:21–22. There isn't a trace of a suggestion that *tsela* was equated with *huppah*.

Talmidah: I concede that point. Sages unanimously read *tsela* in these verses as "rib." However . . .

Mitnagged: Your targum implies that they did just that.

Talmidah: My targum points out that the idea of a marriage ceremony under a *huppah* in the Garden of Eden is not alien to Tradition. In fact, it is quite comfortable with the idea. My translation supports Tradition in its assertion. Now the connection between *huppah* and *tsela* is not as far apart as you think—no more so then the connection between *huppah* and *maseka*. Even if you are totally oblivious at wedding "bashes," you can look in any encyclopedia on Judaica, or any book describing Jewish marriage customs and you will find a couple of interesting connections. First, any child looking at illustrations of various kinds of *huppahs* built throughout the world from medieval times to modern can see that there are two types: the portable outdoor *huppah* and the permanent indoor *huppah*. Portable *huppahs* are typically made of richly-decorated cloth held up by four poles, or they are made of wood, myrtle sprigs, and roses. There are variations, of course. Sometimes an Israeli couple on active military duty will marry under a tallit propped up by rifles.

Mitnagged: The wedding of combat soldiers. A most appropriate *huppah*—the perfect symbol for marital life.

Rabbi: What makes you an expert on marital life, Mitnagged? I don't recall ever seeing a wedding band on your finger.

Talmidah: His face turns red.

Rabbi: She notices a possible weakness in your ego. I hope she does not exploit it.

Talmidah: I shall exploit it at every opportunity . . . half-man.

Mitnagged: I don't see a ring on your finger either, Talmidah.

Rabbi: Now she blushes as well. Once again your faces are in agreement with one another.

Mitnagged: About the *huppah* and its spurious connection with the *tsela*.

Talmidah: So the portable, outdoor *huppah* can easily be imagined in a garden setting. Permanent indoor *huppahs* are three-sided chambers constructed against the side of a wall. It may have cloth overhangings or two sidewalls extending out into the room, or it might be recessed into the wall. In any case, the resemblance to "side-chambers" built into the "sidewalls" of the temple is irresistible.

Mitnagged: I have no trouble resisting it at all. Do you have *any* evidence or *any* commentary by a credible scholar that makes this connection between *huppah* and *tsela?*

Talmidah: None.

Mitnagged: I rest my case.

Talmidah: I'm not finished. The breaking of the Glass of Benediction as part of the wedding ceremony.

Rabbi: A symbol of the destruction of the temple.

Mitnagged: The meaning of this ritual is not certain. There are other possible interpretations.

Rabbi: Reminding wedding guests of the sobriety of this ceremony and to temper their merrymaking during the festivities immediately following.

Talmidah: Some orthodox communities have an additional custom. The bridegroom places ashes on his head while he is under the canopy.

Rabbi: A sign of mourning for the temple.

Mitnagged: That, too, can be interpreted as a warning to wedding guests to temper their merrymaking.

Rabbi: I favor the view that these rituals allude to the destruction of the temple. It is, after all, a *mitzvah*[72] to rejoice with a bride and her groom on their wedding day.

Mitnagged: Her whole speculation about the *tsela* as a *huppah* is just that—speculation. It has no support.

Talmidah: I agree that I am engaged in speculation. I cannot actually prove anything. I *can* point out that my translation is a valid possibility. It is a legitimate alternative to conventional translations of this pericope of Scripture. In fact, I assert that it bears up under intertextual analysis much better than the "rib" story, as I demonstrated earlier.

Rabbi: Mitnagged, do you challenge her textual analysis of *banah,* "built", and *tsela,* "chamber"?

Mitnagged: By itself it makes a credible case. But can you fit these newly-translated words within the verses by which they are contained? Unless you can prove that it makes sense contextually, your "temple" crumbles to the dust.

Rabbi: Explain your polyvalent reading in 2:21 of *wa-yisgor besar tahtenah,* normally translated, "and he closed up the flesh instead thereof," meaning that God healed the wound in Adam's side after taking out his rib.

72. Commandment.

Talmidah: A literal translation of these Hebrew words would be "and he closed flesh instead" or "and he closed flesh below," depending on how you read *tahtenah*. Obviously some editing is required for it to make any sense to an English reader. So translators traditionally add a preposition, *up*, a definite article, *the*, and some kind of nonliteral clarifier, like *thereof*, or *at that spot*.[73] I added a relative pronoun, *whom*, and a preposition, *in*. I also chose "below," rather than "instead," as a meaning for *tahtenah*.

Mitnagged: To compliment your dream of woman coming down from some visionary temple chamber.

Rabbi: Do you challenge this line of her translation?

Mitnagged: Not on technical grounds. I *would* like to point out that it makes little sense. "Whom He enclosed in flesh below"—what does that *mean?* And her other two readings of this phrase manipulate the original text.

Rabbi: As long as she follows acceptable rules for such manipulation, she is justified in doing so. Talmidah, explain how you arrived at your variant readings of this phrase.

Talmidah: We agree that my first reading of this phrase is technically acceptable, because it requires no changes in the Masoretic text. My other two readings of this phrase require revoweling and/or rearrangement of the consonants. Here, I'll write it on the board. The consonants as we have them in the Masoretic text, minus vowel points and accent marks, are

73. JPS. The whole phrase in this translation reads, "and he closed up the flesh at that spot."

grouped as follows: *wysgr bsr thtnh*. The Masoretes voweled it as follows: *wa-yisgor besar tahtenah* which is traditionally translated as "and he closed up the flesh instead thereof." I translated it as "whom He enclosed in flesh below."

Mitnagged: What does that mean?

Talmidah: What does what mean?

Mitnagged: "Enclosed in flesh below." What does that *mean?*

Talmidah: I don't know.

Mitnagged: You don't *know?*

Talmidah: I suppose it could mean a number of things, but it's not important.

Mitnagged: *Not important!*

Talmidah: Let me restate that. It is not important for today's debate. I didn't spend any time hunting down rabbinic commentary or *derashing* biblical exegesis about what this phrase might actually *mean*. That's not the point.

Mitnagged: What *is* your point?

Talmidah: That there are other ways to read this phrase besides the one we've always accepted. It doesn't have to mean that God took a bone out of Adam's side and closed up the wound.

Rabbi: Your other two readings require manipulation of the Masoretic text.

Talmidah: That is correct. The Masoretic text groups the consonants as follows: *wysgr bsr thtnh.* I group them this way: *wysgr bsrt htnh.*

Rabbi: Any objection, Mitnagged?

Mitnagged: Not so far. Letters at the beginning and ends of words can be shifted to adjacent words.

Talmidah: I then voweled these consonants as follows: *wa-yisgor besrat hatanah*/"and he received joyous tidings of marriage," "he" referring to Adam, instead of God. *Besrat* is the construct state of the word *basarah.*

Rabbi: "Good tidings."

Talmidah: And the word *tahtenah,* minus the *tav*, becomes *hatanah.*

Rabbi: "Wedding" or "marriage."

Mitnagged: Quite a feat of mental gymnastics.

Talmidah: Thank you.

Mitnagged: It was not meant as a compliment. You know as well as I do that the more textual emendations required to "invent" a translation, the less credible it is. Now please explain your third reading, because it is a great mystery to me.

Talmidah: My third reading does not require moving the consonants, but voweling it differently so that the last word is a compound word: *wa-yisgor besar ta-hatanah*/"whom He delivered up in flesh to the wedding chamber."

Mitnagged: I looked up *ta* in three different lexicons.

Talmidah: It wasn't there. Actually, the word I have in mind ends with a *heh,* which assimilated to the word it was attached to. That doesn't help you, though, because *tah* isn't in any Hebrew lexicon either.

Mitnagged: You admit it, then. I don't believe it. You *made up a word.* How did you justify making up a Hebrew word?

Talmidah: The word is manifested in Aramaic, with an *aleph* at the end, instead of a *heh. Ta,* in Aramaic, means "chamber."

Mitnagged: Aramaic is *not* Hebrew.

Talmidah: Agreed. But you know that Hebrew words ending in *heh* were commonly transferred to Aramaic, respelled with *alephs* instead of *hehs.* Examples of these are *galah*/"reveal," "*hawah*/"to be," and the familiar *banah*/"build."

Mitnagged: *Galah, hawah,* and *banah* are real Hebrew words, occurring abundantly in the Hebrew text of the Bible. *Tah* does not occur *anywhere.* You work from a strange kind of logic, Talmidah, namely that any word in Aramaic that ends in an *aleph might* have a Hebrew counterpart ending in a *heh.* Rabbi, tell her that this is not a credible basis upon which to make a translation.

Rabbi: Talmidah, this is not a credible basis upon which to make a translation.

Talmidah: I stand corrected.

Mitnagged: I will strike this line for your targum.

Talmidah: Be my guest.

Mitnagged: You don't seem overly brokenhearted.

Rabbi: This case is likened to that in a courtroom. The defense lawyer wishes to introduce evidence legally inadmissible in court. She presents the evidence regardless. The judge strikes the evidence from the court records, sternly reprimands the lawyer and advises the jury to "forget it." But the damage is done. The members of the jury heard the "evidence." It will doubtless have a subtle effect on their verdict.

Mitnagged: What "evidence" did she sneak through . . . "chamber" . . . "wedding chamber" . . . "side-chamber" . . .

Talmidah: The point has been made, Mitnagged. I came up with three different possible readings for this phrase which support my overall translation. One of them is too spurious to be accepted. But that still leaves two uncontested readings. My "temple" yet stands.

Rabbi: Proceed with your challenge, Mitnagged.

Mitnagged: You didn't bother to change or delete 2:23, a glaring contradiction to your entire scenario. Adam points to the woman and says, "This is bone of my bones and flesh of my flesh," which makes perfect sense in the rib account, but not in your fairy tale where they get married and live happily ever after.

Talmidah: They get married, but they don't live happily ever after, as my targum will describe in agonizing detail.

Mitnagged: An agony brought on by the woman, as every man's suffering and pain can be traced to a woman—be it through her weakness or evil inclination.

Talmidah: An agony brought on by the natural course of living. And if you think Scripture portrays Havah as either weak or evil, you are dead wrong.

Mitnagged: It was the woman who was deceived, not the man.

Talmidah: She was *not* deceived. She knew exactly what she was doing. And it was the wise thing to do.

Mitnagged: *Wise?* Hah!

Rabbi: We move away from the topic at hand. You will have your chance to battle over Havah's choice next week.

Mitnagged: I do not wonder that Talmidah leapt at the chance to change the subject. Just how do you interpret 2:23?

Talmidah: Did you know that this phrase occurs elsewhere in Scripture? Seven times.[74] In none of these cases is it possible to suggest that the phrase "bone of my bones, flesh of my flesh" means that the person so addressed was physically created from the bones and flesh of the speaker, not even figuratively. Such a relationship might be conceivable between parent and child, but none of these cases meet this condition. The phrase is used to emphasize the blood ties between uncle and nephew,

74. Genesis 29:14, 37:27; Judges 9:2; 2 Samuel 5:1, 19:12; 1 Chron. 11:1; Isaiah 58:7.

between brothers, between tribesmen or relatives in general. All of these cases involve male relatives, so it is not a formula for putting man over woman in a marriage covenant, either. It is simply the affirmation of familial ties. Following a marriage ceremony, this phrase would declare that the man and woman were now bound together as though they shared the same parentage. They are now kinfolk in the bloodline sense of the word—lateral relatives of equal standing, like siblings, as suggested by the title sung by the groom to his bride repeatedly in Song of Songs, "My sister, my promised bride."[75]

Rabbi: Have you any other arguments against Talmidah's targum?

Mitnagged: Not at the moment. I will think of more in the coming week.

Talmidah: Fine with me.

Rabbi: Meaning that she would rather see you devote time and energy to the piece of targum just debated, rather than next week's "episode."

Mitnagged: "Havah's Failure in the Face of Temptation." Yes, I can see why you want me to be distracted from that piece of Scripture. It is the most damning of all. Don't worry, Rabbi, I shall be *fully* prepared for *next week's* attempt to vindicate Havah.

Rabbi: We shall see.

75. Reference this chapter's targum.

4

"A Desirable Tree" Genesis 2:25–3:7

Targum

Now the two of them were smooth-skinned/naked *Genesis 2:25*
blind in ignorance
the man and his wife
but they were not ashamed
troubled
disturbed
towards one another

The mind is naked when it is clothed neither with vice nor with virtue, but is really stripped of both: just as the soul of an infant child, which has no share in either virtue or vice, is stripped of all coverings of the soul, by which it is enveloped and concealed, good being the garment of the virtuous soul, and evil the robe of the wicked soul.[1]

3:1a Now, the serpent
the adversary
Satan the Serpent
He Who Waits in Ambush
was more smooth-tongued/slier than any other life of the field
any other life of the Almighty

The evil prompter
the Angel of Death[2]
A froward man
a whisperer[3]

Yahweh: One from the order of the archangels deviated, together with the division that was under his authority. He thought up the impossible idea that he might place his throne higher than the clouds which are above the earth, and that he might become equal to my power. He understood how I wished to create another world, so that anything could be subjected to mankind on the earth, to rule and reign over it. The devil is of the lowest place. And he will become a demon, because he fled from heaven: Sotona, because this name was Satanail. In this way he became different from the angels. And he became aware of his condemnation and of the sin which he sinned previously. That is why he thought up the scheme against man.[4]

1. Philo, *Allegorical Interpretation II,* XV.53.
2. *Baba Bathra* 16a, Talmud Bavli.
3. *Bereshith Rabbah* XX.2.
4. 2 Enoch 29:4, 31:4–6, J recension.

He asked the woman 3:1b
"Did Elohim really say:
You shall not eat from any tree of the Garden?"
The woman answered the Serpent 3:2
"We may eat the fruit of any tree in the garden
except the fruit of the tree which is in the middle of the garden. 3:3
Elohim said:
"You shall not eat from it
nor touch it
or you will die."
Then the Serpent said to the woman, 3:4
speaking accusation against his Creator[5]
"You will not die!
But Elohim knows that in the day you eat of it 3:5
your eyes will be opened
blindness/ignorance will be cleared
your springs will be opened
children will come forth
and you will be like gods/divine ones
knowing good and evil
right and wrong
health and injury
joy and misery
pleasure and pain

From this tree the Creator ate and created His world, and He therefore forbade you to eat thereof lest you create another world.[6] Just as He creates worlds and destroys worlds, so will you be able to create worlds and to destroy worlds. Just as He

5. *Targum of Palestine.*
6. *Davarim Rabbah* V.10.

slays and brings to life, so also will you be able to kill and to bring to life."[7]

The Serpent walked over to the tree and touched it. Then the Serpent walked over to the woman and said, "Look, I touched it, but I did not die. You can touch it also and not die." The woman walked over to the tree and touched it, and she saw the angel of death coming towards her.[8] The woman beheld Sammael, the angel of death and was afraid. Yet she knew that the tree was good to eat.[9]

3:6a When the woman perceived
that the tree is good for food/nourishment
that it is beneficial[10] to the eyes
to understanding
beneficial for the springs
for children
that the tree is desirable for gaining wisdom
desirable above grieving childlessness
she took from its fruit
and she ate it
3:6b Then she gave also to her husband who was with her
and he ate

3:7a Then the eyes
the understanding
of them both were opened
enlightened
cleared of blindness/ignorance

---

7. *Pirke de-Rabbi Eliezer,* chap. XIII.
8. *Pirke de-Rabbi Eliezer,* chap. XIII.
9. *Targum of Palestine.*
10. *Targum of Palestine* translates this word as "medicine."

Moses used the expression *eyes* in a figurative sense for the vision of the soul, by which alone the perception of good and evil, of what is elegant or unsightly, and, in fact, of all contrary natures, arise.[11]

and they realized they were naked 3:7b
smooth-skinned
stripped
so they stitched fig-leaves together
and made themselves loin-coverings

They knew they were naked, divested of the purple robe in which they had been created. And they saw the sight of their embarrassment.[12] They realized they were bare of good deeds.[13] So they stitched the leaves of the sweet fig-tree and made clothes and put them on each other, concealing their thoughts because embarrassment had come upon them.[14]

Midrash

> Turn it this way, turn it that way, for everything is in it. Pore over it, grow old and gray over it. Do not stir from it, for you can have no better portion than it.
>
> —*Avot* 5:22

Talmidah: Rabbi is late today.

11. Philo, *Questions*, I.39.
12. *Targum of Palestine.*
13. *The Apocalypse of Moses*, 20.
14. *The Sibylline Oracles*, book 1, lines 47–49.

Mitnagged: He's likely wringing his hands over your targum, afraid to touch it, it drips so profusely with slimy snake oil.

Talmidah: Snakes are not slimy, Mitnagged, nor do they produce oil of any kind, being dry and scaly. If it drips with oil it is *shemen zait,* olive oil, as it is written, "Bring pure olive oil for the lampstand, and keep a flame there continually."[15] It is oil fit for a temple menorah, or the lamps of a woman who welcomes the Sabbath Queen into her home as a light in a world of darkness.

Mitnagged: Must you continually allude to a woman's *mitzvot* in priestly terms!

Talmidah: It bothers you?

Mitnagged: It most certainly does!

Talmidah: Good! Then I shall continue to find such grains of salt to rub into that worm-sensitive skin of yours.

Mitnagged: It is you who wriggles like a serpent, slithering around the hard issues by transforming facts into their opposites, as it is written "Woe to those who call evil good and good evil!"[16] You call sin virtue and weakness wisdom.

Talmidah: "Woe to those who are so wise in their own opinion, so clever in their own judgment!"[17] Who are you to haughtily determine fact from fiction? Particularly in the task

15. Leviticus 24:2.
16. Isaiah 5:20.
17. Isaiah 5:21.

of translating an ancient text whose origins and authors lie obscured in the remote, unseeable eons of the past?

Mitnagged: You are Lilith incarnate![18]

Talmidah: And you are Samuel, the adversary to truth!

Rabbi: Shalom, talmidim. I trust you lovebirds were able to occupy your time constructively in my absence.

Talmidah: Mitnagged has paid me the highest compliment possible, Rabbi.

Rabbi: How so?

Talmidah: He compared my targum to oil, the pure olive oil used for lighting the temple menorahs.

Rabbi: Mitnagged, your uncharacteristic courtesy surprises me. Perhaps there is hope for you yet. I am well-pleased that you were able to acknowledge the merits of your opponent, though compelled by assignment to challenge her work.

Mitnagged: Ugh . . . yes, well . . .

Rabbi: I only hope Talmidah will likewise develop a similar capacity to recognize the merits of her adversary. In any case, I feel most gratified that both of you have moved beyond the childish tendency to demonize those who disagree with you.

Mitnagged: I wouldn't dream of doing such a thing.

---

18. A female demon.

Rabbi: That is wise, considering that demons are the product of certain kinds of dreams.[19]

Talmidah: Nor would I. Mitnagged is most certainly not the man of my dreams.

Rabbi: On to the task at hand.

Mitnagged: Your polyvalent reading of *ayeen* in 3:5 . . .

Rabbi: Pardon me, Mitnagged, but I should like to address her wordplay in 3:1 before moving on to more serious interpretative translation.

Mitnagged: Wordplay?

Talmidah: The word *nachash* or "serpent."

Mitnagged: I do not see a wordplay, only a nonliteral translation which identifies the serpent as Satan. The "Serpent" becomes a derogatory title for a fallen angel determined to destroy mankind.

Rabbi: Rather than a literal talking snake.

Talmidah: But this is not just a nonliteral translation. It's a literal translation of a wordplay on the word *nachash.*

Mitnagged: *Nachash* does not mean "Satan."

---

19. This reflects the folk belief that demons sport with humans while men and women are sleeping at night, thereby reproducing themselves.

Talmidah: It does if you spell it backwards and substitute the middle letter for one that is similar to it alliterally. Here, I'll spell it out on the board for you. This is how you spell *serpent* in Hebrew: נחש. This is how you spell *satan*: שטנ.[20] The middle letters, het (ח) and tet (ט), are very similar to one another in sound in their ancient pronunciation. *Serpent* is a caustic joke on Satan's name.

Mitnagged: I am impressed.

Talmidah: Thank you.

Mitnagged: I am not impressed with your strained attempt to impute to Havah the noble aspiration for motherhood as an incentive to break a commandment expressly given by God, as it is written, "As for the Tree of Knowledge of Good and Evil, you must not eat of it or you will die."

Talmidah: Havah's motivation was more complicated than that. And besides, God did not give this commandment to Havah.

Mitnagged: What are you talking about? I just quoted 2:17 where God explicitly commands the man and woman not to eat from that particular tree.

Talmidah: This commandment was given to Adam when he was alone in the garden. Go back and read it in Hebrew,

20. The letter nun is actually written ן when it appears at the end of a word. It is written as it is above to facilitate an understanding of Talmidah's wordplay.

Mitnagged. The commandment is directed to a second-person male—"you, man."

Mitnagged: Nevertheless, it was meant for both of them. We know from Havah's response to the serpent that Adam told Havah about God's command.

Talmidah: Yes, and he did a great job relaying the message, didn't he? He told Havah that God commanded them not to eat the fruit of the tree *or touch it.* The rabbis point out Adam's deadly mistake in adding to the word of God, for Satan was able to prove quite effectively that nobody was going to die by touching the tree. God said nothing about *touching* it.[21]

Mitnagged: Adam attempted to protect his wife by providing a *siag,* or fence around the law. If she did not touch the tree, she would not eat from it.

Rabbi: But in testing the fence, Satan proved Adam's falsehood, and so caused Havah to doubt the truth of his other words. Thus it is written, "Add not to His words, lest He chastise you and you are found out as a liar."[22]

Talmidah: I assert that Adam not only had no business adding to what God told him, but that he had no business passing it on to Havah at all. It wasn't meant for her, only him.

Mitnagged: If the tree was deadly to Adam, it would be deadly to Havah as well. It was logical for Adam to protect his wife by warning her of its peril.

---

21. *Bereshith Rabbah* XIX.3.
22. Proverbs 30:6.

Talmidah: Doubtless he reasoned in this manner, being unaware of God's mind or purpose. I will concede that it was important for her to know of its mortal effects upon her body, but it was wrong to command her not to eat of it. It was no sin for her to take this fruit for God did not command her not to eat it.

Mitnagged: But it was a sin for Adam?

Talmidah: It would have been a sin for him to eat it first.

Mitnagged: You are making no sense.

Talmidah: It is hard to make sense of a senseless mind. Hopefully it will become clear as we proceed with my translation. Before doing so, it is important to point out that God did give both the man and woman a commandment shortly after their formation and before their temporary separation, "Multiply and fill the earth." In other words, fill the earth with sons and daughters. Adam and Havah were commanded to procreate.

Mitnagged: So? There is no indication that they failed to keep that commandment. As it is written, "They went up as two and came down as four."[23]

Rabbi: Meaning Havah conceived and bore twins—Cain and Abel—in the Garden of Eden. It is also written, "Only two entered the bed and seven left it," meaning she gave birth to a

23. *Sanhedrin* 38b, Talmud Bavli.

set of boy twins, a twin sister for Cain, and a set of girl twins for Abel.[24]

Talmidah: Quintuplets? Are you kidding?

Mitnagged: The girls destined to become the wives of the twin brothers. From this we derive the tradition that had the woman not succumbed to her evil inclinations, the propagation of humanity would have continued within the Garden. If not for her, we would all be living in Paradise today.

Talmidah: But Tradition also says that children were not conceived until after Adam and Havah ate the fruit of the tree of Knowing Good and Evil. The conception and bearing of children is listed as one of several consequences of the "fall."[25]

Rabbi: One might throw in the belief, as reflected in *Jubilees*, that Havah and Adam did not engage in intimate relations while in the garden, even though they were married.

Talmidah: Because in their innocence they did not know how to do so?

Rabbi: No. The reasoning is that since the Garden was a temple and Adam was a high priest, sexual intercourse would have been impossible.

Talmidah: Why?

---

24. *Bereshith Rabbah* XXII.2.

25. 2 *Baruch* 56:6. A pseudepigraphal work written in Syriac, but based on a Hebrew original composed some time in the first or second century C.E.

Rabbi: Mitnagged, you know why. Please explain it to Talmidah.

Mitnagged: But I don't know, Rabbi.

Rabbi: I think you do.

Mitnagged: I do not.

Rabbi: You look uncomfortable, Mitnagged.

Mitnagged: It's a bit hot in this room.

Rabbi: Very well, I'll explain. You see, Talmidah, in the temple cultus, semen is ritually impure. A priest who has experienced a recent ejaculation of semen is therefore "polluted" and cannot officiate in the temple until he has undergone a period of purification outside the temple. Since Adam and Havah were living in a temple they could not have sexual intercourse because that would have defiled temple space. Your hands are trembling, Talmidah. Are you feeling uncomfortable?

Talmidah: No . . . I mean, yes, it's a bit cold in this room.

Mitnagged: Your voice is trembling too.

Talmidah: It is not!

Rabbi: Too hot and too cold. A most uncomfortable room.

Talmidah: By your logic, Rabbi, Havah could not menstruate either.

Rabbi: Ahhh, I see. Menstrual blood is also ritually impure. Do you agree, Mitnagged?

Mitnagged: Makes sense.

Talmidah: Then you admit that she was sterile.

Mitnagged: Sterile!

Talmidah: A woman who does not menstruate is not fertile, Mitnagged. You see, at the beginning of every menstrual cycle an egg is formed in the . . .

Mitnagged: I get the point. So we have two protoadults living in complete innocence.

Talmidah: That is the picture we get from Jubilees, but it is not the one I prefer. I envision a married woman and her husband who enjoy one another sexually, but are unable to conceive children.

Mitnagged: Not consistent with your temple scenario.

Talmidah: But the Garden was a garden of delight, Mitnagged, of pleasure.

Rabbi: I suspect that Talmidah wishes to retain last week's excerpt from Song of Songs in her targum, which celebrates a very adult passion between bride and groom.

Talmidah: I also wish to retain the Zohar's sanctification of marital intercourse as symbolic of the holy union between the male and female presence of God.

Rabbi: Which the Zohar calls the "Father" and "Mother."

Talmidah: Yes, the Shekinah being the "Mother," or presence of God represented by a feminine name. And it is in the Zohar that we read that a holy place is not a holy place unless male and female are found there together, bound as one flesh.

Rabbi: Intercourse then becomes a religious act, as well as a physically pleasurable one. For this reason it is a *mitzva* for a man to give pleasure to his wife on Shabbat.

Talmidah: Or any time she wants it, for that matter.

Mitnagged: But if you allow intercourse, Talmidah, you must allow menstruation as well, and therefore the conception of children. In fact, the conception of children is an expected outcome of the *mitzva* Rabbi alludes to.

Rabbi: It is not unexpected. But it is not the prime reason why marital sex is encouraged and even sanctified. Its prime function is to bond the man and woman to one another emotionally, to make them *yihud,* or one. The pleasure, in and of itself, is important to marriage, regardless of any tangible outcome by way of children. I might also add for your edification, that it is not necessary for a man to produce semen or a woman to menstruate for a couple to enjoy one another sexually. . . . Do not look so puzzled, Mitnagged. You will grow wise with time.

Talmidah: And experience. I wouldn't hold out much hope for him, Rabbi. A little boy can hardly be expected to comprehend the intricacies of hormonal responses.

Rabbi: And a little girl can?

Mitnagged: Hah! In any case, Talmidah, you are inconsistent. Either the Garden is a temple—as you've been insisting all along—and we have a marriage between virginal preadolescents who are naive to the ways of passion, in which case your Song of Songs composition is totally out of place; or the Garden is a place of pleasure and delight, which allows the encroachment of passion along with its fluids forbidden in a temple—those fluids which are the stuff of new life—in which case your entire temple structure of side-chambers and menorah trees crumbles to the dust. You must choose between them, Talmidah.

Talmidah: No, I don't. Remember, the Garden is also timeless. Without the progression of time, neither death nor birth can occur. Old age and fetal development, as well as the growth and maturity of a baby to adulthood, are all dependent on the forward movement of time—of days and months and years. The same principle which prevented death from occurring in the garden, prevented birth as well.

Rabbi: One could also argue that opposites did not exist in the garden. Therefore birth and death, those extreme opposites of mortality, could not exist.

Mitnagged: You refer to the Tree of Knowledge of Good and Evil.

Rabbi: Why didn't God name this tree, the "Tree of Death," a more logical parallel to the "Tree of Lives"?

Talmidah: It did not mean instant death, as we know. The first couple lived well into their nine hundreds—just barely short of a thousand years.

Mitnagged: Which is a day by God's reckoning. But it meant their death, nevertheless.

Talmidah: It meant mortality, a more fitting description of a long life characterized by the vicissitudes brought on by the needs, appetites, and desires of flesh.

Rabbi: Why not call it the "Tree of Mortality" then?

Mitnagged: Perhaps God wished to emphasize the type of knowledge attained through mortality.

Talmidah: That is a most profound thought, Mitnagged.

Rabbi: She is sincere in her compliment.

Mitnagged: A miracle second only to the parting of the Red Sea!

Talmidah: Regardless of whether they enjoyed marital relations or not, a polyvalent reading of the words *ayeen* in 3:5, 6 and *sakil* in 3:6 leaves no question that Havah suffered barrenness.

Rabbi: Do you understand her translation, Mitnagged?

Mitnagged: Of course. I am not stupid. Here, I'll write what she did on the board. The root עין is voweled *ayeen* in the Masoretic text. This means "eyes." It also serves as a metaphor for understanding or knowledge. Let me point out here that the word *eyes* is also a metaphor for bodily appetite, as it is written, "The pleasant odor which the tree emitted inspired in her,

Havah, to eat of it."[26] In other words, she literally succumbed to the weakness of her belly. She ate it because it smelled delicious, thereby demonstrating a complete lack of willpower. *Eyes* is also used to denote carnal desire, or lust, as it is written, "His master's wife cast her eyes upon Joseph, and she said, 'Lie with me!'" From this the rabbis concluded that the woman was tempted by sexual desire for Satan himself.[27]

Talmidah: I agree that *eyes* can serve any number of metaphorical uses, included those base ones unjustly imputed to Havah. But these other meanings do not stand under contextual analysis. What meaning do you assign to the word *eyes* in 3:5 when Satan promised Havah that her eyes and the eyes of her husband will be opened?

Mitnagged: He promises her godhood—an appeal to her pride.

Talmidah: But what was his reasoning? Why would she and Adam become like ministering angels? Because they would know good and evil. Unlike animals, they would have understanding and wisdom. The phrase "knowing good and evil" is a clarification of the previous statement, "your eyes will be opened." We have a similar clarification for 3:6. The phrase "beneficial to the eyes"—yes, I prefer *beneficial* over *pleasing* as a more applicable adjective—is immediately followed by "desirable for gaining wisdom." Moreover, in 3:7, eyes are once again used to describe Adam and Havah's sudden understanding that they were naked.

---

26. *Zohar, Bereshith*, 36a. This version of the Zohar, the Soncino translation, closely follows the original text, as opposed to the version of Matt (see References), who selected a few passages and arranged them by topic in poetic form.

27. *Zohar, Bereshith*, 28b, 49b.

Mitnagged: Verse 3:7 can also be read with sexual overtones, Talmidah. To "see" a person's "nakedness" is a euphemism for sexual intercourse. As it is written, "If a man takes his sister, his father's daughter or his mother's daughter, and sees her nakedness, and she sees his nakedness, it is a wicked thing."[28] This condemnation, by the way, is embedded in a comprehensive list of forbidden sexual relations.[29]

Talmidah: But such an act is not condemnatory between husband and wife.

Mitnagged: It is if performed in a holy place, like the temple.

Talmidah: Alright, let's pursue your reasoning. Let's say that "eyes will be opened" is a cruel joke. Havah thinks he means wisdom, when it really means the awakening of sexual desire. The sin is not in the act itself, but the place where it is performed. That means before that moment, Adam and Havah were ritually pure, were they not?

Mitnagged: Yes.

Talmidah: Then Havah was sterile, Mitnagged, because she was not menstruating.

Mitnagged: OK, forget this preposterous temple scenario altogether and address the *Zohar*'s accusation of adultery. The fruit is symbolic of sexual intercourse, and the one Havah lusted for was her tempter. From this we learn how fickle and easily seduced women are.

---

28. Leviticus 20:17.
29. Leviticus 18, 20.

Talmidah: That is the lowest, most vile accusation leveled against our first Mother, and I vehemently deny it because it is simultaneously an accusation leveled against me personally! Tell me, Mitnagged, how likely is it for a woman to commit adultery with her husband standing there, watching?

Mitnagged: Not at all likely. According to Tradition, Adam was off in his part of the garden.

Talmidah: But not according to the text itself, as it is written, "Then she gave also to her husband *who was with her* and he ate." We conveniently forget Adam's presence during Havah's conversation with the Serpent, because he is silent and passive. But he is there nevertheless. And you might ask yourself, Mitnagged, what Adam was doing, metaphorically speaking, when he ate the same fruit Havah ate. According to your nasty conjecture, Adam likewise would have engaged in sexual relations with the Serpent. What does that make *him?*

Mitnagged: Adam did not take the fruit from the Serpent. It was Havah who gave him the fruit. Therefore it was Havah with whom he had intercourse. Satan gave Havah the fruit.

Talmidah: No he didn't. She took it off the tree herself, as it is written, "she took from its fruit."

Mitnagged: Alright, I'll concede that the accusation of adultery is unsubstantiated.

Talmidah: Thank you.

Mitnagged: The point is, Havah gave Adam the fruit, therefore it was she with whom he had intercourse.

Talmidah: But they were married. Where's the sin in that?

Rabbi: You want to try the logic of temple space again?

Mitnagged: We're going around in circles.

Talmidah: Any thread you take will lead you back to the conclusion that Havah was unable to conceive children, either because they did not have sexual relations or because she was barren. I will complete what Mitnagged began drawing on the board. The Masoretes voweled the root עין to mean "eyes." If we vowel the same root *aiyeen,* we get "springs," which is a metaphor for children.[30] It is possible to treat the root שׂכל in 3:6 in the same manner. The Masoretes voweled להשׂכל as *lehasakil* as an infinitive verb, "for gaining wisdom." We could also vowel the same phrase *lehashakol* as an adjective preceded by a comparative preposition, "instead of/above grieving childlessness."

Mitnagged: *Shakol* is better translated "bereaved of children," meaning the loss of children through violence. This word does not work for simple barrenness, Talmidah.

Talmidah: It works in this case for two reasons. First, it shares the same root as *sakil,* "wisdom," which makes it possible to read the same double message as we did for the root עין, "eyes/springs." It's a brilliant parallel polyvalent reading!

Mitnagged: Your modesty overwhelms me.

---

30. Deuteronomy 33:28.

Talmidah: Not me, the author we call J! Look how neatly the two roots, עין and שכל parallel each other:

beneficial to the עין/*eyes*	beneficial for the עין/*springs*
to the *understanding*	for *children*
desirable for gaining שכל/*wisdom*	desirable above שכל/*grieving childlessness*

This kind of parallel would not be possible with other words for *barren*, because they do not share root letters with *wisdom*. Likewise, there are more common metaphors for children, but *aiyeen*/"springs" shares root letters with the word for eyes, which in turn means "wisdom."

Mitnagged: An incredible stretch.

Rabbi: But workable.

Talmidah: And it fits the pattern of barrenness among the matriarchs in Scripture.

Mitnagged: You compare Havah to the Matriarchs!

Talmidah: If we compare the life stories of Havah and Adam, Sarah and Abraham, Rebecca and Isaac, and Rachel and Jacob, we discover the following common elements:

- The inheritor of the birthright marries a woman of high standing in terms of kinship ties and social status.
- The couple enjoys comparative ideal living conditions: wealth, physical comforts, and comely bodies.
- God promises, or in the case of Adam and Havah, commands numerous posterity.
- The woman is afflicted with barrenness. In Sarah's case

over seventy years. Rebecca suffered seventeen years of long-term infertility, while Rachel endured seven years.

Rabbi: There is an obscure piece of *haggadah* which imputes barrenness to Leah as well.[31]

Mitnagged: Leah! She was anything but!

Rabbi: Nevertheless, the birth of her children was considered miraculous and a sign of God's compassion for Leah, "the hated one."

Talmidah: Why go to great length to prove Leah's barrenness?

Rabbi: Perhaps you are not the first to see this pattern, Talmidah. In fact, one must never assume that anything you think of is truly original. Someone, somewhere has likely thought of it many hundreds of years before.

Talmidah: Is it a matter of finding?

Rabbi: It may not be findable. I suspect many ideas do not survive the era in which they are born. In any case, some unknown rabbi doubtless perceived this pattern among the matriarchs and felt compelled to include Mother Leah in its pattern.

Mitnagged: She being the mother of Judah.

---

31. *Midrash ha-Gadol* (The Great Midrash), ed. Schechter (Cambridge, 1902), pp. 468–469, as cited by Ginzberg, "Jacob," vol. 5, note 171.

Rabbi: Of course.

Talmidah: There is another element to this pattern which is important to the interpretation of Havah's encounter with the Serpent. When it came to bearing and rearing children, the matriarchs took decidedly aggressive roles, while their husbands receded into the background as passive participants. It was Sarah, for example, who insisted that Abraham take a concubine so that she might have children by adoption. Rebecca determined the passage of the birthright through manipulation, which neither Jacob nor Isaac protested with any strength or will power. And of course, Rachel and Leah negotiated aggressively for Jacob's sexual attentions as well as for fertility herbs. In like manner, it was Havah who took the initiative to transform covenant promises into reality.

Mitnagged: Yes, I do see a pattern, Talmidah: "Wife manipulates, deceives, and otherwise tricks her unhappy and unfortunate husband into acts leading to miserable consequences." Sarah browbeats her husband into taking her maid to his bed. Does she thank him for the baby attained in this way? No! She becomes *jealous*. She makes Abraham drive out his firstborn son, much to his sorrow, along with its helpless mother. Rebecca talks Jacob into tricking his father for the birthright. What happens? The older brother is understandably angry and threatens to kill Jacob. So Jacob ends up running away—penniless—to his uncle, where he is enslaved for twenty years, while Isaac remains at home bereaved of son and respect. Then Leah and Rachel have at it at Jacob's expense. They treat him like a stud bull, the object of jealous competition and negotiation. By the time they're done with him he has twelve sons and who-knows-how-many daughters, which he must somehow support with the minuscule wages allotted to him by his stingy uncle. The rest of his life is spent grieving over bloody rivalries among his children begun by their mothers. And now Havah. Her precipitous action leads to expulsion from Paradise and a mortal life filled with painful toil and death. Her action made as little sense as those of the matriarchs who followed her.

Talmidah: It made perfect sense to her . . . and to me.

Mitnagged: Heaven help your future husband! What possible motive could she have to bring upon herself the pain and mortal danger of childbearing?

Talmidah: Motive? The same as Rebecca's. "Give me a child! Give me a child or I shall die!" She experienced a natural and universal feminine emotion—the hunger for a child. I said there were two reasons why the word *shakol* is appropriate for this pericope of scripture. First, was its utility as part of a double reading in parallel with *ayeen*. The second is its emotional implications. Other words for barrenness convey only a physical state of infertility. *Shakol*, on the other hand, is a grieving word. It is a uniquely feminine kind of grief, arising from the anguish of a woman bereaved of her children.

Mitnagged: You suggest misery in Paradise.

Talmidah: Oh yes. Total, abject misery. It was a teaching moment for Havah.

Rabbi: God as Rabbi again. Just as Adam learned that Paradise without Woman was unpleasant and lonely, so Havah learned that Paradise without children was unfulfilling and incomplete.

Mitnagged: But why did they have to leave Paradise to have children, Talmidah? Why not open her womb and fulfill her desires within the Garden as He did for Adam?

Talmidah: But we already talked about that, Mitnagged. Paradise was perfect and timeless. Nothing dies or decays. And where nothing dies or decays, nothing is born or develops. Everything is already fully developed. No death, no birth. Where there is no possibility of dying, there is no possibility of renewing life.

Rabbi: Life's cycle cannot function in a world frozen in time and space.

Talmidah: And now we come to the $40 million question. Why did the Serpent tempt Havah and not Adam?

Mitnagged: Because she was weaker than Adam and therefore more easily persuaded.

Talmidah: No! Because Adam did not have the right to make that choice.

Mitnagged: Didn't have the *right?*

Talmidah: Think, Mitnagged. Why do the rabbis prohibit a man from practicing any kind of birth control, but do not the woman? Why does she decide when to have children and how many?

Mitnagged: Because she is the one who bears the pain of childbearing and most of the burden for childrearing. So . . . I think I'm beginning to see your reasoning. As "Life-giver,"

Havah would bear the most painful and possibly fatal consequences of mortality.

Talmidah: Exactly. Adam had neither the right to hold back the means by which Havah could conceive life—for such action would be cruel to her natural desires—or to force her to bear children, for such action would unjustly subject her to the physical and emotional pain of bearing and rearing children without her consent. That's why God commanded Adam not to eat the fruit. It was not his decision to make. He did not command the woman not to eat the fruit, for it was her right to eat or abstain.

Rabbi: Adam remained silent because it was Havah who had the most to lose from eating fruit that would make her mortal.

Talmidah: And fertile.

Mitnagged: What about the consequences for Adam? You count sickness, toilsome labor, and death insignificant? I'd say he had as much to lose as Havah. More, by your reasoning, because he was perfectly happy with the status quo.

Talmidah: Was he? Does the text say that he was happy?

Mitnagged: It does not comment on his emotional state one way or the other. But I can't imagine him feeling otherwise.

Talmidah: I can. What kind of environment did he live in?

Mitnagged: A perfect one.

Talmidah: A changeless one. Nothing changed, ever. Everything stayed exactly the same—the season, the day, every plant, and every animal. Nothing sprouted, gave birth, grew, or decayed.

Mitnagged: That's not true, Talmidah. We read in the Creation account that plants sprouted up and began to multiply. Living creatures also multiplied and spread across the earth.

Talmidah: That was happening in the "outside world," not inside the Garden of Eden, the "Enclosed Garden," where time and place did not exist. There was no mechanism, Mitnagged, by which the man and woman could grow in knowledge, understanding, or insight, because there was no experience or observation available by which knowledge could be attained. It was *boring*, Mitnagged, insufferably *boring*. I would submit that the status quo is not a joyful experience. Joy—and knowledge—comes from participation in change.

Mitnagged: No flat tires, broken bones, final exams, overdrawn bank accounts, or broken relationships. May the Holy One smite me with such a life!

Talmidah: May He indeed! No inventing of cars, or problem solving of any kind; no dangerous ski trips, or any kind of risk; no challenging courses of study, or any kind of thinking; no working for money, or any kind of self-reliant activity; no outside relationships, or any kind of community life. If that is life to you, you are worse than a half-man. You are a golem.

Mitnagged: A happy golem.

Talmidah: A half-formed, depressed human being.

Mitnagged: Look, Talmidah, knowledge was available in abundance within the Garden. You yourself, quoting Philo, claimed that the Garden was filled with sources of knowledge, as represented by the various types of trees growing there. I'll even throw in Rabbi Eliezer's assertion that Adam studied Torah in the Garden.[32] Recall your own targum quoting the *Targum of Palestine:* ". . . and made him dwell in the garden of Eden, to do service in the law and to keep its commandments."

Talmidah: I do not deny the existence of Torah in the Garden, nor that Adam and Havah "feasted" upon it metaphorically. But of what value is Torah study in a vacuum? When it cannot be practiced or experienced? How could Adam "keep" the commandments if they could not be broken to begin with? It is written, "all study of the Law without labor comes to naught."[33] And again it is said, "Great is Torah, for it gives life to those that *practice* it."[34]

Mitnagged: Torah study in and of itself refines a man and makes him saintly. The rabbis lauded Torah study above any other worldly distraction: "Engage not overmuch in business, but occupy yourself with Torah."[35] It is also written, "He that occupies himself in the study of Torah for its own sake merits many things, and, still more, he is deserving of the whole world. He is called friend, beloved, lover of God, lover of mankind; and it clothes him with humility and reverence and fits him to become righteous, saintly, upright, and faithful."[36]

Talmidah: The sages did not advocate the life of a hermit who removes himself from humanity to devote his life solely to

32. Chap. XII.
33. *Avot* 2.2.
34. *Avot* 6.7.
35. *Avot* 4.10.
36. *Avot* 6.1.

Torah study. As Hillel once said, "Keep not aloof from the congregation."[37] It is true that Torah study guides a person in behavior, but true understanding of its teachings does not come until those teachings are tested in the push and pull of daily life. Torah study involves both intellectual diligence and daily application of its principles. It is written that Torah learning is acquired "by study, by hearing, by reciting, by understanding of the heart, by discernment of the heart, by awe, by reverence, by humility, by cheerfulness, by attendance on the Sages, by association with fellow students, by assiduity, by knowledge of Scripture and Mishna, by moderation in business, worldly occupation, pleasure, sleep, conversation, and jesting; by longsuffering, by a good heart, by faith in the Sages, by submission to sorrows; by being one that recognizes his place and that rejoices in his lot and that makes a fence around his words and that claims no merit for himself; by being one that is beloved, that loves God, that loves mankind, that loves well-doing, that loves rectitude, that loves reproof, that shuns honor and boasts not of his learning, and delights not in making decisions; that helps his fellow to bear his yoke, and that judges him favorably, and that establishes him in the truth and establishes him in peace; and that occupies himself assiduously in his study; by being one that asks and makes answer, that hearkens and adds thereto; that learns in order to teach and that learns in order to practice."[38]

Rabbi: Rabbi Eleazer ben Azariah put it more simply, "If there is no study of the Law there is no seemly behavior, if there is no seemly behavior there is no study of the Law."[39]

37. *Avot* 2.5.
38. *Avot* 6.6.
39. *Avot* 3.18.

Talmidah: Life without Torah is meaningless. Torah without life is also meaningless.

Mitnagged: You are saying that Havah was motivated by a desire to suffer for the sake of gaining knowledge.

Talmidah: No. Havah did not know that knowledge gained through mortality meant understanding gained through suffering. In this she was deceived. She was driven by two powerful needs—the need to bear and nurture a child, and the need for continual enlightenment.

Rabbi: Your parallel polyvalent readings suggest that these two needs are interrelated.

Talmidah: Interrelated? I don't understand.

Mitnagged: I don't either. What does learning new concepts have to do with raising kids? From what I've seen in my home, it dulls the intellect, reducing an adult mind to childish mush.

Talmidah: So you admit that a woman has an adult mind. We're making progress Rabbi! Pity your mother, Mitnagged, whose children are apparently as sharp-witted as stones, thereby necessitating her reversion to a childish vocabulary. What *is* the connection, Rabbi? I share Mitnagged's puzzlement.

Rabbi: You will grow to understand the connection as you experience parenthood. In fact, Havah and Adam's own experiences raising children serve as excellent samples of how knowledge is achieved by this process.

Talmidah: I have not yet translated that pericope of Scripture.

Rabbi: Then we shall save this midrash for a later time. I suggest that you keep the thought in your mind as you compose the remainder of your targum.

Mitnagged: But if Havah's choice was a righteous one, why the shame? When their eyes were opened they became ashamed, and so felt compelled to cover themselves.

Talmidah: The text does not say that they felt any shame, Mitnagged. It says, "Their eyes were opened and they realized they were naked."

Mitnagged: Meaning they were seized with shame.

Talmidah: Not at all! It means they suddenly became conscious of their sexuality.

Mitnagged: Now you're ready to concede my earlier point that 3:7 has sexual overtones.

Talmidah: Yes, but not the kind you suggested. I'm not saying that they had intercourse and then became ashamed of their action. Let's assume for the moment that before they ate the fruit of mortality they were ritually pure, meaning their bodies were not sexually mature. If the fruit represents mortality, with its relentless progression of time and its inevitable effect on the human body, some interesting things would begin to happen to Adam and Havah after eating the fruit—particularly between their legs.

Rabbi: The onset of puberty manifested by menstrual blood and the production of semen.

Talmidah: They became acutely aware, perhaps even embarrassed by their sexuality and so felt the need to cover those areas of their bodies where it was obviously manifest.

Rabbi: With loin coverings.

Talmidah: Right.

Mitnagged: The Garden then becomes a metaphor for childhood.

Talmidah: Childhood. I had not thought of that.

Rabbi: Mitnagged suggests that the Garden can symbolize several ideas simultaneously, including your idea of a holy place where humanity lives in the presence of God, or Mitnagged's idea of the biological and mental state of childhood. As a rabbi, I am tempted to compare it to a *bet-midrash,* particularly in light of our earlier conversation regarding the difference between Torah study and Torah practice.

Talmidah: All of these are workable. This is incredible!

Mitnagged: But God cursed the man and woman for their choice. To say that there was no sin is to say that God was unjustly angry.

Talmidah: The word *aror,* curse, is not used against the man or woman, Mitnagged. Read it again—in Hebrew. God curses the serpent and the earth, but not the man or the woman.

Mitnagged: How can anyone read 3:16–3:19 as anything other than a punishment, meted out by a justifiably angry God!

Rabbi: We shall save that for next week, Mitnagged. We have seen Talmidah's ability to read text and commentary "creatively."

Mitnagged: I'll say. She's turned the text completely upside down. Now instead of a patriarchal reading, we have a decidedly feminist one, which makes the man an inferior being to the woman—passive and indecisive while the woman heroically makes all the right decisions for both of them. That kind of interpretation hardly represents an improvement over previous "male chauvinistic" interpretations.

Talmidah: You are wrong, Mitnagged. This is no vendetta against Adam. God set up a scenario that required Havah to make the choice, for reasons we've already discussed. First of all, Adam had received a commandment directly from God Himself not to eat the fruit of mortality, a commandment not given to the woman. Adam was bound by divine covenant not to break that commandment, whereas Havah was not bound at all. Second, Adam had already made up his mind to go wherever Havah went. He knew that any place without her meant an unhappy existence. This he learned through his experience of terrible loneliness before they were reunited.

Mitnagged: But why did he take the fruit, without any word of protest or warning? Naive trust?

Talmidah: He knew that her choice was the right one. It enabled them, as a couple, to keep the first commandment given to them to multiply and fill the earth with children and to satisfy their need for learning experiences. And I believe he did this also because he loved his wife and wanted her to be happy. Living in the Garden of Delight was not enough for Havah, nor was marriage to a perfect man. It might have been as simple as that, Mitnagged. He ate the fruit, knowing full well what it meant, in order to bring happiness to his beloved. . . . Why are you staring at me like that?

Rabbi: His eyes are opened.

Talmidah: There are any number of ways of interpreting that, Rabbi. Which meaning do you apply?

Rabbi: What meaning do you want it to have?

Talmidah: I have to go now . . . an appointment . . . with a friend. Shalom, until next week.

Rabbi: Shalom, Talmidah.

Mitnagged: How long do I have to keep up this charade, Rabbi?

Rabbi: Until she completes her targum.

Mitnagged: She doesn't strike me as the kind of woman who likes to be deceived. She will be angry when she finds out.

Rabbi: Probably. Does that bother you?

Mitnagged: It does now.

Rabbi: Good.

5

"God Weeps"
Genesis 3:8–3:23

Targum

Then they heard the sound of Yahweh Elohim Genesis
walking about in the garden at the breezy time of day 3:8
for a period of rest
Before man transgressed the Voice sounded to him gentle;
after he had transgressed it sounded to him harsh[1]
The man and his wife hid from the face of Yahweh Elohim
among the trees of the garden

But Yahweh Elohim called to the man, 3:9
"Where are you?"
Adam, where did you hide, thinking that I would not find you?

1. *Bemidbar Rabbah* XI.3.

Can a house hide from its builder?[2]
Is not all the world which I have made manifest before me?
the darkness as the light?
and how did you think in your heart to hide from me?
The place where you are concealed, do I not see?"[3]

3:10 He answered,
"I heard your voice in the garden
and I was afraid because I am naked
and I stood in awe of your might, O Lord,[4]
so I hid myself"

3:11 "Who told you that you were naked?" He asked,
"Did you eat from the tree which I forbade you to eat?"

3:12 And the man replied,
"The wife you gave/consecrated to stand beside me
gave me of the tree
and I ate"

3:13 Then Yahweh Elohim asked the woman,
"What is this you have done?"

And the woman replied,
"The Serpent deceived me
caused me to feel responsible/guilty
and I ate"

2. *The Apocalypse of Moses*, 23.
3. *Targum of Palestine.*
4. *The Apocalypse of Moses*, 23.

Havah: And in the same hour we heard the archangel Michael sounding his trumpet, calling the angels, saying, "Thus the Lord decrees, Come with me into Paradise and hear the sentence which I pronounce on mankind." And the throne of God was made ready where the tree of Eternal Life was.[5]

Then Yahweh Elohim said to the Serpent, *3:14*
"Because you did this you are cursed
bound up
more than any beast
any life of the field
any life of the Almighty
You will crawl on your belly
and you will eat dust all the days of your life
you will eat mortality/death forever
the poison of death shall be in your mouth[6]
I will fix hostility *3:15*
between you and the woman
between your seed/posterity/strength
and her seed/posterity/strength
between your son and her sons[7]
And it shall be when the children of the woman
keep the commandments of the law[8]
they will strike at your head
your chief
your best
but when they forsake the commandments of the law[9]

---

5. *The Apocalypse of Moses*, 23.
6. *Targum of Palestine.*
7. *Targum Onkelos.*
8. *Targum of Palestine.*
9. *Targum of Palestine.*

you will strike at their heel
their least
their weakest
Nevertheless for them there shall be an antidote,
but for you there will be no antidote[10]

The Holy One, blessed be He, said to the Serpent, "I made you that you should be king over all cattle and beasts, but you would not have it, therefore more cursed are you than any beast; I made you that you should walk upright like a man, but you would not, hence you will crawl on your belly; I made you that you should eat the food of man, but you would not, so you will eat dust; you wanted to kill the man and take his wife, therefore I will fix hostility between you and the woman." Thus what he desired was not given him, and what he possessed was taken from him.[11]

3:16 To the woman he said,
"I will make you exceeding great
on account of your painful/toilsome labour in child-bearing.
In anguish you shall bear children.
You will suffer birth pangs and unspeakable pains;
with much trembling you shall bear children
and on that occasion you shall come near to losing your life
from your great anguish and pains.[12]
But your desire will be towards your husband
you will feel passion for your husband
and he likewise in you.

---

10. *Targum of Palestine.*

11. *Bereshith Rabbah* XX.5. A similar passage is found in tractate *Sotah* 9b in Talmud Bavli.

12. *The Apocalypse of Moses,* 25.

Then he said to the man *3:17*
"Because you listened/consented/obeyed the voice of your wife
and ate from the tree which I forbade you to eat,
cursed/bound up is the earth in your harvest.
With painful/toilsome labour you will eat of it
all the days of your life.

Thorns and thistles will she sprout for you *3:18*
and you will eat grain of the plowed field
You will grow weary and not rest;
be afflicted with bitterness and not taste sweetness;
be oppressed by heat and burdened by cold;
you will toil much and not gain wealth;
you will grow fat and finally not be.[13]
By the sweat of your face you will eat bread *3:19*
until you return to the earth
for you were taken from her.
Because you are dust
to dust you will return
for from dust you will arise,
to render judgment and reckoning for all that you have done
in the day of the Great Judgment.[14]

But Awake! Arise! *3:18*
Generation upon generation *(palimpsest)*
will she spring up to you
and you will enjoy the yield of her breast!

Then the man cried out/proclaimed/praised *3:20*
the name of his wife,

---

13. *The Apocalypse of Moses*, 24.
14. *Targum of Palestine.*

"Havah! Life!"
because she was Mother to all living.

Adam gave to the first created woman that familiar name of Life, inasmuch as she was destined to be the fountain of all the generations which should ever arise upon the earth after their time.[15]

3:21 Then Yahweh Elohim provided leather garments
inner garments
garments next to the skin
garments of light
enlightenment
righteousness
for the man and his wife
and clothed them.

The Lord God made for Adam and for his wife vestments of honour upon the skin of their flesh, and clothed them.[16] The Holy One clothed man in garments of high priesthood, since he was the firstborn of the world, the glory of the world.[17]

3:22 Then Yahweh Elohim said,
"Behold, the man has become like one of us,
like one of the ministering angels[18]
knowing good and evil.
He must not reach out his hand now
and also take from the tree of Eternal Life
and eat and live forever/hiding."

---

15. Philo, *Questions*, I.52.
16. *Targum Onkelos*.
17. *Tanhuma Bereshith*.
18. *Bereshith Rabbah* XXI.5.

And the Lord turned and said to Adam, "From now on I will not allow you to be in Paradise." And Adam answered and said, "Lord, give me from the tree of life that I might eat before I am cast out." Then the Lord spoke to Adam, "You shall not now take from it; for it was appointed to the cherubim and the flaming sword which twirls back and forth to guard it because of you, that you might not taste of it and be immortal forever with the strife which the enemy has placed in you. But when you come out of Paradise, if you guard yourself from all evil, preferring death to it, at the time of the resurrection I will raise you again, and then there shall be given to you from the tree of Life, and you shall be immortal forever."[19]

So Yahweh Elohim banished him from the Garden of Eden 3:23
garden of delight
to work/plow/serve the earth
from which he was taken.
And after he drove the man out
He stationed in front of the Garden of Eden the cherubim
divine ministers
and the flaming sword/wasteland/desert whirling
turning about
changing itself
to guard the way to the tree of Eternal Life
and made the glory of His Shekinah to dwell
at the front of the east of the garden of Eden.[20]

Having sent him forth, He began to bewail him, saying, "Where is the man who was as one of us?[21] Behold, mankind!" He

19. *The Apocalypse of Moses*, 28.
20. *Targum of Palestine.*
21. *Bereshith Rabbah* XXI.3.

mourned.[22] "Eykah!" He cried out in lament over him, a howl, if one dare speak thus of God, expressing the ache of His grief.[23]

Jeremiah 3:17 "My soul shall weep in secret for your pride; and Mine eye shall weep sore and run down with tears."

When he transgressed, untimely death came into being, mourning was mentioned, affliction was prepared, illness was created, labor accomplished, pride began to come into existence, the realm of death began to ask to be renewed with blood, the conception of children came about, the passion of the parents was produced and the loftiness of mankind was humiliated.[24]

Midrash

> Five possessions did the Holy One, blessed is He, take to Himself in His world: Torah is one possession; heaven and earth, another possession; Abraham, another possession; Israel, another possession; and the Temple, another possession.
>
> —*Avot* 6.10

Rabbi: Your piece of targum this week is most revealing, Talmidah.

Mitnagged: Yes, indeed! It exposes your contorted style of double-think in all its unsightly nakedness. As it is written, "You stripped the naked of their clothing."[25]

---

22. *Tanhuma Bereshith.*
23. *Pesikta de-Rab Kahan,* Piska 15.
24. 2 Baruch 56:6.
25. Job 22:6.

Talmidah: Quite the contrary. I have "covered the naked with a garment."[26] I do not fear the icy breath of your frigid words "for all my household is clothed in scarlet. I stitched myself coverings of tapestry; my clothing is silk and purple."

Rabbi: The Virtuous Woman of Proverbs 31.

Mitnagged: More the Wanton Daughter of Zion who "walks with mincing steps, jingling the bangles on her feet," draping herself with frivolous adornments like "ornamental chains, medallions, crescents, pendants, bracelets, trinkets, diadems, ankle-chains, necklaces, scent bottles, amulets, finger-rings, nose-rings, party dresses, cloaks, scarves, purses, mirrors, linen clothes, turbans, and mantillas."[27] Reminds me of my sister, who spends most of her time in front of the mirror endlessly adorning herself with makeup, jewelry, and every combination of skirt, blouse, dress, and slacks imaginable.

Talmidah: I clothe Adam and Havah in simple garments of dignity.

Mitnagged: You cover up a naked curse with a fake blessing.

Talmidah: God curses neither man nor woman, Mitnagged. I challenged you last week to find the word *aror,* "curse," in this pericope of Scripture. Show me where God curses either Havah or Adam!

Mitnagged: Chapter 3, Verse 14: "The Lord God said to the serpent, because you did this, you are cursed."

---

26. Ezekiel 18:7.
27. Isaiah 3:16–18.

Talmidah: The Serpent is cursed, not Adam or Havah.

Mitnagged: But why was he cursed? Because of his part in bringing about the fall of man, specifically for deceiving the woman, as it is written in the previous verse, "The Woman said, 'The serpent tricked me.'" If her action was not a sin, why does she try to evade responsibility by claiming that she was deceived? And why would God curse the serpent for persuading the woman to do the "right and noble" thing? Was that not your defense for Havah last week? That her action was "wise"? How can she be wise in her deliberation and duped simultaneously? For the same choice?

Talmidah: Havah understood that eating the fruit would enable her and Adam to procreate and to gain understanding, and that this was desirable. It was good. But she did not understand how this would come about. The Serpent lied to her when he said, "You will not certainly die," for she would most certainly die, and she would suffer much on the way to dying.

Rabbi: He elaborated the benefit of eating the fruit, but cloaked the unpleasant consequences.

Talmidah: Havah's response in 3:13 suggests another reason for the curse on Satan. The phrase *hi-shee-a-ni,* "he deceived me" can also be read *hi-see-a-ni,* "he made me feel guilty/ responsible."

Rabbi: Reading the שׂ symbol as a *sin* instead of *shin.*

Talmidah: Yes, implying that the Serpent laid the responsibility for Adam and Havah's childlessness on her, thus in turn blaming her for their failure to keep the first commandment given to them by God, namely to multiply themselves and fill the earth with sons and daughters.

Mitnagged: Your *hi-see-a-ni* phrase can be read another way, Talmidah: "He caused me to incur guilt," or "He made me guilty." Is that not correct, Rabbi?

Rabbi: Yes, that is correct.

Mitnagged: I read 3:13 as an admission of guilt, Talmidah. She essentially said, "He made me guilty" or "He caused me to sin." *That's* why he was cursed, because he persuaded her to commit a sin for which she is punished. The Holy One may not have used the word *aror* against the woman, but he did curse her. He punished her by saying, "I will multiply your birthing pain."

Talmidah: The word *arbah* does mean "I will multiply." But in Genesis 17:2, when Yahweh makes his covenant with Abraham, it means "I will make you great."

Mitnagged: Your syntax is faulty. The word *arbah* in 17:2 is followed by a direct object pronoun—*otcha,* "you." The two words together mean, "I will multiply you," which can be translated as "I will make you great." But *arbah* in your verse is not followed by a direct object pronoun, *you,* as it would be if our J writer meant to say, "I will make you great." Instead, the word *arbah* is followed by a noun with a possessive suffix, "your pain." The other three occurrences of *arbah* in the Torah are likewise followed by nouns with possessive suffixes, each meaning that God will increase or multiply the object in question.[28]

28. Genesis 16:10, 22:17; Exodus 32:13.

Talmidah: What is the object in question?

Mitnagged: In Genesis 16:10, "your seed."

Talmidah: Meaning . . .

Mitnagged: "I will multiply your seed," or "I will give you numerous children."

Talmidah: What about the other two cases?

Mitnagged: The other two cases? Well, they happen to be the same word—*seed.*

Talmidah: What a coincidence!

Mitnagged: Precisely. A coincidence.

Talmidah: The other two instances of *arbah* in Scripture occur in Jeremiah and Ezekiel. In Jeremiah,[29] God says, "I will multiply the *seed* of David," and in Ezekiel,[30] He promises to restore a devastated Israel by repopulating it.

Mitnagged: Interesting but irrelevant.

Talmidah: The three cases you cited . . . are they part of a curse decreed by an angry God?

Mitnagged: No. They don't need to be.

---

29. 33:22.
30. 36:37.

Talmidah: Is it merely coincidence that all three of your cases are part of covenant promises made by God to Abraham? That they are *blessings*, not curses?

Mitnagged: Just what are you suggesting, Talmidah?

Talmidah: That 3:16 must be read polyvalently, as an honest description of a woman's pain in childbearing, a promise that such pain will give her numerous posterity and that these in turn will make her great. This multiple meaning derives from parallel analogy[31] to the words of the Abrahamic Covenant you cleverly cited.

Mitnagged: What will make her great, Talmidah? The pain or the kids?

Talmidah: You laugh, but the answer is *yes*. Both.

Mitnagged: An odd way to define greatness. In any case, it's not there in the text. Your reading cannot be supported grammatically. I win on this one, Talmidah. Is that not so, Rabbi?

Rabbi: Mitnagged wins the grammatical argument. Talmidah wins the hermeneutical one.

Mitnagged: So which is it? Each contradicts the other.

Talmidah: He's right, Rabbi. It is the difference between curse and blessing, between an angry God and a compassionate one.

---

31. The second of Rabbi Ishmael's thirteen hermeneutical rules is *gezerah shavah*. Scriptural passages containing the same word or phrase may be used to clarify one another.

Rabbi: That you must decide for yourselves. Perhaps you are both right . . . or both wrong.

Mitnagged: Rabbi Eliezer sees no ambiguity in this passage. As he said, "He gave the woman nine curses and death: the afflictions arising from menstruation and the tokens of virginity; the affliction of conception in the womb; the affliction of childbirth; the affliction of bringing up children; her head is covered like a mourner; her ear is pierced like the ears of permanent slaves; like a handmaid she waits upon her husband; her testimony is not believed; and after all these curses comes death."[32]

Talmidah: Rabbi Eliezer was a great commentator, may his memory be blessed, but he was not overly fond of women.

Mitnagged: Talmudic sages preceded him in his judgment that women are cursed for Havah's sin. For example, a woman must hide her shame behind a head covering of mourning because she brought death into the world. A woman is cursed with the blood tokens of virginity and menstruation, a pollution which she must cleanse from herself in a ritual bath, the *mikvah,* before she is worthy to rejoin her husband. A woman must separate the *hallah* from the dough as expiation for defiling Adam, who was the *hallah* of the world. And because Havah extinguished the light of man's soul, it is incumbent upon her to light the Sabbath candles.[33]

Talmidah: Masculine distortion of a woman's *mitzvot,* denying their function as holy rituals performed by a woman who is exalted and sanctified by her status as *ishah*.

---

32. *Pirke de Rabbi Eliezer,* chap. XIV.

33. 2 *Avot de Rabbi Natan* 9, 24–25; 42, 117; *Kiddushin* 2b; *Shabbat* 31b–32a; *Yerushalmi* 2, 5b; *Ketuvot* 2.1, *Yevamot* 114b.

Mitnagged: Let me guess. They're priestly actions.

Talmidah: Of course.

Mitnagged: This is insufferable!

Talmidah: The insufferable are doomed to suffer. Is it not written, "You shall be to Me a kingdom of priests and a holy nation"?[34]

Mitnagged: *Male* priests, Talmidah. The word is *cohanim*—a masculine plural.

Talmidah: You know as well as I do that masculine plurals are ambiguous, Mitnagged. They can be exclusive, meaning all males, or they can be inclusive, meaning both males and females together. Is that not correct, Rabbi?

Rabbi: That is correct.

Talmidah: Let us take each of your so-called curses one at a time. You say a woman who covers her head does so as a sign of mourning and shame.

Mitnagged: That is correct. Because she brought death into the world.

Talmidah: You likewise must be guilty of a shameful crime, Mitnagged.

Mitnagged: What are you talking about?

---

34. Exodus 19:6.

Talmidah: What is that thing you wear on your head?

Mitnagged: My yarmulka? You're not seriously suggesting . . . this is entirely different! My yarmulka serves as a symbol of my Jewishness.

Talmidah: But you said head coverings are symbols of shame and mourning. Does that mean that Jewish identity is a shameful thing?

Mitnagged: Of course not . . . I mean that's not what it means for a man's yarmulka.

Talmidah: *Yarmulka* is a Yiddish abbreviation of *yare me-Elohim,* "stand in awe of God." It's a symbol of respect and devotion to God.

Rabbi: It is said that the custom originated with Rabbi Hanah Ben Joshua, of whom it is said, "He never walked four cubits with uncovered head, for he used to say: The Shekhina, God's Presence, resides above my head."[35]

Talmidah: Meaning that a covered head is a sign of holiness. That is why it is incumbent upon men and women to cover their heads, particularly during religious ceremonies. But Rabbi, the precedent goes further back in time than Rabbi Hanah ben Joshua.

Rabbi: Explain.

35. *Kiddushin* 31a.

Talmidah: It is written in Torah that priests were required to cover their heads while officiating in the temple.[36]

Mitnagged: You can't be equating yarmulkas to mitres and headdresses!

Talmidah: Why not? You say the yarmulka serves as a symbol of Jewish self-affirmation. I agree. But just exactly what does it mean to be a Jew? Somebody who wears odd hats and eats kosher pizza? To be a Jew is to be a member of a holy nation, a nation of priests, Mitnagged. And what does that mean? It means we serve God in serving humanity, providing moral leadership, and intellectual and spiritual enlightenment. We stand for humane ethics and lofty ideals, for self-examination, reverence for life and devotion to the Holy One and His Torah. Whether you cover your head with a yarmulka, a turban, or a scarf, it means the same thing. It means you affirm your allegiance to God and the role you have as one of His chosen, *ahad b'nei Israel*—one of the children of Israel.

Mitnagged: I concede your point regarding the head covering, for whatever I say of the woman's scarf, I say of my yarmulka.

Rabbi: A wise retreat.

Talmidah: That being the case you must also concede the case for the woman's *mitzva* regarding the *mikvah,* the ritual bath.

Mitnagged: No. On that point I stand on firm ground, Talmidah. The woman was cursed with a bloody flow, becom-

36. Exodus 28:36–38.

ing a source of impurity to her husband and any man she comes in contact with. As it is written, "When a woman has a discharge, her discharge being blood from her body, she shall remain in her impurity seven days; whoever touches her shall be unclean until evening. Anything that she lies on during her impurity shall be unclean; and anything that she sits on shall be unclean. Anyone who touches her bedding shall wash his clothes, bathe in water, and remain unclean until evening; and anyone who touches any object on which she has sat shall wash his clothes, bath in water, and remain unclean until evening. Be it the bedding or be it the object of which she has sat, on touching it he shall be unclean until evening. And if a man lies with her, her impurity is communicated to him; he shall be unclean seven days, and any bedding on which he lies shall become unclean. When she becomes clean of her discharge, she shall count off seven days, and after that she shall be clean."[37] That's Torah.

Talmidah: It is also written, "When any man has a discharge issuing from his flesh, he is unclean. His uncleanness means this: Any bedding on which the man with the discharge lies shall be unclean, and every object on which he sits shall be unclean. Anyone who touches his bedding shall wash his clothes, bathe in water, and remain unclean until evening. Whoever sits on an object on which the man with the discharge has sat shall wash his clothes, bathe in water, and remain unclean until evening. Whoever touches the body of the man with the discharge shall wash his clothes, bathe in water, and remain unclean until evening." It goes on for quite a while about the fact that this "unclean" man contaminates everything and everyone he touches. Then finally, "When a

37. Leviticus 15:19–24, 28.

man with a discharge becomes clean of his discharge, he shall count off seven days for his cleansing, wash his clothes, and bathe his body in fresh water; then he shall be clean."[38] That, too, is Torah. When it comes to ritual purity, Scripture equates the status of menstrual blood with semen—or any bodily discharge for that matter. Neither man nor woman with any kind of bodily discharge may enter the sanctuary until they have been cleansed of "impurity." The effects are identical and so is the requirement for purification, namely two turtledoves or two pigeons brought to the sanctuary where they are sacrificed by a priest.[39] The *mikvah* is a separate matter.

Rabbi: Separate matter?

Mitnagged: Well might you be astonished, Rabbi. Every one knows that the *mikvah* requirement is directly tied to a woman's menstrual period!

Rabbi: A woman immerses herself in the ritual bath on the seventh day before the termination of her flow, at the end of her *niddah* period.

Mitnagged: You can't get any tighter than that.

Talmidah: The timing reflects the earliest possible moment when a woman can perform her *mikvah* requirement. We have just read that a woman—or man—is ritually unclean from the time of fluid discharge plus seven days. As you remember, last week we discussed the possible reasons why such fluids were not allowed in the temple.

---

38. Leviticus 15:2–13.
39. Leviticus 15:14–15, 29–30.

Rabbi: Ancient purification laws were not confined to "life's fluids," as you put it, Talmidah. What other elements serve as "polluters" when it comes to sanctity within the Holy Sanctuary, particularly with regard to priestly eligibility to officiate in the temple?

Talmidah: Skin disease, certain animals . . .

Mitnagged: And corpses! The dead bodies of animals and especially human beings were the greatest sources of defilement. In fact, they still are for any member of a priestly family.

Talmidah: Life and death.

Rabbi: Rabbi Adin Steinsaltz taught that purification laws have little to do with hygiene or physical cleanliness, but more with a basic outlook that divided the world into two spheres: "life, the most complete expression of which is anything pertaining to sanctity; and death and void, seen as the opposite of life and sanctity."[40]

Talmidah: Then he agrees with me!

Rabbi: Not precisely. He contends that impurity comes from contact with death: "That which is living and healthy contains no impurity and that impurity increases as an object comes closer to death."[41]

Mitnagged: The greatest pollutant, then, is death.

---

40. Adin Steinsaltz, *The Essential Talmud* (New York: Basic Books, 1976), p. 194.
41. Steinsaltz, *The Essential Talmud*.

Rabbi: That is correct. He did not imply that life, the opposite of death, was likewise a source of ritual impurity. The most impure object is a corpse.

Talmidah: But what about menstrual blood?

Rabbi: One can argue that menstrual blood represents the frustration of life—the failure or even death of an egg.

Mitnagged: You see, Talmidah, at the end of the menstrual cycle, the lining in the uterus . . .

Talmidah: Spare me the details!

Mitnagged: Would that I could, my dear lady, but since you brought it up, you must face the inescapable conclusion that a woman's flow is linked both to death and to Havah's curse for bringing death into the world.

Talmidah: What of childbirth? The biblical requirements for purifying a woman after childbirth are nearly as stringent as those for purifying a priest for touching a corpse. And what do we find today? A woman immerses herself in the *mikvah* following childbirth, as well as her *niddah* period, even though giving birth to a child is the supreme opposite of death.

Rabbi: A point worth considering. One may also argue that blood is life itself and therefore forbidden in temple space for the same reason it is forbidden in dietary law, as it is written, "Take care not to eat the blood, since blood is life, and you must not eat the life with the meat."[42]

42. Deuteronomy 12:23.

Mitnagged: A mass of confusing contradictions. I, too, read Rabbi Steinsaltz's words regarding purification laws. "This legislation is extremely involved and contains a plethora of detail that seems to have been determined at random with no clear rationale."[43] In other words, there is no logical explanation for purification laws.

Talmidah: Faced with a contradiction to your hypothesis, you appeal to the safety net for anything which you cannot explain—"It's a mystery." Very well, you must admit then that there is no justification for listing a woman's *mikvah* requirement as a "curse."

Mitnagged: It is something required of the woman, but not the man. How else can you explain the purification rite, if not to cleanse her from a pollution which is strictly feminine in nature? Why isn't a man required to immerse himself in the *mikvah* following a "discharge"?

Talmidah: That is precisely the point.

Mitnagged: Clear as mud.

Talmidah: If the *mikvah*'s purpose is to cleanse a woman from her impurity, why isn't a man likewise required to immerse himself every time he has a "discharge" of semen?

Mitnagged: Not very practical.

Talmidah: When does a man immerse himself in the *mikvah?*

---

43. Steinsaltz, *The Essential Talmud.*

Mitnagged: He is not bound by any such obligation.

Rabbi: During Mishnaic times a man was required to ritually immerse himself before study or prayer, although this requirement is no longer binding by Talmudic times. Today, in many traditional communities, a pious man will immerse himself three times every Friday evening before he goes to the synagogue.

Talmidah: Male immersion goes further back than Mishnaic times, Rabbi.

Mitnagged: Don't tell me . . . priests officiating in the temple.

Talmidah: Exactly. Ritual purification directly applied only to the sacrificial cult and to those administering it—the priests. Preparatory, and I emphasis the word *preparatory,* to officiating, they necessarily purified themselves from any possible source of pollution—be it semen, bodily discharge, skin disease, or contact with a corpse. Biblical purification requirements for lay Israelites were not the same. The requirement for purifying yourself from a bodily discharge is to wash yourself and everything you touched at home, wait seven days, then go to the temple and make an offering. Nothing is said about a woman having to immerse herself in a ritual bath before she is cleansed from her *niddah* period. She is automatically pure after seven clean days. The same can be said of men.

Mitnagged: Perhaps it is not plainly written in Scripture, but in Oral Tradition the ruling is clear. A woman is *niddah* until she immerses herself properly in a *mikvah.* Until then, she is forbidden sexual relations with her husband. In fact, a virgin is a *niddah* until her ritual immersion shortly before marriage.

Talmidah: Exactly. What does *taharah,* which we clumsily translate as "pure," really mean? "Free flow." And what does *tumah,* "impure," really mean? "Blockage." To be *tumah* is to be blocked from something—entry to the temple or sexual relations with your spouse, both holy actions of utmost sanctity according to our tradition. Under levitical law, the ritual bath served to remove any "blockage" to a priest's worthiness, and then prepared him for acts of holiness.

Mitnagged: Scripture makes no mention of a *mikvah* as a ceremonial bath.

Talmidah: It is called by another name—the *ki'or,* commonly translated as "laver."

Mitnagged: The ten lavers of water in the outer court of the temple? You're kidding!

Talmidah: Whether you call it a *mikvah* or a *ki'or,* it is built the same way and serves the same purpose. Each of them held the same amount of water as our modern *mikvah* today—40 *se'ahs* or 191 gallons.[44]

Rabbi: Actually the requirement is that forty *se'ahs* of water in the *mikvah* must be "pure water"—rainwater or the groundwater of a stream. Additional water may be added for convenience—to heat the bath, for example, or make it easier to immerse oneself totally.

Mitnagged: There is no maximum limit?

---

44. 1 Kings 7:38.

Rabbi: No. As long as forty *se'ahs* are "living waters." For this reason *tevilah,* or immersion, can take place in a stream or even an ocean.

Talmidah: So what was the purpose of the *ki'or* in ancient times? We read in Exodus 40:12 that initiates were washed before they were annointed as priests. In Exodus 30:17–21, we learn that priests were required to wash their hands and feet in a ritual bath before entering the sanctuary.

Mitnagged: Exodus 30:17–21 does not pertain to *tevilah*—total immersion.

Talmidah: The point is that the *mikvah* was intended to prepare priests for entering the sanctuary, to purify them, to sanctify them and make them holy. So also immersion in a *mikvah* prepares a man or woman to resume their exalted duties within the sanctuary of synagogue and home. It is not a symbol of woman's degradation, any more than it is for a man. The requirement is not a "curse" for Havah's so-called sin.

Rabbi: One could say it is a blessing. The rabbis taught that the period of sexual abstinence preceding a woman's immersion in the *mikvah* assures *yehud* between couples, for it causes a man to love his wife as on her bridal day.[45]

Talmidah: That is a beautiful thought. And it occurs to me that it also serves as a reminder to a man that his wife is not his to do with as he pleases, to satisfy his desires anytime he wants. The law allows her to say, "I am not yours. I am myself. I am consecrated and holy in the eyes of God."

45. *Niddah* 31b.

Rabbi: What is the purpose of *tevilah* for a convert to Judaism?

Mitnagged: *Tevilah* is the final step in conversion. In this way he or she becomes a "new Jew."

Talmidah: By immersing themselves three times in the *mikvah,* just like the pious Jew does every Friday.

Mitnagged: In this context, the *mikvah* represents new life, for a person is completely purified by undefiled water in an undefiled container.

Talmidah: In that case, each of us becomes a "new Jew" whenever we perform *tevilah* in a *mikvah.*

Rabbi: Interesting thought.

Talmidah: In any case, the woman's *mitzvah* to immerse herself in a *mikvah* prior to resuming sexual relations with her husband is not a curse. It is, in fact, a blessing of the most sacred nature. It is a preparatory rite to resuming her role as Queen Mother alongside her husband, the "Father," and their symbolic union of God with his Shekinah. As for the *mitzvah* of *hallah,*[46] one only has to read its origin in the Torah to dispute it as evidence that Havah was cursed. In Numbers 15:19–20, it is a gift to the Lord, as it is written, "When you eat of the bread of the land you shall set some aside as a gift to the Lord; as the first yields of your baking." This is a commandment to all the people. In addition, priests are required to burn portions of bread offerings on a number of occasions: for making obla-

---

46. A woman is required to burn a small portion of dough whenever she bakes bread.

tions, thank-offerings, and performing Nazarite vows.[47] Moses was commanded and subsequently performed a similar ceremony as part of the ritual for anointing Aaron and his sons as priests.[48] Are these rituals of shame and admission of guilt? If you are too blind to read, Mitnagged, then listen: "The priest shall remove the token portion from the meal offering and turn it into smoke on the altar as an *offering by fire,* a *pleasing odor to the Lord.* And the remainder of the meal offering shall be for Aaron and his sons, a *most holy portion* from the Lord's offering by fire."[49] In what capacity does a woman make her *hallah* offering?

Mitnagged: There are no priestesses in the Torah!

Talmidah: Not in the ancient temple cult. But there is one in every pious home where a mother's duties are highly valued and couched in holy terms. In this reading the simple act of baking bread becomes an act of devotion and love. I make my burnt offering to God, and then I bake the rest of the dough into hallah loaves and place them on the table—the altar of my sanctuary—as a meal offering for my husband and our children.

Rabbi: That reminds me of another passage in Leviticus regarding the twelve loaves of shewbread. "You shall take choice flour and bake of it twelve loaves . . . place them on the pure table before the Lord . . . arrange them before the Lord regularly every Sabbath day . . . eat them in the sacred

47. Leviticus 2:4–10, 7:12–13; Numbers 6:15–19.
48. Exodus 29:23, Leviticus 8:26.
49. Leviticus 2:9–10.

precinct, for they are his as most holy things from the Lord's offerings by fire."[50]

Talmidah: Without Masoretic voweling you can read that phrase differently, Rabbi.

Rabbi: How so?

Talmidah: "They are his as most holy things from the Lord's offerings by Woman."

Mitnagged: A ridiculous reading. Note that the person baking loaves of shewbread is male, and the people eating it are male priests.

Talmidah: So it was in the ancient temple cult. Now that symbolic rituals and covenants have been transferred to synagogue and home, they are open to every Jew, not just a select caste of priestly families. We have truly become a nation of priests! Not just ten percent, twenty-five percent, or fifty percent of a nation, but a whole nation of priests.

Rabbi: You have neglected an obvious argument, Talmidah.

Talmidah: How so?

Rabbi: Mitnagged quoted a rabbi who claimed that the *mitzvah* of hallah was a curse on woman because she defiled man, the hallah of the world.

---

50. 24:5–9.

Mitnagged: That's true. You yourself inserted commentary from *Tanhuma Bereshith* into your first portion of targum, saying that Yahweh took a portion of the earth to make man, making man himself hallah.

Talmidah: Yes, I'm beginning to see. Incredible!

Mitnagged: A cheerful way to admit guilt.

Talmidah: It is a symbolic act of creation!

Mitnagged: What!

Talmidah: "Once the woman puts water into the dough, she is to remove her hallah. Thus did the Holy One do. Once the Holy One put water on the earth, He immediately removed man as his hallah from the earth." What more appropriate ritual for Woman, Lifegiver to undertake!

Mitnagged: You're comparing yourself to God?

Talmidah: Our rabbis compared God to a woman. Is that any less blasphemous? In any case, I can imitate Him. Hallah symbolizes my role as life-giver to man. Just as God took a portion of the earth to make mankind, so the woman takes a portion of herself to make new life. As for the lighting of Shabbat candles . . .

Mitnagged: You already implied last week that lighting Shabbat candles is parallel to lighting a temple menorah. Spare me a repetition of that claim!

Talmidah: What's the matter Mitnagged? Tired of falling off your horse? This priestly duty is found in Exodus 25:37.

Mitnagged: So why two and not seven? If we are symbolizing the Tree of Life via menorah, where is the sacred number seven?

Rabbi: In some circles it is customary to light seven candles. I suspect that the more widespread custom of lighting two candles is a pragmatic one, it being a hardship for the poverty-stricken Jews of past times to acquire so many candles for Shabbat. Two would have been the minimum requirement to assure its symbolic function. Lighting two candles doubled the light in a home normally illuminated with only one. This added to the luster of the Sabbath Queen, emphasizing her role as a light in a world of darkness.

Talmidah: It occurs to me that this ceremony also reflects a woman's role as life-giver. Is it not written in the Creation account, "Let there be light!"

Mitnagged: As I have already proven, the rabbis interpret this to the contrary. Because a woman extinguished the light of man's soul, she must make expiation by lighting the Sabbath candles.

Talmidah: But Scripture says that God saw the light, that it was good, Mitnagged. You are saying that it is a symbol of shame, death, and mourning.

Mitnagged: You twist my words! Yes, light does symbolize all that is good in the world, particularly on Shabbat, and that is why it was a sin to snuff it out by ushering in death and darkness.

Rabbi: Modern rabbis would side with Talmidah. I recall the words of Abraham Joshua Heschel: "Just as creation began with the word, 'Let there be light!' so does the celebration of creation begin with the kindling of lights . . ."

Talmidah: Celebration!

Rabbi: ". . . It is the woman who ushers in the joy and sets up the most exquisite symbol, light, to dominate the atmosphere of the home."[51]

Mitnagged: Thanks for your support, Rabbi.

Rabbi: Any time.

Mitnagged: If Havah's action was so noble and divine, why the curse on Adam for heeding her voice? It is written, "Because you obeyed the voice of your wife and ate from the tree which I forbad you to eat, cursed is the earth because of you," or "in your harvest," as you chose to translate. Either reading produces a curse upon the man, as your excerpt from the *Apocalypse of Moses* spells out in grim detail.

Talmidah: A single reading of this passage does present unrelieved suffering without hope. But if you read 3:18 as a palimpsest of both mortal consequence and promise, we see, once again, that the benefits of mortal life come through numerous posterity.

Rabbi: Explain your palimpsest, Talmidah.

Talmidah: I shall draw it on the board. This is the passage as we have it in the Masoretic text: תצמיח לך ואכלת את עשב השדה וקוץ נדרדר I modified it thus: ודר דר תצמצח לך ואכלת את עשב השדה וקיץ I substituted a yod (י) for a vav (ו) in the first word, these two letters commonly mistaken for one another. Instead of a

51. *The Sabbath* (New York: Farrar, Straus & Dusahy, 1951), p. 66.

noun, this word can be a verb, specifically a second-person masculine-singular imperative—"Awake!" or "Arise!" Instead of "you shall eat," in a literal sense, *acaltah* means "you shall feast/enjoy" in a metaphorical sense. Instead of reading the root שׂדה as *sadeh*, "field," I read *shad-ah*, "her breast." So here is our palimpsest:

Masoretic Reading	*Alternate Reading*
Thorns	Awake!/Arise!
and thistles	generation upon generation
will she (earth) sprout for you	will she (Havah) spring for you
and you will eat grain	and you will enjoy the yield
of the plowed field	of her breast

Mitnagged: If it works so "beautifully," Talmidah, why the shift in position? Why did you feel compelled to play redactor and split the palimpsest so that its second half occurs two verses later? No need to answer! The problem is self-evident. If you place your palimpsest next to its partner, the passage makes no sense, because your message of hope would be sandwiched in between two halves of a curse. It becomes a glaring intrusion on the text.

Talmidah: This is not merely a partnership between two halves of a palimpsest, Mitnagged. This partnership consists of three parts: two readings of 3:18 plus 3:20. Verse 20 is the strongest evidence that a double reading of 3:18 is not only feasible but indispensable, particularly if you subtract the commentary accompanying 3:19 in my targum. Without the double reading, 3:20 makes no sense whatsoever. Just read it, Mitnagged. God informs Adam that he will live a miserable life and then die. Immediately after that grim pronouncement,

Adam jumps for joy and calls his wife "Life!" because "she was Mother to all living!"

Mitnagged: It does present an abrupt change in story line.

Talmidah: It portrays an impossible reaction on Adam's part. I could have joined the two halves of 3:18 together and left it to the reader to make the causal link between Adam's exclamation of praise and the promise made to him that Havah would bear him generations of posterity. Instead, I chose to place the "hope" side of 3:18 where the connection would be more discernible.

Rabbi: This passage the way you translated it feels familiar.

Talmidah: The Abrahamic Covenant.

Rabbi: Ahhhh. The promise of a multitude of "seed" and the subsequent renaming of Sarah as a mother of nations.

Talmidah: Acknowledging the source of a patriarch's greatness, namely his queenly companion, his life-giver. Havah and Adam, like Sarah and Abraham, would achieve greatness together as a couple, through the painful toil of mortality and the life-nurturing task of begetting and rearing children.

Mitnagged: Why throw them out of Paradise, then?

Talmidah: Our discussion last week provided a number of possible reasons other than punishment. They could not experience mortality or gain understanding in a perfect setting frozen in time and space. Their expulsion could symbolize the necessity for mankind to leave God's holy presence for a time. Otherwise, mankind would have remained eternally untested and never fully complete. Or it could represent the end of childhood, or even graduation from a *yeshiva* with its warm association with a beloved rabbi.

Mitnagged: Then why does God weep, Talmidah? If it was intended all along, why the lament?

Rabbi: I can answer that question from personal experience. It is likened to a Parent who takes his trusting child by the hand and leads him to *kheder*. There He delivers the tender little soul whom He has nurtured for several years into the hands of a harsh stranger who feels no love for His child. He knows that His child will have his knuckles rapped, his ears boxed, and his spirit abused and tortured by teachers and classmates for many long hours of the day. The child weeps and wails and begs the Parent to keep him at His side. Instead, He pushes the child into the cruel world of *kheder* and firmly shuts the door in order to prevent escape. He does this because He loves the child. He knows that this experience is necessary for the child to grow strong in knowledge and understanding. Nevertheless, He stands outside the door and weeps.

Talmidah: Why does He weep, Rabbi?

Rabbi: He weeps because separation from His child is painful. And he weeps because of the suffering of His child.

Mitnagged: I understood that the Holy One grieved because Man had fallen from his former glorious state and had become a degenerate creature, because he lost immortality in a perfect paradise through willful disobedience.

Rabbi: There are many who interpret as you say. Who can say what makes the Holy One grieve when He thinks on mankind?

Talmidah: I believe the answer to that question lies in His dealings with mankind.

Mitnagged: Kicking the man and woman out of His Holy Place.

Talmidah: Personally clothing the man and woman in holy garments, as a symbol of their special relationship with Him. So we drape the tallit over our sons and daughters when they come of age to face the world as adults.

Rabbi: It is traditional in some communities for the father to wrap his child in his tallit and carry him in his arms to the child's first day of *kheder*.

Talmidah: Note that the garments placed next to the skin of Havah and Adam were vestments of honor and glory—not coverings of shame!

Mitnagged: Yes, I also noticed in your targum that only Adam is said to have worn them as priesthood garments, the rationale being that he was created before Havah and therefore entitled to them as firstborn of the world.

Talmidah: From the very beginning, Mitnagged, my targum asserts that man and woman were formed simultaneously, making them equal in their sibling rank. You cannot read the Torah account itself without seeing that Yahweh clothed both man and woman with holy garments. And these were garments placed upon them by a compassionate God, Mitnagged, not an angry one! They would not go out into the world totally unprepared or unprotected. They would keep with them always, a reminder of their worth and esteem and exalted mission in life. The Father did not send His children out into the world naked.

Rabbi: You are leaving, Talmidah?

Talmidah: I promised to meet someone.

Rabbi: Very well. Shalom, until next week.

Rabbi: You look somewhat disturbed, Mitnagged. Are you perhaps wondering who Talmidah may be seeing?

Mitnagged: No, of course not. Why should I care about that? I just don't like this role you've given me.

Rabbi: Because it makes you look like . . . how did she put it? A Neanderthal?

Mitnagged: I don't like doing this to Talmidah.

Rabbi: What would you like to be doing with her instead?

Mitnagged: I hate this game, Rabbi!

Rabbi: Ahhhhh . . . last week you felt uneasy about it. This week you positively hate it. We are progressing quite nicely.

Mitnagged: What are you talking about?

Rabbi: What do you think I'm talking about?

Mitnagged: I don't want to do this anymore, Rabbi. Find somebody else.

Rabbi: No need. I am quite pleased with your performance.

Mitnagged: Well, I'm not at all pleased!

Rabbi: You are not proud of yourself?

Mitnagged: Hardly!

Rabbi: Good.

6

"Good and Evil"
Genesis 3:23–5:3

Targum

Havah: While we were being expelled and lamenting, your father Adam begged the angels, "Let me be a little while so that I may beseech God that he might have compassion and pity me, for I alone have sinned." And they ceased driving him out. And your father wept before the angels in front of Paradise, and the angels said to him, "What do you want us to do for you, Adam?" Your father answered and said to the angels, "See, you are casting me out; I beg you, let me take fragrances from Paradise, so that after I have gone out, I might bring an offering to God so that God will hear me." And they came to God and entreated, "Yael, Eternal King, please command that fragrant incenses from Paradise be given to Adam." So God ordered

Adam to come that he might take aromatic fragrances out of Paradise.[1]

Genesis 3:23 Then Yahweh Elohim drove him out from the Garden of Eden.

When the sun sank, darkness began to set in. Adam was terrified.[2] "Woe is me! Perhaps because I have sinned, the world around me is being darkened and returning to its state of chaos and confusion. This then is the kind of death to which I have been sentenced from Heaven![3] Surely indeed the darkness shall envelop me: shall he of whom it was said, 'He shall bruise thy heel' now come to attack me?"[4] So he sat up all night fasting and weeping and Havah was weeping beside him.[5]

Psalms 22:1 My God, my God! Why have you forsaken me!
The words of my groaning do nothing to save me
22:2 My God! I call by day, but you do not answer,
at night, but I find no respite.
31:12 I am forgotten, as a dead man
Lamentations 3:2 He led me into darkness, not light
3:6 He has set me in dark places
like those long dead
Isaiah 24:11 All joy is darkened
happiness banished from the land
Job 10:21 I go where I cannot return
to the land of darkness
and shadow dark as death
10:22 where dimness and disorder hold sway

---

1. *The Apocalypse of Moses*, 27, 29.
2. *Bereshith Rabbah* XII.6.
3. *Avodah Zarah* 8a, Talmud Bavli.
4. *Bereshith Rabbah* XII.6.
5. *Tractate Avodah Zarah* 8a, Talmud Bavli.

and light itself is like dead of night
Bow down your ear to me! *Psalms*
Deliver me! Quickly! *31:2*
For in death there is no remembering you *6:5*
Who will praise you in the grave?
Will your wonders be known in the dark? *88:12*
Ashes are the food that I eat, *102:9*
my drink is mingled with tears
because of your fury and anger *102:10*
since you have raised me up
only to cast me away.
I am worn out with groaning *6:6*
I drench my head-rest all night
and soak my sleeping place in tears
My eyes waste away with grief *6:7*
Awake! Why do you sleep, Oh Yahweh? *44:23*
Arise! Do not cast us off forever!
Why do you hide your face? *44:24*
Forgetting our affliction and our oppression?
For our soul is bowed down to the dust *44:25*
Our belly clings to the earth.
Why, Yahweh, do you stand far distant? *10:1*
Stay hidden in our time of trouble?
How long, Yahweh, will you forget us? Forever? *13:1*
How long will you turn your face away from us?
How long must we brood in soul? *13:2*
Heart sorrowing day and night?
Look down, answer us, Yahweh our God! *13:3*
Give light to our eyes
or we shall fall into the sleep of death!

What did the Lord do for him? A pillar of fire was sent to him to give illumination about him and to guard him from all evil.

And he said, "Now I know that the Omnipresent is with me." And he put forth his hands to the light of the fire and said, "Blessed art Thou, O Lord our God, King of the Universe, who creates the flames of fire." And when he removed his hands from the light of the fire, he said, "Blessed art Thou, O Lord our God, King of the Universe, who divides the holy from the profane, the light from the darkness."[6]

When dawn broke, he said, "This is the usual course of the world!" He then arose and offered up a bullock.[7] And on that day, he offered a sweet-smelling sacrifice—frankincense, galbanum, stacte and spices—in the morning with the rising of the sun from the day he covered his shame.[8] Adam's offering took place on the Day of Atonement and corresponded to the service of the high priest.[9]

When they were driven out of Paradise they made for themselves a tent and mourned for seven days, weeping in great sorrow. But after seven days they began to hunger and sought food to eat, but found none.[10]

Havah: And it happened that we mourned for seven days. After seven days we were hungry and I said to Adam, "Gather and bring us food that we might eat and live, lest we die. Let us get up and weep on the ground so that God might hear us."[11]

---

6. *Pirke de-Rabbi Eliezer,* chap. XX.
7. *Avodah Zarah,* 8a, Talmud Bavli.
8. *Jubilees* 3:27.
9. *Midrash Tehillin,* XXXIX.3.
10. *Vita Adae,* 1:1.
11. *The Apocalypse of Moses,* 29:7.

So they walked, searching, for nine days and found nothing such as they had had in Paradise, but only such as animals eat.[12]

Havah: And we rose and went through the whole land and did not find food. And I said to Adam, "Rise, my husband, and do away with me that I might depart from you and from the presence of God and from the angels so that they will cease to be angry with you on my account." Then Adam answered, "Why have you been thinking of this evil, that I should commit murder, so that I should stretch out my hand against the image which God made?"[13]

Then the man knew *Genesis 4:1a*
had sexual intercourse
with Havah, his wife
with Life, his holy fire
and she conceived
her springs flowed

And Havah said to Adam, "You live on, my husband. Life is granted to you, but I have been cheated and deceived. And now separate me from the light of such life, and I will go to the sunset and stay there until I die." And she began to walk toward the West and to mourn and to weep bitterly with loud sighing. And she made there a shelter while she was three months pregnant. And when the time of her giving birth drew near, she began to be distressed with pains and cried out to the Lord, "Have mercy on me, Lord, help me!"

---

12. *Vita Adae,* 4:1.
13. *The Apocalypse of Moses,* 29:8–11.

Psalms 30:8 To you, Yahweh, I call!
To my God, I cry for mercy!
Listen Yahweh! Take pity on me!
Yahweh, help me!
22:14 I am poured out like water
my bones all disjointed
my heart turned to wax
melting inside my inward parts
2:15 My mouth is dry as earthenware
my tongue sticks to my jaw
You lay me down in the dust of death
30:9 What point is there in my death?
my going down to the abyss?
Can the dust praise you?
or proclaim your steadfastness?
6:5 For in death there is no remembering of you
Who will praise you in the grave?
31:2 Bow down your ear to me!
Deliver me quickly!
25:18 Look upon my affliction and my pain!

And she said to herself, "Who will give the news to my husband Adam? I beg you, O lights of heaven, when you return to the East, tell my husband Adam." However, at that very moment, Adam said, "Havah's complaint has come to me." And he went forth and came upon her in great distress. And Havah said, "The moment I saw you, my husband, my pained soul was cooled. And now implore the Lord God for me to hear you and to have regard for me and free me from my most awful pains." And Adam prayed to the Lord for Havah.[14]

14. *Vita Adae,* 18–20.

And she bore Cain, "Acquired," saying, *Genesis*
"I acquired a Man of Yahweh *4:1b*
a holy man of God"

And she bore a son, and he was lustrous.[15] She saw his likeness that it was not of earthly beings, but of heavenly beings.[16]

[Havah] Yahweh! My God! *Psalms*
I cried to you for help *30:2*
and you healed me. *30:3*
Yahweh! You lifted me out of the grave
that I should not go down into oblivion
The sorrows of death surrounded me *18:4*
The griefs of Hell enfolded me *18:5*
The snares of death clutched at me *18:6*
In my distress I called upon Yahweh
and cried unto my God
He heard my voice out of his sanctuary
and my wail came before him.
even into his ears
you turned my mourning into dancing *30:11*
you have stripped off my sackcloth
and clothed me with joy
So my glory will sing to you unceasingly *30:12*
Yahweh! My God! I shall praise you forever!
I love Yahweh *116:1*
because he heard my voice
he heard my pleas

15. *Vita Adae,* 21:3.
16. *Pirke de-Rabbi Eliezer,* chap. XXI.

Then Adam brought Havah and the child and led them to the East. And the Lord God sent various seeds by the angel Michael and gave them to Adam and showed him how to work and till the ground so as to have produce by which they and all their generations might live.[17]

Now when a woman sits on the birthstool, she declares, "I will henceforth never have sexual intercourse with my husband again!" Whereupon the Holy One, blessed be He, says to her, "You will return to your desire, you will return to the desire for your husband."[18]

And she bore Awan, "Desire," her daughter.[19]

Genesis 4:2

Then she again gave birth—
to his brother Havel, "Referring to God"[20]
Now Havel was a keeper of flocks
a companion to sheep and goats
a good and docile friend
while Cain was a tiller of earth
a slave of dirt

Havel, the younger, was a lover of righteousness, and believing that God was present at all his actions, he excelled in virtue. But Cain was not only very wicked in other respects, but was wholly intent upon getting.[21]

---

17. *Vita Adae,* 22:1–2.
18. *Bereshith Rabbah* XX.7.
19. *Jubilees* 4:1.
20. This is Philo's midrashic interpretation of Havel's name. *On the Birth of Havel,* II.
21. Josephus, *Antiquities of the Jews,* I.2.

In the course of time 4:3
towards the end of days
of summer days
Cain, "Buy," brought a gift
a grain-offering
a sin-offering
Some of the fruit/harvest of the earth
to Yahweh of the inferior crops
he being like a bad tenant who eats the first ripe figs
but honours the king with the late figs[22]

Havel, "Love of God,"[23] also brought. 4:4a
He brought some of the choicest firstborn females of his flock
along with their fat
their milk

Havel did not bring the same offerings, nor did he bring his offerings in the same manner. He offered what was older and of the first consideration, and instead of what was weak he offered what was strong and fat.[24]

And Yahweh regarded with favor 4:4b
took delight in
Havel and his gift/sin-offering

God turned and inclined to Havel and his offering, and a fire came down from the Lord from Heaven and consumed it.[25]

22. *Bereshith Rabbah* XXII.5.
23. *Hav,* a derivative of *ahavah,* "love," added to *el,* "God."
24. Philo, *On the Birth of Havel,* XXVII.
25. *The Book of Jasher.*

4:5a But upon Cain and his sin-offering
He did not regard with favor

Moses here intimates the difference between a lover of himself, and one who is thoroughly devoted to God; for the one took to himself the firstfruits of his fruits and very impiously looked upon God as worthy only of the secondary and inferior offerings; for the expression, "after some days" implied that he did not do so immediately; and when it is said that he offered of the fruits, that intimates that he did not offer of the best fruits which he had, and herein displays his iniquity. But the other, without any delay, offered up the firstborn and eldest of all his flocks, in order that in this the Father might not be treated unworthily. He accepts the good man, seeing that he is a lover of what is good, and an eager student of virtue; but he rejects and regards with aversion the wicked man, presuming that he will be prone to that side by the order of nature. Therefore he says here with exceeding fitness, that God had regard, not to the offerings, but those who offered them, rather than to the gifts themselves; for men have regard to and regulate their approbation by the abundance and richness of offerings, but God looks at the sincerity of the soul, having no regard to ambition or illusion of any kind.[26]

4:5b Then Cain burned hot with great anger
and his face fell
darkened with resentment

4:6 Yahweh asked Cain,
"Why do you burn hot with anger?

---

26. Philo, *Questions and Answers on Genesis*, I.61.

and why did your face fall
darken with resentment?
Oh that you would do what is right! 4:7
amend your ways!
your head is lifted
you are forgiven
graciously received
exalted
But if you do not do right
amend your ways
sin crouches at the door *of your heart*[27]
hungry to devour you
and you will master it
or you will become like it
And into your hand have I delivered the power over evil passion
and to you shall be the inclination thereof
that you may have authority over it
to become righteous or to sin."[28]

Now Cain said to his brother, Havel, 4:8a
"Let us walk out to the field."

Cain said to Havel, "I perceive that the world was created in goodness, but it is not governed according to the fruit of good works, for there is respect to persons in judgment. That is why your offering was accepted, but mine was not accepted with good will." Havel answered and said to Cain, "In goodness was the world created, and according to the fruit of good works is it governed, and there is no respect of persons in judgment. But

27. *Targum of Palestine.*
28. *Targum of Palestine.*

because the fruits of my works were better than yours, my offering was accepted with good will, and not yours." Cain answered, "There is neither judgment nor Judge, nor another world, nor will good reward be given to the righteous, nor vengeance be taken of the wicked." And Havel answered and said to Cain, "There is a judgment, and there is a Judge, and there is another world, and a good reward given to the righteous, and vengeance taken of the wicked." And because of these words they had contention upon the face of the field. Cain arose against Havel, his brother, and drove a stone into his forehead and killed him.[29] So Cain spilt the blood of his brother upon the earth, and the blood of Havel streamed upon the earth before the flock.[30]

4:8b And while they were in the field
Cain, "Spear," rose up against his brother Havel
and murdered him.

4:9 Then Yahweh asked Cain,
"Where is your brother Havel?"

And Cain replied,
"Am I my brother's keeper/guardian/protector?
Do I keep track of my brother?"

4:10 "What have you done!" Yahweh exclaimed, "Listen!
Your brother's blood *and the blood of his descendants*[31]

29. *Targum of Palestine.*

30. *The Book of Jasher.*

31. *Bereshith Rabbah* XXII.9. This midrash derives the idea of both Havel's blood and that of his descendants spilling into the ground from the fact that the word *blood, dam,* in this verse is in its plural form. It literally reads "bloods."

cries out to me from the earth!
Now you are cursed/banned from the earth which opened her mouth 4:11
to swallow your brother's blood from your hand.
When you work/till the earth 4:12
she will no longer give you her strength/power/wealth.
You will become a *nod*
a staggering/tottering/restless wanderer
a head-shaking griever
in the land."

Then Cain, "Dirge," lamented to Yahweh, 4:13
"My punishment is too great to bear/suffer!
My guilt is too great to lift/forgive!
Look! You drive me out today 4:14
from off the earth's face
and from your face I must hide
and I will become a *nod*
a staggering/tottering/restless wanderer
a head-shaking griever
in the land!
Now anyone who finds me will kill me!"

"That being the case," Yahweh replied, 4:15
"Anyone who kills Cain
will suffer vengeance sevenfold."
Then Yahweh put a mark on Cain
made a token for Cain
established a covenant with Cain
so that no one meeting him would strike him
beat him
kill him

4:16 So Cain left the face/presence of Yahweh,
he and all belonging to him,[32]
and settled in the land of Nod, "Wandering,"
anciently/formerly Eden, "Delight"

So Cain went out from before the Lord and dwelt in the land of the wandering of his exile, which had been made for him from before, as the garden of Eden.[33] And it had been before Cain slew Havel his brother, that the earth multiplied fruits, as the fruits of the garden of Eden, but from the time that he sinned and killed his brother, it changed, to produce thorns and thistles.[34]

God kept Cain in suspense until the Flood came and swept him away.[35]

God himself, with the most perfect wisdom, has laid down the rule of familiarity and intelligence with reference to the first sinner: not slaying the homicide, but destroying him in another manner; since he scarcely permitted him to be enumerated among the generations of his father, but shows him proscribed not only by his parents but by the whole race of mankind, allotting him a state separate from that of others, and secluded from the class of rational beings, as one who had been expelled, and banished, and turned into the nature of beasts.[36]

After these things Adam and Havah were together and when they were lying down to sleep, Havah said to her husband

---

32. *The Book of Jasher.*
33. *Targum of Palestine.*
34. *Targum Yerushalmi.*
35. *Bereshith Rabbah* XXXII.5.
36. Philo, *Questoins and Answers on Genesis,* I.76.

Adam, "My husband, I saw in a dream this night the blood of my son Havel being thrust into the mouth of Cain his brother, and he drank it mercilessly. He begged him to allow him a little of it, but he did not listen to him but swallowed all of it. And it did not stay in his stomach but came out of his mouth." Then Adam said to Havah, "Let us rise and go to see what has happened to them. Perhaps the enemy is warring against them." And when they both had gone out they found Havel killed by the hand of Cain, his brother.[37] The dog which was guarding Havel's flock also guarded his corpse from all the beasts of the field and all the birds of the sky. Adam and his partner were sitting and weeping and mourning for him,

Oh my son! Havel! *2 Samuel 18:33*
My son, my son, Havel!
Would to God that I had died instead of you!
Oh Havel, my son, my son![38]

and they did not know what to do. A raven came, one of its fellow birds dead. It took its fellow and dug in the earth, hid it and buried it before them. Adam said, "Like this raven will I act." He took the corpse of Havel and dug in the earth and buried.[39]

And Adam and his wife mourned four weeks of years on account of Havel, "Sorrow."[40]

---

37. *The Apocalypse of Moses,* 2:1–4, 3:1.

38. This lament is taken from 2 Samuel 18:33, when King David lamented the death of his son, Absalom. Havel's name has been substituted for Absalom's.

39. *Pirke de-Rabbi Eliezer,* chap. XXI.

40. *Jubilees* 4:1. "Sorrow" is a midrashic interpretation of *Havel* by Josephus, *Antiquities,* I.2.1.

Now when Cain had travelled over many countries, he, with his wife, built a city named Nod, which is a place so called, and there he settled his abode; where also he had children. However, he did not accept his punishment in order to amend his ways, but to increase his wickedness; for he only aimed to procure every thing that was for his own bodily pleasure, though it obliged him to be injurious to his neighbors. He augmented his household substance with much wealth, by rapine and violence; he excited his acquaintances to procure pleasures and spoils by robbery, and became a great leader of men into wicked courses. He also introduced a change in that way of simplicity wherein men lived before; and was the author of measures and weights. And whereas they lived innocently and generously while they knew nothing of such arts, he changed the world into cunning craftiness. He first of all set boundaries about lands; he built a city and fortified it with walls, and he compelled his family to come together to it.[41]

Genesis Then Cain knew/had sexual intercourse with his wife
4:17 and she conceived and bore Hanoch, "Dedicated/Consecrated,"
while he was building a city.
So he named the city after his son, Hanoch.

4:18 And to Hanoch was born Irad, "City Dweller/Wild He-Ass";
and Irad begat Mehujael, "God Gives Life";
and Mehujael begat Metushael, "Man of God";
and Metushael begat Lamech, "Strong Young Man."

4:19 Lamech took to himself two wives
married two women

41. Josephus, *Antiquities,* I.2.2.

the name of the first was Adah, "Ornament"
and the name of the second was Tsellah, "Deepening Shadow"

Adah bore Yabal, "Carry Away," *4:20*
who was the ancestor of tent-dwelling herdsmen.
And the name of his brother was Yubal, "Ram's Horn," *4:21*
who was the ancestor of all who skillfully handle lyre and pipe.

And Tsella also bore— *4:22*
she bore Tubal-Cain
"Confusion/Violation of Nature—Metal Worker/Forger"
the ancestor of all who hammer/sharpen
every kind of cutting tool of copper and iron.
And the sister of Tubal-Cain was Naamah, "Pretty."

Lamech warned his wives, *4:23*
"Adah and Tsella, heed my voice!
obey my wishes!
Wives of Lamech, give ear to my word!
obey my command!
For I killed a man for bruising me,
and a boy for striking me!
If Cain will be avenged sevenfold, *4:24*
then Lamech seventy-sevenfold!"

Even while Adam was alive, it came to pass that the posterity of Cain became exceedingly wicked, every one successively dying one after another, more wicked than the former. They were intolerable in war and vehement in robberies; and if any one were slow to murder people, yet was he bold in his profligate behaviour, in acting unjustly, and doing injury for gain.[42]

42. Josephus, *Antiquities,* I.2.2.

4:25a Then Adam yet more/again knew
had sexual intercourse
with his wife
his holy fire

What is implied by Scripture's saying "yet more"? That his desire had been increased by so much more desire than formerly. Formerly he had not felt desire when he did not see his wife, but now he felt desire for her whether he saw her or did not see her.[43]

4:25b and she bore a son
and she named him Shet, "Appointed"
Set, "Exalted"
saying,
"Because Elohim appointed another seed/offspring to me
in place of Havel, because Cain murdered him."

And Adam said to Havah, "See we have begotten a son in place of Havel, whom Cain killed. Let us give glory and sacrifice to God!"[44]

And he begat Azura, "Help/Succor," his daughter.[45]

He had indeed many other children, but Shet in particular. Now this Shet, when he was brought up and came to those years in which he could discern what was good, became a virtuous man; and as he was himself of an excellent character, so did he leave children behind him who imitated his virtues.

---

43. *Pesikta de-Rab Kahana,* Piska 5; *Pesikta Rabbati,* Piska 15.2.
44. *The Apocalypse of Moses,* 4:2.
45. *Jubilees* 4:8.

All these proved to be of good dispositions. They also inhabited the same country without dissension, and in a happy condition, without any misfortunes falling upon them, till they died.[46]

A son was also born to Shet 4:26
and he named him Enosh, "Humanity."
This man was the first to invoke the name of Yahweh
to proclaim/preach in the name of Yahweh

That was the generation in whose days they began to err and to make themselves idols and surnamed their idols by the name of the Word of the Lord.[47] In that time the sons of men began to multiply and to afflict their souls and hearts by transgressing and rebelling against God. And it was in the days of Enosh that the sons of men continued to rebel and transgress against God, to increase the anger of the Lord against the sons of men. And the sons of men went and they served other gods, and they forgot the Lord who had created them in the earth. And in those days the sons of men made images of brass and iron, wood and stone, and they bowed down and served them. And every man made his god and they bowed down to them, and the sons of men forsook the Lord all the days of Enosh and his children. And the anger of the Lord was kindled on account of their works and abominations which they did in the earth.[48]

When Adam saw that his descendants were fated to be consigned to Gehenna, he engaged less in procreation.[49] Adam

46. Josephus, *Antiquities*, I.2.2.
47. *Targum of Palestine.*
48. *The Book of Jashar.*
49. *Bereshith Rabbah* XXI.9

said, "Why should I beget children, when they go to destruction?"[50] What did the Holy One do to Adam? He cast a sleep upon him and showed him Noah and all the unblemished, Abraham and all the proselytes, Isaac and all who sacrifice burnt offerings, Jacob and all tent dwellers, Moses and all the humble, Aaron and all the priests, Joshua and all the community leaders, David and all the Kings, Solomon and all the judges.[51] He had all generations pass before him up until the dead would rise, the righteous and the wicked.[52] While Adam was lying, the Holy One showed him every generation with its teachers, every generation with its righteous, every generation with its wicked, up to the days when the dead are raised. The Holy One showed the first Adam all the generations and put them in his book.[53] He wrote down in His book the names of those He would cause to spring from Adam up to the time the dead are resurrected. And so God read out to Adam all the names of every generation and its teachers, of every generation and its leaders, of every generation and its sages, of every generation and its prophets, of every generation and its scribes and scholars up to the time the dead are resurrected.[54]

5:1 This is the Book of the Generations of Mankind

Then, when he had seen them all, he awakened from his sleep. The Holy One said to him, "Have you seen these? By your life

50. *Tanhuma Bereshith* VII.

51. *Tanhuma Bereshith* VII.

52. *Tanhuma Bereshith* VII. Adam's vision of his posterity is also mentioned in the Talmud (tractate *Sanhedrin* 38b), *Pesikta Rabbati* (Piska 23.1), and *Bereshith Rabbah* (XXIV.5).

53. *Tanhuma Bereshith* I.28, part III.

54. *Midrash Tehillim,* 139.6.

all these righteous are coming forth from you." When He had told him this, his spirit was at rest.[55]

When Shet was born, Adam said, "I did not ascribe my former sons a lineage. Why? Because they were accursed. But to this one I am ascribing a lineage because he is the head of the generations."[56]

Now Adam was a hundred and thirty years old 5:3
when he begat a son in his likeness, after his image
a son like him, who looked like him
and named him Shet, "Appointed"
Set, "Exalted"

Midrash

> According to the suffering, so is the reward.
>
> —*Avot* 5.23

Rabbi: What is this, Talmidah?

Talmidah: I brought a grain-offering for the table of Torah.

Mitnagged: Matza and honey?

Talmidah: It is written, "If you bring an oblation of a bread offering baked in the oven, it must be unleavened cakes of fine

55. *Tanhuma Bereshith.*
56. *Tanhuma Bereshith.*

flour mingled with oil, or unleavened wafers anointed with oil."[57]

Mitnagged: Rabbi, are you going to allow this to go by uncorrected?

Rabbi: You are justified in your criticism, Mitnagged.

Talmidah: But Rabbi . . .

Rabbi: Where is the salt?

Talmidah: Salt?

Mitnagged: *Salt?*

Rabbi: Is it not written, "You must season every oblation of your bread offering with salt; you shall not allow the salt of the covenant of your God to be lacking from your bread offering. You shall add salt to every offering."[58]

Talmidah: I stand corrected.

Mitnagged: This is utterly . . .

Rabbi: Quite delicious. Plain, but tasty. It only lacks salt.

Mitnagged: A common fault with my mother's cooking—totally lacking in seasonings of any kind.

---

57. Leviticus 2:4.
58. Leviticus 2:13.

Talmidah: Perhaps she correctly divined that bland food was most fitting for a son lacking in taste.

Mitnagged: Only a man of taste can discern tasteless food. A case in point is the first course of this week's sequel of Talmidah's fantasy, up through 4:1, which can only be described as a watery stew—a fictional novel in which a mere two lines of scripture float around in a cauldron of nearly 100 lines of fanciful speculation!

Rabbi: You registered your objection to Talmidah's lopsided use of exegesis versus scripture during our first week together.

Mitnagged: But, Rabbi, this is *not* exegesis! It is *aggadah!*

Rabbi: Just what is *aggadah?*

Talmidah: Let me defend myself, Rabbi. I am not helpless.

Rabbi: I think I will enjoy more of this "offering."

Talmidah: Just what is *aggadah?*

Mitnagged: Folk tales, parables, proverbs, and quaint sayings.

Talmidah: And? Mitnagged, you know that *aggadah* is anything that is not *halakah*, or "law." Debate, rulings, and hermeneutical rationale behind civil, ethical, and ritual law is *halakah*. Everything else is *aggadah,* including scriptural exegesis.

Mitnagged: You know what I'm saying, and you know that I am correct. Popular *aggadah* is composed of legends, stories, and folk wisdom. When we hear the word *aggadah*, this is what we think of.

Talmidah: But Mitnagged, by classifying exegesis as *aggadah*, our sages wisely infer that these so-called legends, stories, and bits of folk wisdom are themselves exegesis.

Mitnagged: Impossible.

Talmidah: In rabbinic thinking, telling a story is as valid in interpreting a biblical text as arguing its meaning outright. *Aggadah* fills gaps left by scriptural accounts with "missing" plot fillers, inspired by questions naturally arising from the text: How did Adam and Havah respond when they were told to leave the garden? What was it like for them that first day out in the "real" world? How did they learn to survive? What did Havah think when she experienced pregnancy? What did Havah mean when she said that she "acquired a Man of God"? Why did God reject Cain's offering? We can answer these questions a number of ways; by hashing them out in midrashic debate, or by retelling the story in a way that answers our questions. In either case, we are expressing what the text "means" to us. Instead of a watery stew, I would compare it to whipped meringue.

Mitnagged: An appropriate analogy. The yolk of Torah ripped, torn, and distorted by empty air.

Talmidah: Expanded and sweetened by popular *aggadah*. There are several versions of the Havah and Adam narrative available—both ancient and modern—each entirely different from the others. Which is the "correct" one?

Mitnagged: Not yours!

Talmidah: There is no "correct" one, Mitnagged, for each is really commentary on what this narrative means to the person who composed it.

Rabbi: One could say that the way in which a person interprets or retells this story does not so much reveal the original intent of the text, as it does the attitudes and world-view of the interpreter himself . . . or herself.

Mitnagged: You're not even pretending to be an objective observer today, Rabbi.

Rabbi: I find Talmidah's unsolicited offering of matza and honey to be "sweet" and "savory." Therefore, I am inclined to view her favorably.

Mitnagged: A strong allusion to Cain and Havel's offering. Very well, let us go to 4:3. How did you justify translating *minha* as "sin-offering"? The literal meaning of this word is "gift," secular or ritual, and in Leviticus applies to a number of different types of sacrificial offerings.

Talmidah: Including "sin-offering"

Mitnagged: But not exclusively.

Talmidah: An interpretive choice. In this way I tie 4:3 to 4:7, where sin and *teshuvah*, "returning," are major themes. In this translation, the Holy One pleads with Cain to "amend" his ways, implying that Cain's offering was rejected because of Cain's personal unworthiness, not because God prefers meat over fruits and vegetables.

Mitnagged: You take many liberties with *set,* which simply means "uplift." At most, you can say, "uplifted head." From this you get "forgiven," "exalted"?

Talmidah: To be lifted up or to hold your head high are idiomatic terms for "exalted" or "honored," Mitnagged. As it is written, "He was important to his lord and uplifted/exalted to his favor."[59] In other words, "highly esteemed." So the penitent is highly esteemed, or exalted, in the eyes of the Holy One. *Set* also means "to take away" or "carry off," and is utilized often in Scripture to mean "take away guilt," as it is written, "Carry away/forgive,[60] I beg you, the offense and guilt of your brothers."[61] Forgiveness, acceptance, and exaltation are all promises given to anyone who "returns" to God.

Rabbi: Explain your double-reading of *timshal-bo.*

Talmidah: *Timshal* is a conjugated form of *mashal,* which can either mean "to master/rule" or "be like/similar." The word *-bo* is a preposition with a direct object pronoun suffix, which, among several possibilities, can mean "over it" or "as it." Since this phrase refers directly to sin, reading it both ways—"to master it" or "become like it"—teaches us that there is a choice laid before us when confronted with an evil inclination.

Mitnagged: We can make ourselves stronger by overcoming it.

---

59. 1 Kings 5:1.

60. The Hebrew word in this verse is *sa,* which derives from the same root from which *set* is conjugated, namely *nasa.*

61. Genesis 50:17. See also Exodus 32:32, 10:17, 34:7; Numbers 14:18; 1 Samuel 15:25, etc.

Talmidah: Or be overcome by it and find ourselves retrograding to a state identical to that of our tempter—lower even than an animal.

Rabbi: In regard to this phrase, Rabbi Berekiah quoted Rabbi Simeon as saying, "Happy is he who is master over his transgressions, but his transgressions are not master over him."[62]

Mitnagged: It is also written, "If one indulges his evil inclination in his youth, it will eventually rule over him in his old age."[63]

Rabbi: In light of his degeneration, Cain's name is tragically ironic.

Talmidah: Yes, indeed! When Havah holds her firstborn infant in her arms, she is filled with wonder, joy, and hope. The baby is glorious and beautiful, full of promise. So she calls him "Acquired" because she acquired an *ish*-man of God.

Mitnagged: But according to your multireading of his name scattered throughout the text, "acquired" turned out to be most appropriate after all, for the word *kana,* "acquired," also means "buy."

Rabbi: Hence the popular belief that Cain hoarded his wealth and bent all his mind and effort to gaining more and more property.

---

62. *Bereshith Rabbah* XXII.6.
63. *Bereshith Rabbah* XII.6.

Talmidah: A belief at least as old as Josephus.[64] But I read "buy" differently in this context, Rabbi.

Rabbi: How so?

Talmidah: Cain sought to "buy" Yahweh with a gift, thereby justifying whatever sin or transgression he committed.

Rabbi: He lacked sincerity of heart.

Talmidah: Yes, as opposed to his brother, who made his offering for the love of God.

Mitnagged: So the issue is one of *kavannah,* "intent." Cain failed to perform his duty of the heart.

Rabbi: You refer to that famous commentary called "Duties of the Heart," written by Rabbi Bachya ben Joseph ibn Paquda.[65]

Mitnagged: Yes, in which he distinguishes between outward duties and duties of the heart, between ritual obedience and the inward life.

Rabbi: And what are the duties of the heart?

Mitnagged: Rabbi Bachya wrote that "the duties of the heart are to believe that the world had a Creator and that there is none like unto Him; to accept His Unity; to worship Him with our hearts; to meditate on the marvels exhibited in His

---

64. *Antiquities,* I.1–2.

65. Written about 1050 C.E. "Duties of the Heart" was originally written in Arabic. It was subsequently translated into Hebrew 1120–1190 C.E. by Jehuda ibn Tibbon.

creatures, that these may serve us as evidences of Him; that we put our trust in Him; that we humble ourselves before Him, and revere Him; that we tremble and be abashed when we consider that He observes our visible and our hidden activities; that we yearn for His favor; that we devote our works to the glory of His name; that we love Him and love those that love Him, and thus draw nigh to Him."[66]

Talmidah: He went so far as to say that "no work is complete without the assent of the soul."[67] Cain's offering was incomplete, because, as you said, it was made without proper *kavannah,* or intent.

Mitnagged: It is written, "Does the Lord delight in burnt offerings and sacrifices as much as in obedience to the Lord's command? Surely obedience is better than sacrifice, compliance than the fat of rams."[68]

Talmidah: Your sword is sheathed today, Mitnagged. Are you weakened from prolonged battle, or do you think to insult me by humoring me in a patronizing manner?

Mitnagged: I was attempting to play my pipe before the king.

Rabbi: Hoping you would respond by playing the lute in countermelody. Are you blushing, Talmidah?

Talmidah: No! Of course not!

---

66. Moses Hyamson, trans. (Jerusalem: Boystown Jerusalem Publishers, 1965), p. 19.

67. Hyamson, 21.

68. 1 Samuel 15:22.

Rabbi: Perhaps she is embarrassed for you, Mitnagged. It is painfully apparent that you have not had a great deal of practice in this gentle art.

Mitnagged: Doesn't *kavannah* count for anything?

Talmidah: If it exists. I am not so easily "bought."

Rabbi: Nor was God, apparently, in the case of Cain and Havel.

Talmidah: Cain's naming of his son, "dedicated," suggests that he continued in his attempt to "buy" Yahweh.

Rabbi: By dedicating his son to God?

Talmidah: Possibly. In any case, the character of his line of descendants proved the hypocrisy of his "dedication."

Mitnagged: How is hypocrisy indicated, Talmidah? Their names suggest otherwise: "God gives Life," "Man of God," "Strong Young Man." These names suggest sincere piety, at least on the part of the fathers who named their sons.

Talmidah: There is no indication which parent, father or mother, named their child. If anything, Scripture favors the woman. For as we read in the text itself, Havah named her firstborn, as did the matriarchs who followed her. Perhaps these names reflect the hopeful piety of the unfortunate women imprisoned by the harshness of Cain's new order of male tyranny.

Mitnagged: Where do you read of such an order!

Talmidah: Why that "Strong Young Man" of which you spoke as an example of great piety—Lamech. How did Lamech treat his wives, Adah and Tsella? He threatens to kill them if they don't run to do his every bidding!

Mitnagged: Where is this found!

Talmidah: In 4:23.

Mitnagged: This verse tells of a secret Lamech entrusts to his wives—how he accidentally killed his son, as well as his great-grandsire Cain, much to his grief and anguish.

Talmidah: A laughable reading, Mitnagged!

Mitnagged: If you laugh at me, you laugh at the sages, as well. According to them, Lamech used to go out hunting even when he had become a blind old man. And so one of his young sons would lead him about the field and point out game for him to shoot at. One day, Lamech's son mistook Cain for game because of the horn growing from his head—the horn being the identifying mark which Yahweh put on him. So Lamech shot at the "animal," only to discover at close inspection his mistake. Upon this terrible realization, he swung his arms together, inadvertently killing his son. It was a tragic accident.[69]

Talmidah: Not very convincing.

Rabbi: One could read this verse to mean that Lamech boasted to his wives regarding his exploits as a warrior.

---

69. *Tanhuma Bereshith.*

Talmidah: Just the kind of thing a braggart like him would do. But that is not how I read this verse. This "Strong Young Man"—doubtless named so by his despairing mother who hoped that her son would prove to be strong enough to see through his unimpressive role models and stand against his evil inclinations—used his strength to terrorize his women. The phrases "Hear my voice!" and "Give ear to my word!" are constructed as imperatives—strong commands, not whimpering confessions. And what does it mean to command someone to "Hear my voice!"?

Mitnagged: "Please listen to what I have to say."

Talmidah: "Obey me!" For it is written, "*Hear,* O Israel, to the laws and commandments which I teach you! *Do* them that you may live!"[70] The words *hear* and *do* are in parallel to one another. Israel is commanded to obey the laws and commandments of God.

Rabbi: This meaning puts a different slant on the *shema.* "Hear, O Israel!/Be obedient, O Israel! The Lord our God, the Lord is One."

Talmidah: The imperative command of *shema,* "Listen!", with *koli,* "my voice," is nearly always used in the context of a command to obey, as is clearly the case when Rebekah commands her son, "Therefore, my son, hear/obey my voice according to that which I *command* you." Likewise, God commands Abram to listen to the voice of his wife. In other words, "do what she says."[71]

---

70. Deuteronomy 4:1.

71. Genesis 27:8, 15:2, 21:12. Other examples: Genesis 27:13, 43;

Mitnagged: Yes, we've already discussed the consequences which happen to a man who listens to his wife. "Because you listened/obeyed the voice of your wife, the earth is cursed."

Talmidah: You plow a field already sown.

Mitnagged: I'm making a different point from the same series of unfortunate episodes in the lives of our patriarchs. You consistently argue that it is no sin for a husband to listen/obey the voice of his wife. In fact, it is the height of "wisdom" (*hah*) to do so. Yet you say it is deplorable for a woman to listen/obey her husband.

Talmidah: No, that is not the condemnatory part of 4:23. Lamech commands his wives to listen/obey him *or else.* He threatens them with violence, even death. He terrorizes them into submission. Rabbi Hisda said, "A man should never terrorize his household."[72]

Rabbi: Rabbi Abbahu further said, "It is better to punish immediately or say nothing" than to threaten.[73]

Talmidah: Meaning that a hanging threat, particularly one of violence, is an evil way to treat those under your roof, for they live in constant fear and apprehension.

Mitnagged: Perhaps that is the only way a man can control his wife and children.

Exodus 18:19; Deuteronomy 5:1; 1 Samuel 8:7, 9, 22; 28:22; 1 Kings 15:1; Jeremiah 38:20.

72. *Gittin* 6b.

73. *Gittin* 7a.

Talmidah: That being the case, he is counted among the descendants of Cain. For such behavior occurs in his line of doomed posterity, rather than Shet's, the Head of Adam's posterity. Physical abuse and domination is the mark of Cain, not that of an *ish*-man of God.

Mitnagged: Why the mark?

Talmidah: The mark?

Mitnagged: Yes, the mark God put on Cain for his protection. In fact, you went so far as to say that Yahweh made a *covenant* with *Cain,* of all people. A covenant with a *murderer* to protect him from justice.

Talmidah: It was not a covenant to protect a homicide from the consequences of killing another human being.

Mitnagged: No? It certainly reads that way to me.

Talmidah: Verse 4:15 tells you why the Holy One made a covenant with Cain: "So that no one meeting him would kill him."

Mitnagged: Or so much as hit him, according to your translation. Sounds like protection to me.

Talmidah: It *is* protection, Mitnagged, but not for Cain. It protected others from committing the same crime that drove Cain permanently from the presence of God. From this we learn that taking a life, for any reason—even for just compensation for murdering an innocent person—killing a human life is far worse than being killed. As Golda Meir of blessed memory once said, "The only thing I cannot forgive them for is that they forced our sons to kill their sons."

Mitnagged: But a murder cannot go unpunished!

Talmidah: If you go back and reread my targum, you will see that according to Philo, Cain was justly destroyed by God Himself, in that he was castrated from the society of mankind altogether, and his posterity cut off so that he had no descendants left in name or blood.

Mitnagged: We read of six generations directly descended from Cain. I see no "cutting off."

Talmidah: A truncated genealogy, doomed to perish ultimately in the flood.

Rabbi: Legend has it that Cain himself was swept away in the flood, a victim of his own unrighteousness.[74]

Mitnagged: Legend also has it that he was killed by Lamech, as I have already pointed out. So it is written, "I killed a man to my wounding, a young lad to my hurt." That interpretation would seem to support your exegesis regarding the sanctity of life, Talmidah, without villanizing Lamech.

Talmidah: Your persistence in following the King James translation for 4:15 is tenacious if not stubborn. Modern versions universally translate Lamech's words to reflect his belligerent attitude: "I killed a man for wounding me,[75] a lad

---

74. *Bereshith Rabbah* XXXII.5.
75. JPS, Anchor, NEB, RSV, NIV.

for bruising me[76]/a boy for injuring me[77]/a young man for striking me."[78] The message is the same: "Look, you women, I've *killed* people for slight offenses. I'll do the same to you if you don't do as I say. And do you think anything is going to happen to me? If Cain got protection for what *he* did, then *I'll* get even *more* protection for doing something worse." Contrast this attitude with that of Adam, who respects what Havah tells him, comforts her when she grieves, cares for her when she is incapacitated and prays for her when she suffers childbearing pain—a pain he is otherwise helpless to share or alleviate. And for this she loves him. She is glad to see him in her hour of near-death travail; she weeps beside him in dark hours of fear or grief; she confides in him, trusts him, shares her joy of giving birth to a righteous child with her *ish*-man.

Rabbi: And what do they learn from these experiences together?

Talmidah: What do they learn?

Rabbi: Your targum suggests, as we pointed out earlier, that knowledge of Good and Evil is interrelated somehow with raising children.

Talmidah: But I didn't understand the connection.

Rabbi: Do you understand now?

Talmidah: Not really.

---

76. JPS.
77. Anchor.
78. RSV.

Rabbi: Mitnagged?

Mitnagged: They saw murder, violence, and decadence in operation, through their own son.

Talmidah: They also saw good in their son Havel.

Mitnagged: Yes, and they saw that evil can kill goodness.

Talmidah: But that good eventually shines through, as it did in the lives of Shet and his children.

Mitnagged: But evil is easier and therefore more dominant in the real world.

Talmidah: Good brings happiness and exaltation; evil brings misery and estrangement from God.

Rabbi: A promising beginning. But what of themselves, as parents and spouses? Are they mere spectators, this father and mother? This husband and wife? What did they learn that they could not have learned by watching humanity through a telescope from some safe vantage point above?

Mitnagged: I suppose they learned that children will bring happiness and grief, depending on the choices they make. As it is written, "A wise son makes a glad father; but a foolish son is the sorrow of his mother."[79]

---

79. Proverbs 10:1.

Talmidah: Yes, and "a foolish son is a grief to his father, and bitterness to her that bore him."[80]

Mitnagged: "Children's children are the crown of old men; and the glory of children are their fathers."[81]

Rabbi: How does this understanding assist men and women to become "like one of us"?

Mitnagged: Like a ministering angel?

Talmidah: Or God Himself?

Rabbi: Consider the following: "I reared children and brought them up, but they have rebelled against me. An ox knows its owner, an ass its master's crib; Israel does not know, my people do not understand. Ah, sinful nation! people weighed with guilt! brood of evil doers! depraved children!"[82] and "Woe to rebellious children, the Lord says, taking counsel against my wishes!"[83] and further, "Children, heed the discipline of a father; listen and learn understanding. For I give you good instruction, forsake not my teaching."[84]

Mitnagged: These passages compare God to a father who loves his son.

Talmidah: Or a mother who loves her child.

---

80. Proverbs 17:25.
81. Proverbs 17:6.
82. Isaiah 1:2–4.
83. Isaiah 30:1.
84. Proverbs 4:1–2.

Rabbi: Who are His children?

Mitnagged: *Bnei-israel,* the children of Israel.

Talmidah: Or all humanity. So . . . to experience the raising of children is to understand more fully the dealings of Yahweh with his covenant people.

Rabbi: "My son, reject not the chastening of the Lord; neither be weary of his correction. For whom the Lord loves, He rebukes; even as a father the son in whom He delights."[85]

Talmidah: To love a child is to understand how God loves us.

Rabbi: And why, at times, He weeps.

Mitnagged: Or punishes.

Talmidah: Or praises.

Rabbi: Or protects the *nephesh,* "soul," of one child by insisting that justice for certain capital crimes be left to Him, just as a parent will forbid an innocent child to "punish" a sibling who has wronged him. There is much in this richly-expanding experience that you cannot begin to comprehend at this moment, my children. But to be a parent is to understand, just a little, what it is to be God, and to comprehend with heart as well as mind the Torah itself as a record of a Parent's travail, struggle, and wrestling with His children. You knew this all along, Talmidah.

85. Proverbs 3:11.

Talmidah: I did?

Rabbi: The way you structured 5:3. Compare it to 1:26.

Talmidah: "He begat a son in his likeness, after his image." "Let us form mankind in our image, after our likeness."

Mitnagged: "Likeness" and "image" are reversed.

Rabbi: To avoid irreverent comparisons.

Talmidah: But the presence of both words in a nearly identically structured phrase suggests a connection.

Rabbi: What kind of connection?

Talmidah: Perhaps after many years of struggle and disappointment, Havah and Adam had achieved a status more elevated and holy than when they began.

Mitnagged: But the sages insist that Adam began as a glorious being and subsequently lost that glory when he fell.[86]

Talmidah: But over time he regained his glory.

Rabbi: Or perhaps achieved a different state of holiness not otherwise possible.

Talmidah: It occurs to me that the man and woman, as husband and wife, would have also progressed as a couple as

86. *Bereshith Rabbah* XII.6.

well. These experiences would have knit their souls inseparably together, achieving true *yihud.*

Mitnagged: It didn't seem to work that well for Lamech and his wives.

Rabbi: It is written, "His name was called *ish*-fire, and she was called *ishah*-fire. What did the Holy One, blessed be He, do? He put His name, Yod (*i*) *Heh* (*h*) between their names, saying: "If they go in My ways and keep all my precepts, behold My name is given to them, it will deliver them from all distress. If they do not walk in My ways, behold I will take away My name from their names, and they will become fire. And fire consumes fire."[87]

Mitnagged: Are you saying that sincere piety acts like some kind of "glue" for a marriage?

Talmidah: Without it, the relationship falls apart?

Rabbi: It burns to ashes.

Talmidah: Depending on the choices you make, then, mortality will move you toward light or darkness, joy or grief, strength or weakness, *yihud* or separation. So you are correct, Mitnagged, when you said that the Tree of Good and Evil represents the kind of knowledge acquired through mortality.

Mitnagged: You come to know the good or the evil.

Rabbi: By experiencing both.

---

87. *Pirke de-Rabbi Eliezer,* chap. XII.

Mitnagged: I'm sorry to be leaving so soon, but my car is being repaired and I must catch the next bus if I am going to get to work on time.

Rabbi: Shalom, Mitnagged, until next week.

Talmidah: Peace be with you, Mitnagged.

Talmidah: He hardly tried today.

Rabbi: Are you disappointed?

Talmidah: A little. It seemed more like a conversation than a debate.

Rabbi: Nothing to sharpen your claws against? From my vantage point, it appeared that both of you had put up your lances and were having a picnic under a pleasant fig tree.

Talmidah: It is written, "A knife can be sharpened only on the side of another knife."[88] One can hardly joust without an opponent, Rabbi. And it's too bad, because I felt invigorated by our midrashic debates. He's usually pretty sharp.

Rabbi: For a Neanderthal.

Talmidah: Neanderthal? I wouldn't call him *that!*

Rabbi: Ahhhh, but you did, scarcely six weeks ago.

---

88. *Bereshith Rabbah* LXIX.2.

Talmidah: I might have misjudged him. He really isn't that . . . bad. Today he seemed distracted, though.

Rabbi: Apparently. Not unusual for a young man his age.

Talmidah: Are you saying it might be . . . a girl?

Rabbi: I would not be surprised. He is a healthy young man, after all, and likely to have certain natural inclinations. Does that bother you?

Talmidah: Bother me? Why should it bother me?

Rabbi: A question worthy of meditation.

7

"DEATH AND HOPE"
Genesis 5:4,5

Targum

Adam lived 800 years after the birth of Shet — *Genesis 5:4*
and he begat sons and daughters.
Adam fathered thirty sons and thirty daughters.[1]

All the days of Adam were lived lively/active — *5:5a*
He lived going straight
happy
blessed
930 years

After Adam had lived 930 years, he became ill and he knew his days were at an end. Crying with a loud voice he said, "Let all

1. *The Apocalypse of Moses*, 5.

my children be gathered to me, that I may bless them before I die, and speak with them." And they all came to the door of the house in which he used to enter to pray to God. And they asked him, "What is it with you, Father, that you should gather us together? And why are you lying on your bed?" And Adam answered and said, "My children, I am sick with pains." And all his children asked him, "What is it, Father, to be sick with pains?"

Then his son Shet said, "Lord, perhaps you have longed for the fruit of Paradise of which you used to eat, and that is why you are lying in sadness. Tell me and I will go to the entrances to Paradise and will put dust on my head and throw myself to the ground before the gates of Paradise and mourn with great lamentation, entreating the Lord. Perhaps he will hear me and send his angel to bring me the fruit you desire." Adam answered and said, "No, my son, I do not long for that, but I have weakness and great pain in my body." Shet responded, "What is pain, O lord Father? I do not know; do not hide it from us, but tell us."[2]

They asked Adam, "Who brought death to you?" He replied, "I brought it upon myself." They asked him, "Was it not the Holy One who caused you to die?" He replied, "No! Do not speak like that! I am like the sick man who was confined to his bed. When the physician came and looked at him, he enjoined him, 'You may eat such-and-such thing, but do not eat such-and-such thing, which will be bad for you and fatally dangerous.' But the sick man ate and was about to die. The people asked him, 'Was it perhaps the physician who is causing you to die?' He replied, 'I myself have caused my death. If I had given heed to what the physician enjoined me, I would not be dying.'"[3]

2. *Vita Adae,* 30–31; *The Apocalypse of Moses,* 5:1.
3. *Midrash Tehillim,* 92:14.

Adam said this to all his children while he was seized with great pains, and he cried out with a loud voice, "Why should I suffer misery and endure such agony!"[4]

Hear my prayer, Oh God! *Psalms*
Give ear to the words of my mouth! *54:2*
My heart writhes within me *54:4*
the terrors of death come upon me
Fear and trembling overwhelm me *54:5*
and shuddering grips me
My days are vanishing like smoke *102:3*
my bones burning like an oven
My heart is withering like grass *102:4*
I forget to eat my meals
My bones stick out through my skin *102:5*
from the effort of voicing my groans

And when she saw him weeping, Havah herself began to weep. "My husband Adam, rise, give me half of your illness and let me bear it!" Adam said to Havah, "Rise and go with my son Shet to the regions of Paradise and put dust on your heads and prostrate yourselves to the ground and mourn in the sight of God. Perhaps he will have the oil of life and will give you a little of it with which to anoint me, that I may have respite from these pains by which I am wasting away."

So Shet and his mother walked toward the region of Paradise for the oil of mercy, to anoint the sick Adam. And they arrived at the gates of Paradise, took dust from the earth, and put it on their heads, prostrated themselves to the ground on their faces and began to mourn with loud sighs, begging the Lord God to

4. *Vita Adae,* 35:1.

pity Adam in his pains and to send his angel to give them the oil from the tree of mercy. Then God sent Michael the archangel, and he said to them, "Shet, Man of God, do not labor, praying with this supplication about the tree from which the oil flows, to anoint your father Adam. It shall not come to be yours now, but at the end of times. Return to your father, since the measure of his life is fulfilled, that is, in three days. And as his soul departs, you are sure to witness its fearful upward journey."

While Adam was lying ill, having one more day before going out of the body, Havah asked Adam, "Why are you dying and I live? And how long have I to live after you die? Tell me." Then Adam answered Havah, "Do not worry about this, for you shall not be long after me, but we shall both alike die, and you yourself shall be laid in my place. But when I die, leave me alone and let no one touch me, for God will not forget me, but will seek his own vessel which he has formed. But rather, rise to pray to God until I shall give back my spirit into the hands of the one who has given it."[5]

Genesis 5:5b And then he died
and was gathered from the midst of the world[6]

While Havah was still on her knees praying, behold the angel of mankind came to her and lifted her up, saying, "Rise, Havah, for behold Adam your husband has gone out of his body. Rise and see his spirit borne up to meet its maker."

So Havah rose and put her hand on her face and the angel said to her, "Lift yourself from earthly things." Havah gazed into

5. *The Apocalypse of Moses,* 13; *Vita Adae,* 31, 36, 40.
6. *Targum Yerushalmi.*

heaven and saw a chariot of light coming, drawn by four radiant eagles of which it is not possible for anyone born from the womb to tell their glory or to see their faces, and angels went before the chariot. Now the body of Adam was lying on the ground in Paradise, and Shet was mourning greatly over him.[7]

Havah: And I wept from fear and cried out to my son Shet, "Shet! Get up from the body of your father, Adam, and come to me, that you may see things which no eye has ever seen!"

Then Shet got up and came to his mother. And he said to her, "What is the matter? Why are you weeping?" She replied, "Look up with your eyes and see the heavens opened, and see with your eyes how the body of your father lies on its face, and all the holy angels are with him, praying for him and saying, 'Forgive him, O Father of all, for he is your image.'"

Then Yahweh Elohim said, "Adam, your sorrow shall be turned into joy. I will establish you in your dominion on the throne of your seducer. But that one shall be cast into this place, so that you might sit above him. Then he himself and those who listen to him shall be condemned, and they shall greatly mourn and weep when they see you sitting on his glorious throne." Then he spoke to the archangel Michael, "Go into Paradise in the third heaven and bring me three cloths of linen and silk. Cover Adam's body with the cloths and bring oil from the oil of fragrance and pour it on him." And thus they did and prepared his body.[8]

7. *The Apocalypse of Moses,* 32, 33, 39.
8. *The Apocalypse of Moses,* 34, 35.

And in that place all the children of men made a great mourning and weeping on account of Adam. It has therefore become a custom among the sons of men to this day.[9] And all of his children buried him in the land of his creation. He lacked seventy years from one thousand years, for a thousand years are like one day in the testimony of heaven and therefore it was written concerning the tree of knowledge, "In the day you eat from it you will die." Therefore he did not complete the years of this day because he died in it.[10]

You told him, "In the day that you eat thereof you will surely die." But did you not afterwards give Adam one day of yours—a day which is a thousand years? Otherwise, how could Adam have united with his wife and begotten children? Hence it is said, "Your tender mercies and your loving-kindnesses have been ever of old," that is, "ever since the days of Adam."[11]

Six days after Adam died, Havah, aware that she would die, gathered all her sons and daughters, Shet with thirty brothers and thirty sisters, and Havah said to them all, "Listen to me, my children! Make now tablets of stone and other tablets of clay and write in them all my life and your father's which you have heard and seen from us. If he should judge our race by water, the tablets of earth will dissolve and the tablets of stone will remain; but if he should judge our race by fire, the tablets of stone will break up and those of clay will be thoroughly baked."

---

9. *The Book of Jasher.*
10. *Jubilees* 4:29–30.
11. *Midrash Tehillim,* 25.8.

While living, she herself wept about her death, because she did not know where her body was to be placed. And Havah, in the hour of her death, implored that she might be buried where Adam her husband was, saying, "My master, Lord and God of all excellence, do not separate me from the body of Adam. Just as I was with him in Paradise and not separated, so also let no one separate us now." Therefore after she prayed, she looked up to heaven, rose, beat her breast and cried, "God of all! Receive my spirit!" And immediately she gave up her spirit to God.

After this, all her children buried her with great weeping. Then, when they had mourned for four days, the archangel Michael appeared to them and said to Shet, "Man of God, do not prolong mourning your dead more than six days, because the seventh day is a sign of the resurrection, the rest of the coming age, and on the seventh day the Lord rested from all his works." Then Shet made the tablets.[12]

Shall the decree which was decreed against Adam continue forever? Surely not! Shall his transgression make him desolate in the grave? Shall he and his descendants be trampled down by the angel of death? When the morning of the nations of the world turns to evening, and the evening of Israel to morning, at that time I will declare him clear of that decree. Behold! Let the man become as one of us![13]

Then all flesh from Adam up to that great day shall be raised, such as shall be the holy people; then to them shall be given every joy of Paradise and God shall be in their midst, and there

12. *Vita Adae,* 49–51; *The Apocalypse of Moses,* 42:3–8.
13. *Bereshith Rabbah* XXI.3.

shall not be any more sinners before him, for the evil heart shall be removed from them, and they shall be given a heart that understands the good and worships God alone.[14]

Enoch: And I ascended to the East, into the paradise of Eden, where rest is prepared for the righteous. And the guards are appointed at the very large gates to the east of the sun, angels of flame, singing victory songs, never silent, rejoicing at the arrival of the righteous. When the last one arrives, he will bring out the couple Adam, together with the ancestors; and he will bring them in there, so that they may be filled with joy; just as a person invites his best friends to have dinner with him and they arrive with joy, and they talk together in front of that man's palace, waiting with joyful anticipation to have dinner with delightful enjoyments and riches that cannot be measured, and joy and happiness in eternal light and life.[15]

Happy are the righteous!
Their days are all stored up with the Holy King,
woven into radiant garments to be worn in the world that is coming.[16]

In the future the faces of the righteous will resemble seven joyous things: the sun, the moon, the firmament, the stars, lightning, lilies, and the lampstand of the Temple. "And behold, ye are this day as the stars of heaven for multitude." Behold, you are as eternal as the day.[17]

---

14. *The Apocalypse of Moses,* 13:5.
15. 2 Enoch 42:3–5, J recension.
16. *Zohar,* 92.
17. *Sifre Deuteronomy,* Piska 10. This same midrash of Proverbs 1:10 is found in *Ve-Yikrah Rabbah* XXX.2.

This is the Book of the Generations 5:1
begettings
accounting
of the couple, Adam

In the likeness of Divine Ones He shaped them 5:2
male and female
man and woman
He fashioned them
He blessed them and called their name Adam
red/blood earth/dust
Humanity

Midrash

> Provide a teacher for yourself; and for yourself acquire a study companion.
>
> —*Avot* 1.6

Rabbi: What are these, talmidim?

Mitnagged: Free-will offerings, Rabbi! Shavuot is tomorrow and we wish you *hag sameach!*

Talmidah: Yes, happy holiday, Rabbi! I brought the two loaves of leavened bread,[18] along with strawberry jam and honey.

Mitnagged: And I brought the firstfruits.[19]

---

18. Leviticus 23:17. The one offering of leavened bread, rather than unleavened, was brought to the temple during Shavuot.

19. Deuteronomy 26:1–11. The firstfruits of the harvest were also brought at this time. Traditionally, nuts and fruits are eaten in commemoration of this offering.

Rabbi: A generous variety of nuts and fruits, Mitnagged: almonds, walnuts, peanuts, pistachios . . . ahhh, dates, figs, peaches, pineapple, oranges, and bananas. A grand feast for three people! May the Holy One enlarge this door for a rabbi who must pass through it greatly enlarged by His goodness. One thing lacking.

Talmidah: What are you taking out of your coat, Rabbi?

Mitnagged: Wine! Ah-hah!

Rabbi: Before we celebrate the giving of Torah on Mount Sinai, let us honor it by completing our study of Talmidah's targum. Mitnagged?

Mitnagged: I have no questions. Can we open the wine now?

Talmidah: No questions? What trickery is this?

Mitnagged: No trickery. Your targum is perfectly delightful. Nothing objectionable or controversial about it at all. The wine?

Talmidah: You liar!

Rabbi: She is angry, Mitnagged.

Mitnagged: OK, I do have a question.

Talmidah: I thought so. I am prepared for anything you have to throw at me.

Mitnagged: What are you doing for dinner tonight?

Talmidah: What?

Mitnagged: My family is having our traditional supper of milk dishes and cheese cake tonight for the eve of Shavuot. Would you like to join us?

Rabbi: Or just the two of you could celebrate it. I know a *kashrut* restaurant not far from here that serves excellent *blintzes.*

Talmidah: Are you asking me for a *date?*

Mitnagged: My mother expects all of us home for the holiday, Rabbi. But she would welcome a guest like Talmidah.

Talmidah: Just look at you smiling into your beard! You planned this all along, Rabbi!

Mitnagged: She is angry.

Rabbi: Not any more. Her eyes are laughing. And if you look closely at the corners of her mouth, you will see that they are slightly turned up. You will learn to read her face with time.

Talmidah: This is outrageous! You old matchmaker! Did you really expect me to get under the huppah with this . . . this . . . *adam*-man!

Rabbi: How else can he hope to become an *ish*-man?

Mitnagged: He does have a point.

Talmidah: He is an insufferable, narrow-minded, chauvinistic boor!

Mitnagged: Tell her, Rabbi, please.

Rabbi: He is not altogether what he seems to be.

Talmidah: Undoubtedly worse—a rotten apple with a fat worm squirming around at the heart of it.

Rabbi: A golden orange disguised as an apple.

Talmidah: What are you talking about?

Rabbi: Mitnagged is squirming with impatience for me to sing his merits. Understandable, considering his fervent desire to impress you.

Mitnagged: Rabbi!

Rabbi: Where to begin. Ahhh, yes. His parents. As it is written, "An apple does not fall far from the tree."[20]

Talmidah: An apple. Thought so.

Mitnagged: Rabbi, please.

Rabbi: No need for groaning, Mitnagged. I shall vindicate you as best as I can. His father, Talmidah, is the head of Judaic Studies at the university.

Talmidah: He has a father? And it's Dr. Zucker? *The* Dr. Zucker?

20. A folk proverb.

Rabbi: His mother is an ordained rabbi.

Talmidah: His mo . . . an ordained rabbi! Wait a minute, there's only one . . . Rabbi Zucker? Your *mother* is Rabbi Zucker? I didn't even know they were married to each other!

Rabbi: Small world.

Talmidah: This is the woman whose cooking you have maligned for seven weeks?

Mitnagged: She's an attentive mother and a great rabbi, Talmidah, but she is the worst cook on God's planet, may the Holy One protect us! Fortunately, my father is the chef tonight, so our table will be doubly blest with words fit for angels as well as good food.

Rabbi: Where was I? Ahhh, yes. His sister recently graduated from law school, first in her class. She will be specializing in criminal law.

Talmidah: This is the same sister who primps in front of the mirror?

Mitnagged: An exaggeration.

Rabbi: You never look in a mirror, Talmidah? His brother . . . too young for laudation, I'm afraid.

Mitnagged: I wouldn't say that, Rabbi. He and his partner just took the state championship in debate. You'll never guess how he did it! He constructed a foolproof case proving that if we eliminated the electoral college, human civilization as we know it would be destroyed in a worldwide flood.

Talmidah: I would like to hear this "foolproof" case.

Mitnagged: If anybody can outmaneuver him, you can. But I must warn you, none of us have been able to crack his logic.

Talmidah: Your table conversations must be incredible!

Mitnagged: To say they are lively would be an understatement.

Rabbi: Now for Mitnagged himself. Hmmmm . . . well, you know there's one in every family.

Mitnagged: Rabbi!

Rabbi: His name is not Mitnagged. What Jewish mother would call her son such a name? His name, Talmidah, is Jacob . . . or Yaacov, depending on his preference on any given day. It is an appropriate name, don't you see? All this time you thought he was Esau, the red-necked, hairy "Neanderthal" of your nightmares. But take off the goat skin and smelly clothing foisted upon him by his scheming rabbi and you have Jacob.

Talmidah: The smooth-skinned coward.

Jacob: Rabbi!

Rabbi: Smooth-skinned, yes, except the hair on his face. But coward? No, one cannot call a young man a coward who champions social causes the way our Jacob does.

Talmidah: What do you mean?

Rabbi: Why, Jacob is president of Students Against Hunger, Poverty, and Injustice, an ambitious organization which gathers food for the homeless shelter, solicits jobs and education funds for indigent workers, counsels unwed mothers about welfare benefits and childcare options, and lobbies for legislation favorable to women, minority groups, and the handicapped.

Talmidah: You do all that? This is too good to believe.

Rabbi: There is hope for you yet, Jacob. See, she is beginning to feel impressed.

Jacob: She doesn't believe you, Rabbi. Could you sing my merits a little less freely?

Rabbi: Aside from these laudable humanitarian efforts, Jacob is preparing for a brilliant career in psychotherapy. He has nearly completed his graduate studies and will no doubt be a guiding light in his field. A catch if there ever was one!

Jacob: You neglect the most important achievement, Rabbi.

Rabbi: Patience, patience, my young man. Do you think I have forgotten? Would I ever forget such a thing?

Talmidah: Out with it, Rabbi.

Rabbi: See, she laughs. Your old rabbi knows more than Torah. As it is written, "Look, Listen, and Learn."

Jacob: You're sounding like Tevye the Dairy Man.

Rabbi: I purchased two bottles of wine for this occasion. As you can see, there is one left. Where were we? Ahhh, yes. Jacob will not only be a good provider and great humanitarian, but he is destined to be a rabbi-of-sorts himself.

Talmidah: What do you mean?

Rabbi: He leads a group on campus called, "Torah le Kol."

Talmidah: "Torah for All"?

Rabbi: Yes, a study group composed not only of men and women, but Jews and gentiles.

Talmidah: Gentiles? Why would a bunch of *goyim* be interested in Torah? Of what possible benefit could it be to them?

Jacob: It appears you are not without biases of your own, Talmidah. Is it not written in the Talmud, "Where do we find the proof that even a Gentile who pursues the study of Torah is like a high priest? From the assertion about Torah's ordinances that 'by pursuing their study man shall live,'[21] where Scripture speaks not of priest, Levite, or Israelite, but of 'man.' So you learn that even a Gentile who pursues the study of Torah is like a high priest."[22]

Rabbi: Two members have already come under the wings of the Shekinah.[23]

21. Leviticus 18:5.
22. *Sanhedrin* 59a.
23. A euphemism for conversion to Judaism.

Jacob: You'd enjoy it, Talmidah. Come join us next time and see for yourself. We meet every Wednesday night at 7:00 in the conference room next to my father's office.

Talmidah: So it was all a great joke. At my expense. You were totally convincing, Mit . . . Jacob. Congratulations. I feel like a complete fool.

Rabbi: Come now, Talmidah. If Jacob were really the sort of man as Mitnagged pretended to be, would he talk to you at all, let alone argue with you about Torah? Would he sit down with you at the same table? Would he even look at you?

Talmidah: He would not have given me a chance to prove myself.

Rabbi: Exactly. The opportunity to express your viewpoint on an important pericope of Scripture which directly impacts your life would never have been given to you by a real Mitnagged.

Jacob: Something else you have to think about—why would I pick *him* for my rabbi?

Rabbi: That is correct. A student will acquire for himself a rabbi who takes him where he . . . or she . . . wants to go.

Jacob: But I must confess something to both of you. I actually enjoyed my role as Mitnagged, at least through most of our debates. I mean . . . I *relished* it. So you were not deceived, Talmidah. I think I really was Mitnagged. Deep down I was a self-righteous Mitnagged pretending to be a liberal-minded activist. And maybe he's still there, just under the skin.

Talmidah: So you were a jerk pretending to be a hero pretending to be a jerk.

Jacob: Something like that.

Rabbi: Humility, Talmidah! Think what you could do with someone so teachable and eager to improve.

Jacob: I readily concede to your superior wit and understanding.

Rabbi: Well?

Talmidah: Well, what?

Jacob: Will you have dinner with me tonight?

Talmidah: Your parents sound like a fascinating couple. I would like very much to meet them.

Jacob: Then it's settled! I will come for you at 6:00.

Talmidah: You look pleased with yourself, Rabbi.

Rabbi: I am not disappointed. Let us celebrate.

Jacob: Not yet! I need to get something.

Rabbi: Where is he going?

Talmidah: You'll see.

Talmidim: "*Hag Sameach,* Rabbi!" "*Shalom Aleichem!*" "Surprise!" "*Yom Tov,* Rabbi!"

Rabbi: All my students! And more food!

Jacob: And wine. Anybody bring music?

Talmidim: "I brought 'Havah Nagila.'" "I brought Itzhak Perlman." "I brought Israeli folk music." "I brought the sound track to Animal House!"

Rabbi: Excellent! Let us celebrate the Feast of Revelation. "Blessed be He who in His Holiness gave the Torah to His people Israel. May it be thy will to open my heart to thy Torah and to fulfill the wishes of my heart and of the heart of all thy people Israel for happiness, life, and peace."

Talmidah: Amen!

Jacob: Amen!

Talmidim: Amen!

Bibliography

Bet ha-Midrash. Jerusalem: Wahrmann Books, 1967. (Hebrew)

Bible Translations into English:

(JPS) The Jewish Publication Society

(NEB) The New English Bible

(NJB) The New Jerusalem Bible

(NIV) The New International Version

(KJV) The King James Version

(Anchor) The Anchor Bible

Elliger, Karl, and Wilhelm Rudolph, eds. *Biblia Hebraica Stuttgartensia*. Germany: Deutsche Bibelgesellschaft Stuttgart, 1967/77.

Brown, Francis, S. R. Driver, and C. A. Briggs. *Hebrew and English Lexicon of the Old Testament*. Oxford: Clarendon Press, 1906.

Evan-Shoshan, Avraham. *Konkordantzia Hadasha le-Torah, Nevaim ve-Ketuvim*. Jerusalem: Kiryat-Sefer, 1992. (Hebrew)

Ginzberg, Louis. *The Legends of the Jews, vols. 1 & 5*. Philadelphia: The Jewish Publication Society of America, 1925.

Josephus, Flavius. *The Antiquities of the Jews*. Trans. William Whiston. Grand Rapids, MI: Kregal Publications, 1960.

Midrash Bereshith Rabbah. Jerusalem: Wahrmann Books, 1965. (Hebrew)

Freedman, H. and Maurice Simon, trans. *Midrash Rabbah*. London: Soncino Press, 1939.
Bereshith (Genesis)
Ve-yikra (Leviticus)
Bemidbar (Numbers)
Devarim (Deuteronomy)
Tehillim (Psalms)
Qohelet (Ecclesiastes)

Danby, Herbert, trans. *Mishnah*. Oxford: Oxford University Press, 1933.

Charlesworth, James H., ed. *Old Testament Pseudepigrapha*. Garden City, NY: Doubleday, 1983.
F. I. Anderson, trans. 2 *Enoch*.
G. MacRae, trans. *The Apocalypse of Adam*.
O. S. Wintermute, trans. *Jubilees*.
M. D. Johnson, trans. *Vita Adae*.
M. D. Johnson, trans. *The Apocalypse of Moses*.
J. J. Collins, trans. *The Sibylline Oracles*.
A. F. J. Klijn, trans. 2 *Baruch*.

Braude, William G. and Israel J. Kapstein, trans. *Pesikta de-Rab Kahana: R. Kahana's Compilation of Discourses for Sabbaths and Festival Days*. Philadelphia: Jewish Publication Society, 1975.

Braude, William G., trans. *Pesikta Rabbati*. New Haven, CT: Yale University Press, 1968.

Yonge, C. D., trans. *The Works of Philo*. Peabody, MA: Hendrickson Publishers, 1993.
"On the Creation"
"Allegorical Interpretation, I & II"
"Questions and Answers on Genesis, I"
"On the Birth of Abel and the Sacrifices Offered by Him and by His Brother Cain"

Seder Olam Rabbah. Jerusalem: 1931. (Hebrew)

Sifre Deuteronomy. New Haven, CT: Yale University Press, 1986.

Epstein, Isidore, ed. *Talmud Bavli: Hebrew-English Edition*. London: Soncino Press, 1988.

Mishcon, A., and A. Cohen, trans. "Avodah Zarah."

Simon, Maurice, and Israel W. Slotki, trans. "Baba Bathra."

Simon, Maurice, trans. "Beracot."

Slotki, Israel W., trans. "Eruvin."

Abrahams, I., trans. "Hagigah."

Slotki, Israel W., trans. "Ketuvot."

Slotki, Israel W., trans. "Niddah."

Freedman, H., trans. "Sanhedrin."

Freedman, H., trans. "Shabbat."

Slotki, Israel W., trans. "Yevamot."

Talmud Yerushalmi. New York: E. Grossman, 1959. (Hebrew)

"Kiddushin"

"Peah"

Townsend, John T., trans. *Tanhuma Bereshith*. Hoboken, NJ: KTAV Publishing House, 1989.

Etteridge, J. W., trans. *The Targums of Onkelos and Jonathan ben Uzziel on the Pentateuch with the Fragments of the Jerusalem Targum from the Chaldee*. New York: KTAV Publishing House, 1968.

Sperling, Harry, and Maurice Simon, trans. *The Zohar*. London: The Soncino Press, 1931.

Matt, Daniel Chanan, trans. *The Zohar: The Book of Enlightenment*. New York: Paulist Press, 1983.

Index

Abbahu, Rabbi, 271
Abel. *See* Havel
Adam, 91
  characteristics of, 190, 198
  consequences of "fall" for, 205–206, 231–233
  forbidden fruit commandment given to, 173–175, 191
  as prophet, 96, 142
  and temptation by serpent, 167–169, 173–175, 184, 190
Adam
  as representative, 71–72, 145–149
  meanings of, 13, 35
Adam and Havah
  as representation of men and women, 63–64, 101
Adultery, and temptation of Havah, 182–184
Aggadah, vs. law, 261–262
Androgyne, Adam and Havah as, 98
Angels, 34, 143–144, 148, 206, 286–287
  and Garden of Eden, 74–75, 239
Appearance, of consonants, 15–16
Aramaic, vs. Hebrew, 5–7, 160
Ascension, 87–88, 143–144
Awan, birth of, 246
Azariah, Rabbi Eleazer ben, 193

Barrenness, of Havah, 178, 185–189, 210–211
Baths, ritual, 217–226

Blessings
from God, 126, 213–214
mikvah as, 225–226
Boring, Garden as, 191–193
Bread
Adam as *hallah,* 35–36
mitzvah of the *hallah,* 214, 226–229
Building, in creation of Havah, 136–139

Cain, 265, 272–273
birth of, 175–176, 243–245
children of, 254–255
death of, 269, 273–274
and Havel, 246–251
Chariot of God, 59, 88–90
Cherubim, guarding Garden of Eden, 206–207
Childbearing, 185–186, 190, 233
as consequence of "fall," 205–206, 212–213
and fathers, 188–189
and Havah eating forbidden fruit, 167–168, 173
pain of, 190–191, 203–204
Childrearing, 233, 274–276
Children, of Adam and Havah, 175–176, 243–246, 252–253, 256–258, 274, 283–284, 288
Commandments, 270–271
to multiply, 39, 175–176, 210–211
not to eat from Tree of Knowledge, 167, 173–175, 198
Commentaries, 3–4
dangers of, 6–8
select use of texts for, 102–109
in targums, 29, 53–54
vs. translation, 18–20
Consonants
interchangeability of, 13, 15
regrouping of, 159–160
Creation, 33–41, 74, 167–168
accounts of, 49–50, 56–58, 93, 106–107
of Havah, 121–124, 133–141
location of, 82–85, 92
and women's *mitzvot,* 229–231
Curses, of God, 197–198, 209–215, 231–233

Death, 230, 271–273. *See also* Mortality
of Adam and Havah, 283–289
as impurity, 220–221
lack of, in Garden, 180, 190
Debate
and commentaries, 8–9, 18–20, 108
purposes of, 64–65

of sages, 47–48, 99
settings for, 18–20
Descent, in account of creation, 57–60, 82–85
Desire, sexual, 181–183, 204, 225
Documentary Hypothesis, 22–23, 141
Duties of the heart, 266–267

Earth, Adam and Havah given dominion over, 39–40
Eleazar ben Arak, 89–90
Eliezar, Rabbi, 15, 91, 97–99, 214
Eliezer, Rabbi, on Torah study, 42–43, 193
Elijah, and holy fire, 146–147
Elohim, significance of number of, 61, 67–68
Enosh, 257
Eternal, translation of, 61
Ethics, from sacred literature, 26
Exile, and writing of Torah, 23–24
Eyes, translations of, 168, 181–183, 185–186
Ezekiel, visions of, 144
Ezra the Scribe, redaction by, 23–24, 51

"Fall," consequences of, 176, 180–181, 202–208
Fire
God as, 143–144, 145, 241–242
holy, 146–148
Flood, end of Cain's line in, 273
Fragrances, in Garden, 113–114, 181–182, 239–240
Free will, in Garden of Eden, 80
Fruit, forbidden, 173–175, 198–199
and temptation of Havah, 167–168, 182–184

Garden of Eden, 73–80, 95, 197, 252, 290
expulsion from, 207, 233, 239–241
nature of, 178, 180–181, 189–194
procreation in, 175–176
as temple, 112–120
Garments
of Adam and Havah, 14–15, 39, 206, 235–236
of high priests, 116–117
Gender, in pronouns, 66–71
Gnosticism, 99–100, 109
God, 178, 229
and Adam, 79–80, 287
and Cain, 247–249, 266–268, 272–273
God, (*continued*)

and human mortality, 234–235, 276–278
names of, 61, 67
relation with Adam and Havah, 240–243
response to eating of fruit, 197–198, 201–208
visions of, 143–144
Good and evil, 181–182, 274–276. *See also* Tree of Knowledge of Good and Evil
Grief, 287–288
for childlessness, 185, 189
of God, 208, 234–235
Guilt, 227
of Cain, 264
for eating fruit, 202, 210–211

Ha-Meiri, Menahem ben Solomon, 44
Hanah ben Joshua, Rabbi, 216
Hananiah, Rabbi, 45–46
Havah, 166–168, 204. *See also* Adam and Havah
creation of, 121–124, 133–141, 157–158
and death, 285–286, 288–289
images of, 101, 186–189
Havel, 175–176, 252
and Cain, 246–251
Head coverings, 214–217
Hebrew, 140
consonants in, 13, 16
polyvalency of, 11–13, 57, 94–95
pronouns in, 66–71, 215
shifting letters in, 16, 70, 159–160
vowelization in, 12–13, 15, 69–70, 157–158
vs. Aramaic, 5–7
Hekhalots, 87
Heschel, Abraham Joshua, 230
High priests
Adam and Havah as, 116–117
Adam as, 96, 176, 206
Ishmael as, 87–88
Hillel, School of, 105–106
Hisda, Rabbi, 271
Holiness, 91–92
achievement of, 87, 278–279
Esh vs. adam, 146–148
Ish vs. adam, 146–148
of males and females, 178–179
Intent, 47
and duties of the heart, 266–268
in interpretations, 24–25, 27, 65–66, 263
Interpretations, 6–8, 13–15, 62, 108
in targums, 2, 9–10, 13, 53–54

true, 20, 25, 262–263
Intertextuality, 102
Ish, meanings of, 145–150
Ishah, 148–151, 214–215
Ishmael, Rabbi ben Elisaha, 86–88
Israel, rival Torahs in, 23

Jeremiah, 23, 42
Johanan, Rabbi Yose Ben, 43
Judah the Prince, Rabbi, 105

Kabbalah, 59, 62
Kahana, Rabbi Abba bar, 91
Knowledge. *See* Wisdom

Labor, 205, 207, 246
Lamech, 254–255, 269–271, 273–274
Languages
meanings of, 7–8
and targums, 4–5
and translations, 11–13, 29
Leah, barrenness of, 187
Levi, Rabbi, 98–99, 125
Light, in creation of Adam and Eve, 38–39
Loneliness, 134
of Adam for Havah, 101, 121–123, 198–199

Markers, added to consonants, 16
Marriage, 101–102, 149–150, 188–189
of Adam and Havah, 121–131, 278–279
of Lamech, 269–271
and parenting, 233, 274
passion in, 225, 246, 256
Masoretes
alternative interpretations than, 159–160, 185, 231–232
vowelization by, 12, 15, 157–158
Matriarchs, Havah compared to, 186–189
Maturity, of Adam and Havah, 165, 178, 180, 196–197, 234–235
Menorah, as Tree of Life, 113, 229–230
Menstruation, 197
as curse on women, 214, 217–222, 225
impurity of, 177–178
Merkavah literature, 58–59, 63, 86
Michael, 286, 289
Midrash, 52
vs. targum, 7–9, 20, 53–54
Mikedem, translations of, 94–95, 119
Mishna, 104–105, 108
Mortality, 180–181, 190–191, 231, 233–234

and death of Adam, 284–288
and maturity, 196, 279
Moses, 20–21, 248
Motherhood. *See* Childbearing; Procreation
Mount Moriah, "descent" from, 83–85
Mysticism, 59, 62

Nachimanides, 16
Nakedness, 182–183, 196
of Adam and Havah, 165–166, 169, 202
Natan ha-Bavli, Rabbi, 102–103, 107–109
Nod, Cain in, 251–252, 254

Obedience, in marriage, 270–271
Offerings, 81, 87, 239–240, 242, 259, 263
of Cain and Abel, 266–268
of Cain and Havel, 247–250
of *hallah,* 226–228
to rabbis, 291–292
Olive oil, 112, 170–171

Palimpsest, splitting of, 231–233
Paquda, Rabbi Bachya ben Joseph ibn, 266–267
Paradise. *See also* Garden of Eden
after death, 118, 285–286, 290
Philo, 62, 91, 95
Philosophy, and mysticism, 62
Pleasure
bringing to beloveds, 178–179, 199
in Paradise, 74–76, 290
Plural. *See* Singular and plural
Polyvalency, of Hebrew, 11–13, 57, 185
Priests. *See also* High priests
rituals of, 214–217, 223, 225, 227–228
Procreation, 150, 179
and commandment to multiply, 39, 175–176, 210–211
as consequence of "fall," 199, 210–213, 243–245
and forbidden fruit, 173–176
Prophecies, 95–96, 142
Purity, 196
and cleansing, 217–227

Rachel and Jacob, 186, 188
Rashi, 43–44
Rebecca and Isaac, 186, 188
Redaction, 23–24, 51–52, 55
Responsibility, and Havah eating fruit, 202, 210
Resurrection, in vision of Adam, 258
Rib, translations of, 123–124, 133–141

Rituals
of priests, 214–217, 227–228
of women, 214, 217–231
Rivers, in Garden of Eden, 77–78, 114–116

Sabbath, 229–230
Sages, 26
and achievement of holiness, 87–88
antagonisms among, 47, 66
Samuel, Rabbi, 99
Sarah and Abraham, 186, 188, 233
Satan, 166–168, 172–173, 182. *See also* Serpent
School of Hillel, *vs.* Shammai, 105–106
Scribes, errors by, 15–16, 70
Scriptures
interpretation of, 9–10
reading in services, 5–7
and Torah, 4, 54–55
Semen, 197
impurity of, 177, 217–227
Separation, of Adam and Havah, 97–99, 101, 124
Serpent, 172–173
and Havah, 166–168, 182–184
punishment of, 202–204, 209–210
Services, synagogue, 6–7, 12, 18–20
Sexual intercourse, 177–179, 183
and passion, 204, 208, 225
Shame, 196, 215–217, 227
Shekina, 179
Shet, 256–257, 283–288, 289
Simeon, Rabbi, 45–46
Singular and plural, 61, 97
in pronouns, 66–71, 215
Sin-offerings, 263
Sins, 257
of Cain, 247–252, 263, 265
of Cain's children, 254–255
eating fruit as, 80, 173–175, 210–211
and intercourse, 184–185
of murder and violence, 271–273
resisting, 264–265
Speiser, Dr. E. A., 67–68
Springs, translations, 185–186
Steinsaltz, Rabbi Adin, 220, 222
Suffering, 189, 284–285
of childbirth, 190–191, 204
as consequence of "fall," 195, 204, 231–233, 240–243

Tabernacles, as temples, 84
Tablets, with story of Adam and Havah, 288–289
Talmud, writing of, 108–109
Talmud Bavli, 104–105

Targums, 1–10, 13, 48–49
scriptural passages in, 52–53, 55–56
writing of, 27–31
Temples
"descent" from, 83–86, 92
Garden of Eden as, 78, 112–120, 176–177
purity and cleansing for, 219–221, 223, 225
side chambers of (tsela), 135–141, 151–155
Texts, 3, 102–103
selection of, 102–109
shifting letters in, 16, 70
Time
before Creation, 95
in Garden of Eden, 118–119, 180–181, 190
Torah, 6–7, 76
definitions of, 3–4, 53–54
study, 42–46, 87–88, 193–195
text of, 48–52
writing of, 17, 20–28
Tradition, 2–4, 22, 26
Translations. *See also* Hebrew
to Aramaic, 5–7, 160
errors in, 15–16, 70
literal *vs.* non, 10–11, 17–18
in targums, 2–4, 56–61
Tree of Knowledge of Good and Evil, 76–77, 80, 180
forbidden fruit on, 167, 173–175
Tree of Life, 76, 206–207. *See also* Tree of Knowledge of Good and Evil
Tree of Mercy, 77, 112
Trees, in Garden of Eden, 75–77, 80, 95–96, 112, 113, 167
Tribes, histories told by, 22

Violence, in marriage, 270–271
Visions, 95
of Adam, 123, 141–144, 148–149, 258
Vowelization, 12–13, 15, 69–70, 157–158

Wedding, of Adam and Havah, 124–131, 133–134, 152–156
Wellhausen, Julius, 22–23
Wisdom, 185–186
from eating forbidden fruit, 167–169, 210
of eating forbidden fruit, 162, 168, 198
gained through childrearing, 195, 274–276
in Garden of Eden, 75–77, 95–96, 192–193
and mortality, 180–181
Women, 65–66, 202–203, 268
in account of creation, 92–93

characteristics of, 42–43, 182–184, 190
curses on, 214, 226–231
relations with men, 63–65, 133–134, 150
Torah study by, 42–46

Yarmulka, symbolism of, 216
Yohanan ben Zakkai, Rabbi, 88–90

About the Author

Shira Halevi is the author of three books and is a student of traditional Jewish texts. She has both an undergraduate and graduate degree in Hebrew, as well as a degree in Middle Eastern studies.